opposing viewpoints® SOURCES

death/dying

1988 annual

David L. Bender, *Publisher*
Bruno Leone, *Executive Editor*
M. Teresa O'Neill, *Senior Editor*
Bonnie Szumski, *Senior Editor*
Janelle Rohr, *Senior Editor*
Lynn Hall, *Editor*
Susan Bursell, *Editor*
Julie S. Bach, *Editor*
Thomas Modl, *Editor*
William Dudley, *Editor*
Robert C. Anderson, *Editor*

greenhaven press, inc.
San Diego, CA

© 1988 by Greenhaven Press, Inc.

ISBN 0-89908-536-9
ISSN 0748-285X

HQ1073
D28
1988

contents

Editor's Note   ***Opposing Viewpoints SOURCES*** provide a wealth of opinions on important issues of the day. The annual supplements focus on the topics that continue to generate debate. Readers will find that *Opposing Viewpoints SOURCES* become the barometers of today's controversies. This is achieved in three ways. First, by expanding previous chapter topics. Second, by adding new materials which are timeless in nature. And third, by adding recent topical issues not dealt with in previous volumes or annuals.

Viewpoints

Infant Euthanasia

1. **Disabled Newborns Can Be Allowed To Die** by *Arthur L. Caplan*   1

   Treatment decisions for disabled newborns should be handled on an individual basis, considering the best interests of the child. For children whose future lives will be filled with pain, it may be ethical to withdraw or withhold treatment.

2. **Disabled Newborns Must Not Be Allowed To Die** by *Patrick Wiseman*   7

   The decision to withdraw treatment from Baby Doe, a handicapped infant born in Indiana, was wrong. Receiving life-saving treatment is always in a disabled child's best interest.

Euthanasia

3. **Ethical and Medical Issues in Euthanasia: An Overview** by *Arthur Zucker*   11

   Euthanasia poses many ethical questions, none of which are easy to decide. Decisions about specific euthanasia cases rest on individual moral philosophies about death.

4. **Physicians Should Practice Active Euthanasia** by *Phillip J. Miller*   17

   Death is a natural part of life. Physicians should help patients die rather than rely on intrusive and unnatural technology to keep them alive.

5. **Physicians Should Never Practice Active Euthanasia** by *D. Alan Shewmon*   21

   Active euthanasia is a morally dangerous policy. No physician has the right or obligation to help a patient die.

6. **Withdrawing Treatment Violates Professional Ethics** by *Edward R. Grant & Clarke D. Forsythe*   25

   Conscience and the law demand that physicians provide appropriate care for their patients. Physicians who withdraw life-sustaining treatment are acting unethically and their actions should be ruled illegal.

7. **Withdrawing Treatment Does Not Violate Professional Ethics** by *Marsha D. Fowler*   29

   Physicians must be able to withdraw treament from their patients when it becomes more burdensome than beneficial to the patient.

8. **Nutrition May Be Withheld from Dying Patients** by *Norman L. Cantor*   31

   Food and water should be regarded as medical treatments that may be withheld at a dying person's request.

9. **Nutrition Should Not Be Withheld from Dying Patients** by *Jacqueline M. Nolan-Haley & Joseph R. Stanton*   37

   Withholding food and water from dying patients amounts to assisting suicide.

10. **Critically Ill Patients Have a Right To Die** by *Howard Moody*   43

    Individuals have the right to choose how and when they will die. Courts and medical authorities cannot prevent them from exercising that right.

11. **Critically Ill Patients Do Not Have a Right To Die** by *Robert Barry & Frank Morriss*   47

    The right to die is really a euphemism for suicide. Natural law dictates that society try to prevent suicide. Society should also, then, prevent seriously ill people from taking their own lives.

LIBRARY
SAINT MARY'S COLLEGE
NOTRE DAME, INDIANA

Coping with Death, Case Study: AIDS

12. Critically Ill Patients' Right To Die Is Limited by *Ruth Macklin* — 51
The right of patients to decide their own deaths should be balanced with legal and moral prohibitions. In some circumstances, patients have a right to die.

13. AIDS Should Be Faced with Hope by *Tom O'Connor* — 55
People with AIDS should not resign themselves to dying. By taking control of their lives and maintaining hope and self-esteem, many AIDS patients have lived longer than predicted.

14. AIDS Should Be Faced with Acceptance by *Elisabeth Kübler-Ross* — 61
By accepting the fact that they will die, AIDS patients can prepare themselves psychologically for death by working through the states of the grieving process.

15. Accepting AIDS as Fatal Helps Victims by *George Whitmore* — 67
Most AIDS patients die within eighteen months of their diagnosis. Talking about death can help AIDS sufferers and their loved ones cope with grief.

16. Accepting AIDS as Fatal Harms Victims by *Michael Callen* — 75
There is a significant minority of AIDS patients who have lived for as long as five years after their diagnosis. Telling all AIDS patients that they must face death robs them of the hope they need to survive.

17. Support Groups Help AIDS Victims Cope with Death by *Bob Russell* — 81
Going to support groups helps victims realize that although they have AIDS and will die, they can make the most of their last years by caring for others.

18. Focusing on the Self Helps AIDS Victims Cope with Death — 85
by *George Melton, interviewed by Lese Dunton*
AIDS can be an opportunity for victims to examine their identity and self-esteem. By improving mental and spiritual health, they can feel better physically as well.

19. Hospices Help AIDS Victims Cope with Death by *Herman Kattlove & Jeannee Parker Martin* — 89
Hospice programs provide support personnel including health aides, social workers, nurses, therapists, and community volunteers who help AIDS patients cope with the illness in their final days.

Organ Donation

20. Infant and Fetal Transplants Are Ethical by *Arthur L. Caplan* — 93
Fetuses, anencephalics, and brain-dead infants are needed for organ and tissue transplants. It is more ethical to use these handicapped babies to save the lives of people who need transplants than it is to let those people suffer or die meaninglessly.

21. Infant and Fetal Transplants Are Unethical by *Leslie Bond* — 99
Using organs and tissue from aborted fetuses or anencephalic infants is morally wrong and further devalues human life.

22. Anencephalic Infants Should Be Used as Organ Donors — 107
by *Michael R. Harrison*
Organs are needed for children with fatal diseases. Anencephalic infants would be ideal sources for these organs. Since anencephalics lack a brain and have no chance of survival, harvesting their organs in acceptable.

23. Anencephalic Infants Should Not Be Used as Organ Donors — 111
by *Mary Senander*
Though anencephalics have only a brain stem, they are still living persons. Their organs should not be taken for transplants while they are alive; nor should they be kept on life support machines to keep their organs viable for transplantation.

24. Aborted Fetal Tissue Should Be Used for Transplants — 113
by *Mary B. Mahowald, Jerry Silver & Robert A. Ratcheson*
Using tissue from aborted fetuses is a morally defensible option if those fetuses are dead or if they have no chance of survival. Fetal tissue can cure diseases in other people.

25. Aborted Fetal Tissue Should Not Be Used for Transplants — 117
by *Dave Andrusko*
Using the tissue of aborted fetuses is unethical. No benefit to other patients suffering from diseases can justify using the remains of aborted babies.

Bibliography — B-1

Index — I-1

"An infant's best interest can lie in withholding or withdrawing medical treatments, resulting in death."

viewpoint 1

Disabled Newborns Can Be Allowed To Die

Arthur L. Caplan

Developments within clinical pediatrics in the last few years have reinforced the governmental impetus toward aggressive treatment of all imperiled newborns. Neonatal treatment in the 1980s now includes the use of respirators, sensitive monitoring of blood pressure, oxygenation, blood flow and biochemical parameters, and other evolving nursing and medical technologies. In addition to these intensive care measures, new techniques have been developed in heart, intestine, liver, kidney, and brain surgery to correct congenital anomalies. Intravenous techniques of "total nutrition" now allow infants to gain weight and grow with normal development for weeks, months, or years with minimal oral intake. Research on new therapies for neonates includes trials of kidney, liver, and heart transplantation and the use of extracorporeal membrane oxygenation (ECMO) to replace temporarily the function of damaged lungs.

These new technologies as well as the application of modern medical and nursing techniques are largely responsible for dramatic increases in neonatal survival rates. Full term infants with nonlethal congenital abnormalities survive at rates of greater than 99 percent throughout the country. Infants as young as twenty-six weeks of gestational age weighing 600 grams survive at a rate of at least 20 percent in most centers in the United States. Yet it is true that a small number of infants survive the neonatal period only to be left technology-dependent—permanently on a respirator, attached to an intravenous line for feeding, or chronically in need of dialysis.

However, the most common cause of major long-term morbidity rarely results in the high drama of technology dependence. Instead the problem is one of neurologic sequelae, such as spasticity, learning disabilities, or profound mental retardation. These cases often involve the small premature infant with intraventricular hemorrhage. Such bleeding in the brain is present in almost half of very low birthweight infants, but the outcome for each varies significantly. A small amount of bleeding can lead to major impairments; a large amount of bleeding can result in almost no impairments. There are some predictors of poor outcome, but they are far from absolute.

Technology Creates Uncertainty

Thus technological success has bred more uncertainty and options than previous physicians and parents faced. Uncertainty is initially associated with survival but, if a child survives, the uncertainty becomes associated with the level of morbidity and the quality of future life for the infant.

This latter form of uncertainty is a product of many factors. One is the inescapable biological variability of the individual patient. The impact of variability is exacerbated by a lack of information concerning the efficacy of some of the newest forms of intensive care technology and of some post-nursery interventions. This has led some to argue that clinical trials ought to be undertaken for all new interventions and that such trials should be controlled and randomized in order to assess adequately the usefulness of proposed interventions. Although theoretically ideal, this approach has been constrained by ethical concerns about withholding possibly effective treatments from those infants who would serve as "control" subjects. Thus many interventions become part of the armamentarium of the practicing professional without ever having been proven to be effective.

Decisions regarding treatment of imperiled newborns, like decisions in any medical context, have two components: the data on which to base the

Arthur L. Caplan, ed., "Imperiled Newborns," *The Hastings Center Report*, December 1987. Reproduced by permission. © The Hastings Center.

decision, and the personal values one applies to the analysis of the data. Yet, medicine is inherently a probabilistic profession. Diagnoses are rarely 100 percent certain and in spite of the traditional jargon, very few diagnoses are ever "ruled out." Prognosis, as mentioned, is rarely certain at the time that a diagnosis is entertained because all treatments vary in their efficacy from patient to patient and from time to time. Furthermore, the risks of treatment are not always predictable....

Responding to Uncertainty

There are several ways to respond to the uncertainty in neonatal medicine. One approach is for physicians or other decisionmakers to make an across-the-board determination that infants fitting a particular statistical profile are unlikely to benefit from treatment and that it should therefore not be initiated for them. We shall call this the *statistical approach*. According to this decision strategy, if a premature infant were to fall below a cut-off for age and size, aggressive treatment would not be provided. This approach has been said to characterize that used in most institutions in Sweden, where infants below 750 grams are rarely given artificial ventilation.

A contrasting approach is to begin treatment for every infant that is even potentially viable, and to continue active treatment until it is certain that a particular baby will either die or will be so severely impaired that under any substantive standard, parents could legitimately opt for termination of treatment. We shall call this the *wait until near-certainty* approach. While it is difficult to generalize about treatment policies in the United States, it appears that an increasing number of American physicians and institutions employ this strategy.

"The 'sanctity of life' standard remains a vague slogan, rather than a meaningful guide to decisionmaking."

An intermediate approach, which has been said to characterize British neonatal practice, is to begin treatment for every infant, but to allow parents the option of termination before it is absolutely certain that a particular infant will either die or be so devastatingly disabled that he or she will be unable to relate to others or to the environment. Under this strategy, which we shall call the *individualized approach*, doctors will periodically reassess an infant's probable prognosis, taking into account such factors as severe intraventricular hemorrhages or other indicators of probable neurological impairment, and will allow termination of treatment if there is a high chance (though not certainty) of severe disability....

As parents and clinicians evaluate specific strategies for responding to uncertainty, it is essential to ask how they should determine whether treatment is *ethically right* for a particular infant. The ethical questions can only be resolved by establishing reasonable standards of judgment against which to measure strategies and procedures.

Many critics of the practice of selective nontreatment argue that we must concentrate on the *sanctity* of life. But what does it mean to base our decisions on the sanctity of each child's life? Does it mean that caregivers may *never* forgo treatment, or that they may do so only for the most catastrophically afflicted newborns? Without further specification, the "sanctity of life" standard remains a vague slogan, rather than a meaningful guide to decisionmaking.

Vitalism. The most extreme sanctity of life position would hold that "where there is life, there is hope," and that so long as a child continues to cling to life, he or she must be treated. According to this view, which we shall call "vitalism," the mere presence of a heartbeat, respiration, or brain activity is a compelling reason to sustain all efforts to save the child's life. Only the moment of death relieves caregivers of their duty to treat. An adherent of this vitalist philosophy would accordingly hold that, except in cases where the child has been declared dead, all withholding and withdrawal of treatment is ethically wrong.

This most extreme sanctity of life position has few advocates. Its major flaw is that it would insist upon aggressive treatments even for those children who are deemed to be in the process of dying. If responsible physicians have concluded that a particular child cannot be saved, that he will soon die, then it seems pointless and cruel to continue to treat the child with medical interventions that are by no means benign. By insisting on treatment even in such hopeless cases, the vitalist can justly be accused of worshipping an abstraction, "life," rather than focusing on the concrete good of the patient. As theologian Paul Ramsey has cogently argued, the appropriate response to a dying patient is not the futile imposition of painful medical treatments, but rather kind and respectful *care* designed to ease the child's passing.

Another Position

The Medical Indications Policy. A more reasonable sanctity of life position has been proposed by Paul Ramsey and adopted (with some modifications) in various versions of the Department of Health and Human Services so-called "Baby Doe Rules." According to this standard, each child possesses equal dignity and intrinsic worth (i.e. "sanctity") and therefore no child should be denied life-sustaining medical treatments simply on the basis of his or her "handicap" or future quality of life. Such treatments must be provided to all infants, except (1) when the infant is judged to be in the process of dying, or (2) when the contemplated treatment is itself deemed to be "medically contraindicated." As Ramsey puts it, *treatments* may be compared in order to see which will be medically beneficial for a child, but abnormal *children* may not be compared with normal children in order to determine who shall live.

> *"Even though treatment might be withheld from . . . a grievously afflicted infant 'solely on the basis of his handicap,' such a decision would in no way count as* unjust *discrimination."*

This policy is supported by two complementary ethical principles. First, the "nondiscrimination principle" states that children with impairments may not be selected for nontreatment solely on the basis of their "handicapping condition." If an otherwise normal child would receive a certain treatment—for example, surgery to repair an intestinal blockage—then a child with an abnormality must receive like treatment. Failure to do so discriminates unfairly against the child with impairments.

Second, the "medical benefit principle" states that caregivers are obliged to provide any and all treatments deemed, according to "reasonable medical judgment," to be "medically beneficial" to the patient. This means that if a certain medical or surgical procedure would be likely to bring about its intended result of avoiding infection or some other fatal consequence, then it must be provided to the child.

An Inadequate Guide

Although this medical indications policy was obviously well intended, insofar as it attempted to prevent instances of *unjust* discrimination against newborns with impairments, we believe that it is an overly rigid and inappropriate guide to decisionmaking. The first problem is that the nondiscrimination principle would have decisionmakers ignore, not just relatively mild handicaps of the sort encountered in most children with spina bifida and Down syndrome, but also impairments that are genuinely catastrophic.

Consider, for example, the child suffering from severe birth asphyxia who also happens to have a grave heart defect. Although surgeons would be willing to operate to fix the heart of an otherwise normal infant, the fact that this particular infant will never be sufficiently conscious to interact with his environment would appear to be a factor that the child's caretakers might permissibly take into consideration. Should the child be subjected to major and painful cardiac surgery only so that he might subsist in a permanently unconscious state? Even though treatment might be withheld from such a grievously afflicted infant "solely on the basis of his handicap," such a decision would in no way count as *unjust* discrimination precisely because the child's handicap is so severe that he can no longer meaningfully be compared to an "otherwise normal" infant.

The second problem with the medical indications policy lies in its "medical benefit" principle. Although this principle works well in many cases—for example, mild to moderate spina bifida—it does so because we think that the treatment confers a benefit, not merely upon the child's spine, but rather upon the whole child.

Quality of Life Standards

Although we conclude that quality of life judgments are ethically proper, and indeed inevitable, a great deal of care must be given to specifying why quality of life matters and what qualitative conditions might justify the denial of treatment. Merely invoking the phrase "quality of life" will get us no farther than invocations of the "sanctity of life."

The phrase "quality of life," as used in medical contexts, is ambiguous and frequently misunderstood. It is sometimes used to denote the social worth of an individual, the value that individual has for society. According to this interpretation, a person's quality of life is determined by utilitarian criteria, measured by balancing the burdens and benefits to others, especially family members. It is this meaning of the phrase that gives rise to the greatest worries about undertreatment of newborns with impairments.

This interpretation of quality of life has been defended on the grounds that external circumstances are crucially important in the outlook for certain newborns and because of the increased stress families undergo in raising children with disabilities. Despite the recognition that these external factors play a role in parental attitudes toward treatment, the consensus of this report is that "quality of life" should refer to the present or future characteristics of the infant, judged by standards of the infant's own well-being and not in terms of social utility.

Another way of understanding "quality of life" is as measured against a norm of "acceptable" life. Yet it is often noted that what would not be acceptable to some people, for themselves, is clearly acceptable to others. A danger lies in drawing the line too high, thereby ruling as "unacceptable" the life of a person with multiple handicaps or with mild-to-moderate mental retardation. When quality-of-life assessments are made for newborns with impairments, caution must be exercised to avoid this pitfall.

An example of drawing the line of "acceptable" life too high is "the ability to work or marry," a factor cited by the British pediatrician, John Lorber. An example of a very low standard is permanent coma, a criterion appearing in the 1984 Child Abuse Amendments. This threshold is so low as to be noncontroversial.

The Best Interest of the Child

A subset of the quality of life standard and an alternative to a medical indications policy is the standard known as the "best interest of the child." Traditionally, this standard has been employed by courts in making child custody determinations and other decisions involving placement of an infant or child.

Unlike the medical indications policy, the "best interest" standard does incorporate quality of life considerations. This standard holds that infants should be treated with life-sustaining therapy except when (1) the infant is dying, (2) treatment is medically contraindicated (the two exceptions built into the medical indications policy), and (3) continued life would be worse for the infant than an early death. The third condition opens the door to quality of life considerations, but requires that such considerations be viewed from the infant's point of view. That is, certain states of being, marked by severe and intractable pain and suffering, can be viewed as worse than death. Thus, according to the best interest standard, there is room to consider the possibility that an infant's best interest can lie in withholding or withdrawing medical treatments, resulting in death.

"The prevailing 'best interest' notion presupposes that all infants have interests, but for some, the burdens of continued life can outweigh the benefits."

Care must be taken, however, not to employ a standard based on the sensibilities of unimpaired adults; for example, one in which adult decisionmakers judge, from their own perspective, that they would not want to live a life with mental or physical disabilities. An infant-centered quality of life standard should be as objective as possible, in an attempt to determine whether continued life would be a benefit, from the child's point of view. An impaired child does not have the luxury of comparing his life to a "normal" existence; for such a child, it is a question of life with impairments versus no life at all.

The greatest merit of the best interest standard lies precisely in its child-centeredness. This focus on the individual child will aid decisionmakers in avoiding the twin evils of overtreatment, sanctioned by the medical indications policy, and undertreatment, which might result from allowing negative consequences for the family or society to determine what treatment is appropriate for the infant.

Limits of the Best Interest Standard

Although we believe the best interest of the infant should remain the primary standard for decisionmaking on behalf of newborns with impairments, it has limits. In addition to the undeniable problem of vagueness, there is the further question of the applicability of this standard to some of the most troubling dilemmas in the neonatal nursery. As one critic has noted about the standard suggested in the President's Commission report, *Deciding to Forego Life-Sustaining Treatment:*

> The fact that the child-based best-interest standard would mandate treatment even in the face of a prognosis bereft of any distinctly human potentiality reveals a feature of that standard that has so far gone unnoticed. In such extreme cases, the best-interest standard tends to view the absence of pain as the only morally relevant consideration. No matter that the infant is doomed to a life of very short duration, and lacks the capacity for any distinctively human development or activity; so long as the child does not experience any severe burdens, interpreted from her point of view, the fact that she can anticipate no distinctly human benefits is of no moral consequence.

In an article published in 1974, Father Richard McCormick explained and defended a quality of life viewpoint that differs from the best interest standard. Noting that modern medicine can keep almost anyone alive, he posed the question: "Granted that we can easily save the life, what kind of life are we saving?" McCormick admits this is a quality of life judgment, and holds that we must face the possibility of answering this question when it arises.

McCormick's guideline is "the potential for human relationships associated with the infant's condition." Translated into the language of "best interests," an individual who lacks any present capacity or future potential for human relationships can be said to have no interests at all, except perhaps to be free from pain and discomfort.

A Better Way

Our conclusion is that there is a need for two different standards embodying relational potential considerations. The prevailing "best interest" notion presupposes that all infants have interests, but for some, the burdens of continued life can outweigh the benefits. The alternative "relational potential" standard focuses on the potential of the individual for human relationships, and presumes that some severely neurologically impaired children cannot be said to have interests to which a best interest standard might apply. In employing these two standards, decisionmakers should first determine whether the best interest standard applies to the case at hand. For the large majority of infants this standard is applicable, and should be used to determine whether life-sustaining treatment should be administered. However, if an infant is so severely neurologically impaired as to render the best interest standard inapplicable, then the alternative standard, lack of potential for human relationships, becomes the relevant criterion, placing decisionmaking within the realm of parental discretion.

When the best interest standard is applicable, because the infant's best interest can be determined, decisionmakers are obligated either to institute or to forgo life-sustaining treatment. In contrast, the relational potential standard is nonobligatory: it permits the withholding or withdrawing of therapy from infants who lack the potential for human relationships, but it does not require that treatment be forgone. Continued treatment would not benefit such infants, but neither would it harm them. An example might be an infant born with trisomy 13. Most such infants do not survive beyond the first year of life, are severely or profoundly mentally retarded, and have multiple malformations. Their chances of being able to experience human interactions are minimal. Unlike the best interest standard, which is infant-centered, the relational potential standard allows the interests of others—e.g., family or society—to weigh in the decision about whether to treat.

Whereas the honest and informed application of these standards in the Baby Doe case should have yielded a clear mandate to treat a life-threatening condition, cases involving much more severe impairments may resist any straightforward application of normative standards. Although the precise medical facts in the celebrated Baby Jane Doe case remain mired in controversy, cases *resembling* that of Baby Jane regularly pose problems for decisionmakers attempting to apply either a "best interest" or a "relational potential" test.

Waiting for Enough Evidence

Suppose an individualized decisionmaking strategy were combined with our preferred "best interest/relational potential" substantive standard. Clearly, the most important result would be a tendency to apply the substantive standard to a somewhat different category of child in settings removed from the exigencies of the delivery room. The strategy of waiting for evidence to accumulate on the prospects of individual children will have the practical effect of postponing decisionmaking, so decisions will be made for somewhat older infants. Waiting for the evidence to come in will also mean that the question of withholding or withdrawing treatment may have to be raised for many children who have bonded with their parents and caregivers and left the neonatal ICU [intensive care unit] for other settings, such as the general pediatrics service, a long-term care facility, or even the child's home.

Notwithstanding its evident merits, this particular conjunction of substantive standard and decisionmaking strategy will have its costs. First, it will tend to be more expensive than the statistical approach, since it will usually require the initiation of costly medical treatment for all children whose best interests and relational potential cannot be judged at delivery or in the neonatal ICU.

"The relational potential standard permits the withholding or withdrawing of therapy from infants who lack the potential for human relationships."

Second, it will most likely exacerbate the anguish and pain of parents and health care providers, because decisions will more often be made after the child's caregivers have bonded with the child and come to regard him or her as more than a mere bundle of possibilities. Once a child has achieved some sort of identity and entered into a well-defined social role, decisions to terminate life-sustaining treatments will no doubt be even more disturbing and anxiety-producing than they are at present. Still, considering what is at stake, perhaps a heightened sense of anxiety is appropriate for such exceedingly difficult decisions.

The Best Policy

In spite of these difficulties, we conclude that a "best interest/relational potential" standard combined with a strategy of "individualized approach" is the best policy. Endorsing this combination does not answer in the abstract the question of how reliable predictions must be in order to justify withdrawing treatment in particular cases. Nor does it do away with the inevitable trade-offs entailed by these dilemmas. But the only way to avoid tragic results is to oversimplify these dilemmas. Because parents will be the ones who have to live with the result, whether it is fortunate or is something everyone concerned would rather have avoided, there must be some range within which parents can choose how much risk they can tolerate and how much pain they, and their baby, can bear.

Arthur L. Caplan is the director of the Center for Biomedical Ethics at the University of Minnesota.

"It is invariably in the child's best interest to provide life-saving medical treatment."

viewpoint 2

Disabled Newborns Must Not Be Allowed To Die

Patrick Wiseman

The death, just over five years ago, of an infant in Indiana known to the public only as "Infant Doe" was noteworthy almost as much for the furor it occasioned as for the tragedy of the event itself. The debate over withholding treatment from handicapped infants continues today with as much vigor as ever, and courts address ever more difficult questions of life and death.

Infant Doe was born with "reparable esophageal atresia and tracheoesophageal fistula," a condition in which the esophagus is obstructed, thus preventing normal eating. The surgery to correct this condition is relatively simple. Infant Doe was born, however, with Down syndrome, a genetic condition frequently associated with mental retardation. Whether a child born with Down syndrome will have retardation, and, if so, to what degree, cannot be determined at birth. Nonetheless, Infant Doe's parents, operating on the assumption that their son would be retarded, and following the advice of physicians, decided to withhold from their son the surgery which would have permitted him to eat normally and the intravenous feeding which would have kept him alive in the interim. The Indiana courts deferred to the parental judgment that life with retardation is worse than death. As a consequence, Infant Doe died six days after his parents declined to authorize surgery.

The death of Infant Doe was by no means an isolated event. Withholding treatment from "severely defective newborns" has probably long been standard medical practice. In 1973, [Raymond S.] Duff and [A.G.M.] Campbell reported on the frequency with which decisions not to treat were made in the special-care nursery of the Yale/New Haven Hospital, thus documenting the extent of the practice.

Patrick Wiseman, "Denial of Treatment to Handicapped Newborns: In Whose Interest?" *Georgia State Law Review*, Spring/Summer 1987. Reprinted with permission.

Infant Doe's death provoked national debate on the morality and legality of decisions to withhold medical treatment from infants born with significant potentially handicapping conditions. In response, several state legislatures passed bills regulating the practice. The Infant Doe case also provoked a flurry of activity from the federal government, including the issuance by the Department of Health and Human Services of detailed regulations prohibiting the discriminatory denial of treatment to handicapped newborns.

A Poor Decision

Despite all the legislative activity and the extensive commentary, the justification for deciding to withhold treatment from children such as Infant Doe remains obscure. It is this author's judgment that the Indiana courts, in deferring to a parental judgment that life with retardation is worse than death, decided wrongly. The purpose of this contribution is to articulate some reasons for this conclusion and to persuade others of the cogency of those reasons. In the following sections the context in which decisions to withhold treatment are made is briefly described, and the competing interests of the various parties to the decision are examined. It is concluded that, in cases like Infant Doe's, it is invariably in the *child's* best interests to receive defect-correcting medical treatment even though the child will probably be handicapped....

Our ability to decide whether to treat babies who are born with various physical problems is, in many cases, a very recent phenomenon. With advances in medical science and technique, children now survive who, not many years ago, would have died. The decision, as one commentator has expressed it, has become not whether we can treat, but whether we should. Thus, having the power to treat, the question has arisen whether we should always exercise it, or whether we may be selective. In this context, the

death / dying 7

question naturally arises, if we may be selective, on what basis and by what standards may we make the selection? Some commentators have proposed criteria for deciding not to treat and others have devised models of decision making. Still others have proposed procedural plans which should be followed to ensure that the decision not to treat be the correct one.

As a practical matter, the decision not to treat a child born with a significant potentially handicapping condition is usually made by parents acting on the advice of physicians. The physician, already a powerful figure to whom patients and families frequently defer, is highly influential in the parents' decision-making process. Furthermore, physicians, faced with a situation similar to that of Infant Doe, will frequently defer to parental judgment that treatment be withheld. When physicians were invited to assume "complete anonymity" and "no constraint by existing laws," only five percent of them, presented with a case similar to Infant Doe's, expressed the preference that everything possible be done to preserve life; twenty percent would have opted for active euthanasia. Furthermore, most of the physicians surveyed not only expected that an infant born with Down syndrome would "present a clear threat to family integration" and "experience a poor quality of life with little social value," but also viewed these expectations as justification for allowing the child to die.

Doe Would Have Lived

Infant Doe was a child who, if treated, would have enjoyed a life of relatively normal span, and who would have been, in one way or another and to some degree or another, handicapped. It is with such cases that this article is concerned. Not addressed are other related issues, such as whether treatment may be withheld from a child or adult who has a terminal illness and who will therefore die in a short period of time whether treated or not. Also not discussed are questions concerning the right of terminally ill patients to be withdrawn from life-support systems. Although some of the considerations may be similar, courts have recognized that the situations are different in several relevant respects: the newborn child has had no opportunity to express a desire concerning treatment, and the purpose of treatment of the newborn infant is to cure or alleviate a condition, not merely to prolong life. Also not discussed are cases alleging "wrongful life" or "wrongful birth," even though the acknowledgment of such causes of action by some courts is perhaps indicative of the trend evidenced in cases such as that of Infant Doe, showing a judicial willingness to evaluate the quality of a person's life. The discussion is restricted to children born with a fatal but treatable medical condition who, if treated, would enjoy lives of relatively normal span, and who would be, in one way or another and to some degree or another, handicapped. The question squarely presented by such cases is whether the potential handicap justifies a decision not to treat the medical condition.

The decision to withhold treatment, whether or not made explicitly on the basis of handicap, is usually characterized as a medical decision, based on such factors as diagnosis, prognosis, and feasibility of treatment. But the decision is not simply a medical one. As Robert Veatch has noted, the decision whether to treat does not rest solely on prognosis. "The decision," says Veatch, "must also include evaluation of the meaning of existence with varying impairments." He describes the presumption that the decision is a medical one as a "fallacious generalizing of the physician's expertise [in technical matters] to matters of moral and other value choices. . . ." The decision, then, far from being simply a medical decision, is a moral decision to which some medical information may be relevant. Even assuming accurate and infallible prognosis, the relevance of that prognosis to the treatment decision is mediated by social considerations. For example, if it could be known at the birth of an infant with Down syndrome and a reparable heart defect that he or she would have profound retardation, what significance does the likelihood of retardation have for deciding whether to repair the heart? There clearly are some relevant medical considerations, such as the child's strength and capacity to withstand surgery, but it is not clear how or why the fact that the child will most likely be profoundly retarded is one of them.

"Infant Doe . . . , if treated, would have enjoyed a life of relatively normal span."

The situation, if medically characterized, will evoke only medical responses: treat or not. Perhaps it would be better to characterize the situation to emphasize the social nature of the problem: some children are born whose condition at birth is such that they will require, in order to grow and develop, greater than ordinary supports and responses from the environment, and who also have a medically treatable condition which, if left untreated, will cause early death. This characterization of the situation has the advantage of bringing into sharper focus the medical and non-medical interests of the child and the relationship between the child's condition and the societal response to it. . . .

Most important among the interests of the child is the interest in life itself, an interest which enjoys constitutional recognition. As a constitutionally protected interest, the child's interest in life may not be denied without some semblance of due process, although what process is due may be open to debate. At the very least, however, due process requires that the child's interests be represented, perhaps by a guardian ad litem [in a suit or action], if the issue is litigated; by a surrogate parent; or by some other disinterested party (disinterested, that is, with respect to those interests which compete with the child's interests). Arguably, neither parent nor physician is in a sufficiently disinterested position to represent properly the interests of the child. The parents, quite appropriately, must consider the interests of the family; and the physician, being responsible to both mother and child as patients, ought not to be placed in the position of having to resolve any conflict of interest which may arise between parent and child. The same considerations suggest that neither physician nor parent can objectively decide that treatment should be withheld. Due process may require that any decision to withhold or withdraw treatment be subject to review by an interdisciplinary panel (such as a hospital ethics committee), a judge, or some other independent decision maker able to acknowledge the relevent interests. In any event the child has a constitutionally protected interest in being given the treatment which will preserve life.

But is it always in the child's best interest to live? Could it be that some kinds of life are, or would be, not worth living, and that it would therefore be in the child's interest to withhold treatment and so to allow him or her to die? Some commentators have indeed argued so. In distilled form, the argument is: (1) There is some, perhaps minimal, quality of life without which life is not worth living; (2) people with sufficiently severe handicapping conditions will, if they live at all, live lives which lack even this minimal quality; (3) their lives accordingly, are not worth living; (4) therefore, we may appropriately deny infants with these handicapping conditions the medical treatment which would keep them alive.

Quality of Life

Is there some quality, the lack of which, may make life not worth living? As [John A.] Robertson has noted, the claim that death is a better fate than life cannot be sustained in most cases. But, he says, some infants are so handicapped that their response to love and care, in fact their capacity to be conscious, is always minimal. "Although mongoloid and nonambulatory spina bifida children may experience an existence we would hesitate to adjudge worse than death, the profoundly retarded, nonambulatory, blind, deaf infant who will spend his few years in the back-ward cribs of a state institution is clearly a different matter."

What is it about the life of "the profoundly retarded, nonambulatory, blind, deaf infant who will spend his few years in the back-ward cribs of a state institution" which would lead us to have no hesitation in deeming that life to be worse than death? Is it his slowness to learn, his inability to walk, to see, or to hear? Or is it, perhaps, that his life will be spent "in the back-ward cribs of a state institution," a fate we should not wish on anyone?

Anthony Shaw has suggested a formula for estimating "quality of life": "QL=NE x (H+S), [where QL represents the quality of life and NE represents the natural endowment, physical and mental, of the individual under consideration and] where H and S represent the contributions *to* the infant under consideration from home (family) and society respectively."

"The child has a constitutionally protected interest in being given the treatment which will preserve life."

Shaw proposes the following application of his formula: "Clearly if the family of a baby with a Down's syndrome [sic] refused to care for it, and society's sole contribution is a crowded, filthy, understaffed warehouse, that infant's quality of life equals zero (NE x (0+0) = 0) just as surely as if it has been born an anencephalic."

In such a situation, says Shaw, "one might seriously question the desirability of correcting a duodenal atresia in such a baby." If the child did not have Down syndrome, the parents decided that they were either unwilling or unable to care for the child, and society's only response was a crowded, filthy, understaffed orphanage, would Shaw still question the desirability of treatment? If not, one wonders on what basis he would make the distinction. Reporting the results of a survey of physicians, Shaw concludes, "It is not surprising then that the degree of effort made by many physicians on behalf of some defective newborns is directly related to the willingness of families and/or communities to provide sufficient resources and support to compensate for these infants' deficient NE [natural endowment]."

A "Happiness" Criterion

Not all commentators so explicitly connect "quality of life" to society's response to a child's need for greater than ordinary support. [Richard] Brandt, for example, proposes for argument's sake a criterion which is not so explicitly based on "quality of life." Brandt calls his criterion a "happiness" criterion: "If a person *likes* a moment of experience while he is having it, his life is so far good; if a person *dislikes* a moment of experience while he is having it, his life is so far bad."

Based on such reactions we might construct a "happiness curve" for a person, going up above the indifference axis when a moment of experience is liked—and how far above depending on how strongly it is liked—and dipping down below the line when a moment is disliked. Then this criterion would say that a life is worth living if there is a net balance of positive area under the curve over a lifetime, and that it is bad if there is a net balance of negative area.

Applying this criterion to the prospective life of "the seriously defective newborn," Brandt concludes: "On the whole, the lives of such children are bad according to the happiness criterion," and so, "the lives of some defective newborns are destined to be bad on the whole, and it would be a favor to them if their lives were terminated." A person's "happiness," however, is, at least in part, a function of his environment even if, as Brandt maintains, a seriously defective newborn "will presumably suffer from severe sensory deprivation." Therefore, the "happiness criterion" does not escape the criticism that it places a burden on the handicapped child which ought properly to be placed on his social environment. Furthermore, the happiness criterion turns on a *prediction* that an infant's life will be "bad on the whole," a prediction which cannot reliably be made without reference to the child's environment.

Provide Life-Saving Treatment

Both Robertson and Shaw, and to a lesser degree, Brandt, apparently are prepared to contemplate denial of life-saving treatment to an infant with varying degrees of handicap on the basis that the response of family and society to handicapped people is to place them in "back-ward cribs" or in "crowded, filthy, understaffed warehouse[s]," or to make them unhappy. But allowing the decision whether to treat to turn on the adequacy of the family's or society's response, far from being in the child's best interests, simply begs the question as to the relative weights of the competing interests. A life cannot be legally deemed to be lacking in some necessary quality because society or family has made or deemed it so.

"The argument that it is in the child's best interest to withhold treatment fails to survive careful scrutiny."

The argument that it is in the child's best interest to withhold treatment fails to survive careful scrutiny. Insofar as all such arguments turn on the "quality" of the child's life and insofar as that quality is within society's and the family's control, and not within the control of the child, "allowing" the child to die begs the question of which of the competing interests is to be given the most weight.

Without the illegitimate reference to the inadequacy of social or familial responses to the child's need for greater than ordinary supports, then, it is invariably in the *child's* best interest to provide life-saving medical treatment.

Patrick Wiseman is assistant professor of law at Georgia State University College of Law, Atlanta.

"'What counts as a good reason for choosing death?'—given that in general death is an evil—is the question at the heart of the issue of euthanasia."

viewpoint 3

Ethical and Medical Issues in Euthanasia: An Overview

Arthur Zucker

Very few of us look forward to dying. No matter what we may believe about what happens after death, we do know that once dead, our earthly options are ended. It is this lack of future potential that is probably responsible for the feeling that death is an evil—an evil to be avoided at just about any cost. Yet there are exceptions to this belief. Some people risk death in order to intensify their enjoyment of life. Some people risk death as part of a chosen profession. Still other people actually choose death rather than face the certain travails of life. The question "What counts as a good reason for choosing death?"—given that in general death is an evil—is the question at the heart of the issue of euthanasia. But it is not the only question at the heart of the euthanasia issue....

Some Euthanasia Cases

Following the philosopher [Ludwig] Wittgenstein, who emphasized how difficult it was to find definitions for fuzzy concepts, we shall begin with cases which exemplify the "problem of euthanasia."

> I was called to the newborn nursery to see Baby C, whose father was a busy surgeon with three teen-aged children. The diagnoses of imperforate anus and microencephalus were obvious. Doctor C called me after being informed of the situation by the pediatrician. "I'm not going to sign that op permit," he said. When I didn't reply, he said, "What would you do, Doctor, if he were your baby?" "I wouldn't let him be operated on either," I replied. Palliative support only was provided, and the infant died 48 hours later.
>
> Brother Fox was an alert and active 83-year-old priest when he was hospitalized for the surgical repair of an inguinal hernia. As the procedure was nearing its conclusion, Brother Fox suffered a cardiac arrest. In spite of [prompt treatment] Brother Fox sustained substantial brain damage. He became comatose and showed little signs of ever regaining a state of sapience or consciousness.... Father Eichner, who had known Brother Fox for many years, asked the hospital to discontinue the respirator.
>
> A young, ex-marine pilot, who thrived on his good looks and athletic ability was severely burned in a freak gasoline accident. In that accident, his father, to whom he was very close, was killed. After a year of painful treatment for his burns, the young man was just as adamant as he was when first taken to the hospital: Please let me die. The pain of the treatment would in no way be compensated for by the low quality of life in store: little vision, little mobility, and very severe scarring.
>
> An elderly man, dying of cancer of the jaw, asks for enough pain killer to be fatal. He sees no difference between being unconscious and pain free and being dead. Since these have become the only real options for him, he asks for a swifter death....

A traditional four-fold distinction is almost always made at the beginning of every discussion of euthanasia. When a person asks for euthanasia, we refer to this as voluntary euthanasia in contrast to involuntary euthanasia. Perhaps some instances of capital punishment by lethal injections can be considered involuntary euthanasia. When the euthanasia involves a clear action, e.g., firing a shotgun at one's brother who has Alzheimer's disease, the euthanasia is classified as active. This is to be distinguished from less clear cases of direct action, e.g., writing the order on a patient's chart "No Code." This, in turn, can be distinguished from deciding (with or without the patient's consent) never even to begin treatment. These sorts of cases are classified as passive....

Passive vs. Active Euthanasia

In a now classic article, James Rachels argues as follows. The distinction between active and passive euthanasia will not hold up to analysis. It is easy to show that morally the two are equivalent. He shows this by example. Consider Smith, who stands to gain a fortune should his six-year-old cousin die. Smith murders his cousin by drowning him while he is

Arthur Zucker, "The Right to Die: Ethical and Medical Issues," *Dying: Facing the Facts*. New York: Hemisphere Publishing, 1988. Reprinted with permission.

taking a bath. Now suppose that with the same plan, Smith enters the bathroom, but before he can do a thing, the little boy slips in the tub, hits his head, goes under the water, and drowns. Smith makes no attempt to save his cousin. Rachels claims that Smith is equally as immoral in both cases. Thus, the active/passive distinction fails to hold water.

K.D. Clouser, in a veiled reply, points out that what makes the case of a physician different from the case of the uncle is that it is clear that the uncle has a moral duty to save his nephew from drowning. It is precisely the fact that there is a clear duty to save that makes both styles of killing wrong. Often, in cases of euthanasia, it is not clear what the duty on the part of the physician is. It is in these sorts of cases where active (killing) and passive (letting die) may not be moral equivalents. If there is even the hint of a duty to save, then a clear action (to kill) almost certainly must be different from a passive (letting die). A case will help make this point.

"The moral standing of euthanasia is in part a function of how particular physicians view their duties and responsibilities."

Consider an 83-year-old diabetic woman. The disease has been getting worse and worse. She is losing her vision to diabetic retinopathy and now one of her legs is gangrenous. Her leg must be amputated, or she will die. When she enters the hospital, she is lucid and determined. She will die, i.e., she will refuse the option of surgery. Her life is getting more and more restricted by her disease and by the resulting circumstances. Moreover, she now will become even more of a burden on her son and daughter-in-law with whom she lives. Her son has mixed feelings about whether to respect his mother's wishes. The resident in charge of the case feels that she definitely has a moral and legal right to die. The attending physician believes that she has a right to die but not on his service, when her life can so easily be saved. It is not obvious that she should be allowed to die. It, therefore, cannot be the case that she should be killed, e.g., given an overdose of morphine. This particular case also shows that the moral standing of euthanasia is in part a function of how particular physicians view their duties and responsibilities.

Crossing the Line

Another case will illustrate even more clearly that the doctor's obligations are involved in deciding when and how physicians should hasten the deaths of their patients. Emma was a 64-year-old retired department store executive. She was suffering from the last stages of emphysema. Although the use of a ventilator had been put off as long as possible, it was felt that she now needed the ventilator. She agreed; she also agreed to a tracheotomy. However, this sort of existence soon depressed her. After a few weeks, she asked to be taken off the respirator. Her physician said that this would be her decision. Emma, who realized that her death off the ventilator would be difficult, asked her physician for "a drug or something" to ease the discomfort. The physician refused.

Catch Phrases

The physician had no trouble withdrawing life-sustaining therapy (the respirator) but could not administer a drug to make the death "easy." He couldn't give the drug because it would be, in his mind, tantamount to killing her because it became clear that she wouldn't let herself die otherwise. (The physician was not punishing the woman. He agonized over his feelings. He wanted to give her the drug, but he just couldn't do it.) To this physician there was a real line between active and passive euthanasia—a line which he just could not cross. To him, anything that was clearly a killing could not be part of medicine. It did not matter that the killing would make dying easier. For this physician when the principles, "do not kill" and "alleviate suffering," clashed, the choice was clear. "Do not kill" took precedence even if it caused (resulted in) suffering. The clash of moral rules will almost always create problems. . . .

Sometimes in discussion of euthanasia the expression "death with dignity" occurs. Tacked onto rights talk, one gets "Isn't there a right to a death with dignity?" Dignity is probably a very idiosyncratic concept. To some people, dying is not dignified and that is the end of the matter. To others, getting undressed and being probed by physicians is the height of indignity. It is not at all clear that there is anything intrinsically undignified about being hooked to monitors, machines, intravenously delivered drugs, etc. Whatever indignity there is as a result of such treatment is related to the patient's not wanting the treatment or to having little chance of restoring the health (even for a short while) of the patient. Death with dignity is likely best filled out as a death in the style chosen (or negotiated for). Usually, the indignity is a violation of a patient's desire to be left alone; a violation of autonomy or a violation of good sense, i.e., the patient's privacy is invaded by medical technology when there is not sufficient reason for believing that the gains, given the cost, would be chosen by the patient.

Opposed to death with dignity is another catch phrase, the sanctity of life. Sanctity of life is used to mean that each and every life has infinite importance and value and, therefore, that it is always wrong to take life or to hasten death. Embedded in this position is the idea that we do not have the moral authority to set the value of our lives. In a way, what this principle suggests is that we do not own our lives in any way analogous to the way that we own our cars and television sets. Cars can be trashed if they upset us enough. But our lives can't be snuffed out even for the (apparently) best reasons. A physician who held a sanctity-of-life principle would be opposed to all forms of euthanasia. It is important to recognize that the sanctity-of-life principle, while ruling out euthanasia as legitimate, does not imply that the physician is "in charge" of lives. It is rather that no one is "in charge" except to save and to prolong....

We find lack of a mental life, especially total lack, to be such a detriment that it seems to lead inexorably to a decision to let die. Thus, it is not surprising that if we discover that the *entire* brain is dead, then we find the fact that the rest of the body can be supported not enough reason to begin or even to continue life support. This claim needs some emendations. We have to be quite convinced that the medical criteria for whole brain death are accurate and precise, and that, of course, they have been met. We also need consent from the patient or from the next of kin. Naturally, one cannot get consent from a patient whose brain is dead. However, there are situations where the patient made his/her wishes known. There are also cases where there was a known risk of brain damage and, therefore, the issue was specifically discussed with the patient.

"What I might want, whether I am physician, husband, father, or daughter, can be relevant only if I am reasonably certain that my desires, feelings, emotions, etc. are relatively like those of the patient."

Irreversible coma differs from brain death in that the criteria for whole brain death are not met. Rather criteria are met which indicate that the patient will never again regain what we understand as full consciousness. Often it is said that the patient is in a permanent vegetative state. What makes irreversible coma more troublesome than whole brain death is that such patients may have some mental states.

If science proceeded to the point where it was possible to say that only the part of the brain responsible for mental life was destroyed, then we might feel that such a patient was no longer a person. That is, as the expression "vegetative state" implies, there is a distinction between a person and a vegetable in that (presumably) the main difference is the possibility of self-consciousness, what has been called "mental life," in the person. Turnips and carrots may have some similarity in anatomical structure and physiological mechanism to humans. But the similarity (most likely) ends there. Just as "person" has a legal meaning, so it might be claimed, does it have a moral force? A person, by virtue of being a person, has certain rights and expectations. But when the biological basis of personhood is lost forever and there is no longer any possibility for a mental life, then we have not a person but a body. It is not at all clear that bodies, qua bodies, have or ought to have rights, e.g., to be kept "alive."

Deciding on Life-Support

A problem has been skirted in this discussion. How can we decide that a body with no mental life is not worth life support? There are at least four ways. 1) It just may not be worth the effort—in solely economical terms. This may sound harsh. But in a world where not everything can be done at once, this sort of consideration cannot be postponed forever. 2) We can perform three sorts of thought experiments: (a) Would this patient, given what we know, want to continue in a vegetative state? (b) Would I want to continue in a vegetative state? and (c) Would anyone want to continue in a vegetative state? The three thought experiments require some further analysis.

Clearly (a) calls for a good doctor-patient relationship. Especially where the question was not specifically asked, the opinion of the physician will have to depend on information gleaned from knowledge of the patient (and family). Naturally, we are assuming that the physician has been asked something like "What should we do?" by the family, for it is their decision to make unless there are specific requests by the patient.

What I might want, whether I am physician, husband, father, or daughter, can be relevant only if I am reasonably certain that my desires, feelings, emotions, etc. are relatively like those of the patient. What anyone would want seems to have the advantage of being general. But this generality carries problems with it. Does "anyone" refer to the average person? Does anyone mean all people like the patient? Or does anyone mean any rational person? The last question brings with it all the difficulties of deciding what is the best characterization of rational.

The point of this philosophical diversion is this. Sometimes we are forced to make important judgments for other people. It is essential to understand the principles involved in making decisions for others. In other words, we have come to the issue of paternalism, an issue which many authors see as the central one for understanding many of the more difficult medical-ethical cases.

In general, how do we justify what we do for others when we aren't sure whether they want to be left alone by us or not? This question ranges from a forced Caesarean in the interests of the fetus to withholding some frightening information from a patient about to undergo surgery. The middle ground is faced more often. When do we try to influence others even if they do not ask for help? Nozick defines paternalism as a *prima facie* infringement on liberty. In his *Anarchy, State and Utopia,* he says:

> My nonpaternalistic position holds that someone may choose (or permit another) to do to himself *anything* unless he has acquired an obligation to some third party not to do or allow it.

The rider is meant to show how to justify paternalism. The justification would include a discussion of obligations, both professional and general, and how they are acquired. In general, where liberty is restrained, the burden should be put on the restrainer to justify interference. Otherwise, morality would become the morality of the strong.

[B.] Gert gives the following characterization of paternalism:

> A is acting paternalistically toward S if and only if A's behavior (correctly) indicated that A believes that (1) his action is for S's good; (2) he is qualified to act on S's behalf; (3) his action involves violating a moral rule (or will require him to do so) with regard to S; (4) S's good justifies him in acting on S's behalf independently of S's past, present, or immediately forthcoming (free, informed) consent; and (5) S believes (perhaps falsely) that he (S) generally knows what is for his own good....

Gert goes on to say:

> Being deprived of freedom is simply being deprived of an indefinite number of opportunities. Being deprived of an opportunity is simply being deprived of the freedom to do some particular thing.

Gert offers the following as a justification for paternalistic intervention:

> (A necessary condition is that) it must also be true that the evils that would be prevented to S are so much greater than the evils, if any, that would be caused by the violation of the rule, that it would be irrational for S not to want to have the rule violated with regard to himself. But even this is not sufficient: To make it sufficient one must also be able to universally allow the violation of this rule in these circumstances, or, in somewhat more technical terminology, be able to publicly advocate this kind of violation....

With even more technical philosophy on line, we can move on to our next set of cases.

Terminal Patients

Let us examine the category of terminal patients first. Obviously, we should settle on a characterization of terminal: A disease is terminal when cure is unlikely given the a) survival time of similar patients from time of diagnosis and b) research state of the art at the time of diagnosis. There is a relatively direct causal chain, so it can be established that death was due to the disease and that death occurred sooner than would have been expected or predicted if the disease had not been present.

We immediately have a further distinction. Some terminal patients are not near death. If they are not near death and if they have some "quality of life" ahead, should we—as physicians—accede to their request to be left to die? That is, suppose such a patient prefers no treatment, where treatment will extend life. Should a physician agree and do nothing else? Is it part of the professional or general moral obligation of a physician to make some effort to persuade this patient to undergo therapy? Is it (usually) the patient's legal right to refuse treatment? When treatment has already been started, then it is usually more difficult for the physician to stop treatment, when requested, without also attempting to change the patient's mind. Perhaps it should be easier to "give in" to the patient's wishes because at least he or she has tried.

"Part of the decision will be the kind of dying in store for the individual."

Naturally, part of the decision will be the kind of dying in store for the individual. Life shortly after diagnoses and initiation of treatment may be acceptable, whereas the prognosis may hold in store a relatively long and painful death—even a short but intensely painful death is exceedingly unpleasant as one's inevitable future. Shouldn't it be the patient's right to decide that the pain of the dying just isn't worth the quality of life up until that time?

Is the best reason for euthanasia in these cases a) being terminal; b) the perception of unpleasantness and the pain that lies ahead; c) the actual unpleasantness and pain? If one chooses a) or b), then euthanasia would seem to be justified before the point of closeness of dying is reached. If one chooses c), then euthanasia, it would seem, would have to wait until the time of dying....

Rejecting Life

What of patients who are so unhappy with their physical conditions that, even though they are not terminal, they wish to die? Cases will help here, since this is a category not obvious to those outside the medical profession. Some patients have chronic diseases that get more and more debilitating, e.g., diabetes. As we saw, a patient with advancing diabetes might choose to die rather than to have life-saving surgery for a gangrenous leg. The thought of an even more crippling existence can be just too much. Other patients, often because of trauma, are forced to realize that to remain alive will be to accept a totally new lifestyle. For example, in the play (and movie) "Whose Life Is It Anyhow?" a young sculptor is injured in a car accident. Once vigorous, he now can move only his head. What lies ahead for him is a life of total dependence—certainly a life devoid of sculpting. Should he reject this "new" life before he actually gives it a try? What are the obligations of his physicians?

Instead of asking "Does he have a right to reject this new life?" we ask, "Should he reject the new life without giving it a try?" Isn't he giving up in the face of adversity and asking the medical profession to give up as well? On the other hand, is it the job of the medical profession to create moral fiber in such patients?

Applying the quality-of-life principle and assuming that it is a judgment to be made by the patient yields one answer: let him die. Applying the sanctity-of-life principle that any life is inestimably precious and, therefore, to be saved at all costs, yields another answer: don't let him die. These two ways of approaching the problem yield conflict, which is not surprising, since, in a sense, they are principles constructed in such a way that they must conflict.

There are other approaches. A cost-benefit analysis would give an answer. Flipping a coin would give another answer. The point of using two approaches which give conflicting results is to remind ourselves that moral problems often come from choices of principle and that those choices rarely lead to compromise, since principles are so often stated in absolutist terms. Loosening the concept of a moral principle to "other things equal, do X (or don't do Y)" helps, but only if we can clearly spell out the riders—"other things equal" or "within reason." For example, if we considered the principle, "Within reason, don't let mentally alert and physically stable patients die," would we apply it in this case? a) Is such a patient truly stable? b) Is such a rule really meant to apply to such severely injured patients? c) Can we ignore the rule when a mentally alert patient asks us? That is, isn't this patient too depressed to be considered competent? Obviously, a teenager who could no longer play tennis and asked to be allowed to die for that reason alone, would be rebuffed, but the sculptor and the burn victim (from the introduction) may have compelling reasons. The rules and the riders don't supply answers.

Searching for a Middle Ground

Is there a middle ground, a way to avoid choosing between the application of conflicting principles? Wouldn't it be at least rational to suggest to such a patient that a new life is worth a try? If it turns out to be as dismal as it now appears, then "letting die" can again be discussed as a live option. The importance of this strategy is that it shows to the patient that the medical profession can be supportive and not merely adversarial. While this strategy does not yield total control to the patient, neither does it emphasize what is often felt as a total lack of control. Indeed, some requests for euthanasia can easily be reinterpreted as requests for return of some self-control—a return of autonomy and, in this sense, dignity. The very offer may be enough to change an intended course of action. It may not, but at least it makes discussion real and more than just talk.

The cases of terminal patients can be handled in a similar fashion. As long as there is a trustworthy doctor-patient relationship, there can be an agreement to the effect that if the dying becomes unbearable, especially due to pain, then the idea of "letting die" will be seriously considered. It should be clear, however, that this strategy will not satisfy someone who wants to die now or, at least, soon. Before dealing with "direct" killing, let us deal with the question of when, if ever, it is permissible to withhold food and water from a patient, since it will lead us to one approach to an answer about "direct killing."

In 1986, in New Jersey, a judge ruled that food and water could be withheld from a 31-year-old woman who had been in a vegetative state for six years. Her husband had petitioned the court for the right to stop "treatment." Withholding food and water, unlike stopping chemotherapy for cancer, will necessarily lead to death. Because of this, it can be held that withholding food and water is equivalent to active killing. Since active killing is never allowed neither should the withdrawing of food and water. It may be that legally there is no difference between mechanical ventilation and "artificial" feeding. Still, there is a moral difference based on the inevitability of death when feeding is discontinued.

"Applying the quality-of-life principle and assuming that it is a judgment to be made by the patient yields one answer: Let him die. Applying the sanctity-of-life principle . . . yields another answer: Don't let him die."

What has to be understood in evaluating this argument is that when life-sustaining treatment, e.g., a ventilator, is removed, one has every good reason to expect that death will ensue. Surprises occur. But surprises cannot be used to claim that the reasoning was fallacious or that one should never act on good reasons. For then, no action would ever be possible. Thus, the argument that withholding food and water is of a different moral ilk from withholding mechanical ventilation is, at best, a weak argument.

There is, however, another sort of argument to shore-up the claim that food and water must never be withheld or withdrawn. This argument turns on a characterization of medicine as a profession.

According to this line of reasoning, medicine's primary goal is to preserve life at all costs. Lives should be saved and bettered, if at all possible; but above all, lives must never be ended by interfering with the natural course of events. Since feeding is natural (as is breathing), it follows that just about any mechanical intervention is justified and may never be withdrawn once started. Indeed, they must also be started whenever available. Without the presumption that lives must be preserved, the trust which makes up the core of the doctor-patient relationship would be corroded to the point where medicine as a profession would be impossible. At least, without the idea of "preserve all lives" at its core, we would no longer recognize the profession of medicine. . . .

"The perplexing questions surrounding euthanasia are certainly ones for moral philosophy."

Can we kill a patient directly? Here we are being told "no," and the reason has to do with the nature of the medical profession and its role in society. This complex line of reasoning is difficult to analyze. It turns on facts, e.g., how do residents in oncology really feel about patients near death? It turns on values, e.g., what is the proper attitude worth instilling in young physicians? It turns on a view of the goals of medicine as if those goals can be determined only by the practitioners. Although this pattern of reasoning should not be dismissed out of hand, it is clear that if patients have some say in what the goals of medicine should be, then much of the force of the above argument is lost. Again, we are reminded that medicine as a profession should grow out of an agreement between two parties. Once the doctor-patient relationship is opened to negotiation, then some physicians might be persuaded to kill and still others might find a different ground of agreement with the patient. The value of seeing the source of the disagreement and being willing to deal with the disagreement is that it is the only real way to ensure an open, nondogmatic approach, not only by the physician but also by the patient.

The perplexing questions surrounding euthanasia are certainly ones for moral philosophy. Yet it must be remembered that these perplexing questions grow out of personal relationships, out of deeply felt needs, desires, emotions, and fears. It would be easy to forget these factors while concentrating on the conceptual analysis of moral philosophy. . . .

Rights and Duties

If X is right, then people with that right have another right: the right not to have their right to X interfered with. The right creates in the rest of us a duty not to interfere. On a different view, if X is a right, then those with that right have another right: the right to have help in exercising their right to X. This right creates in the rest of us a positive duty to help others exercise their rights. As if this weren't complex enough, some rights are probably more central than others. The right to park in my allotted parking space is not nearly as important as my right to be treated by, and not turned away from, an emergency room when I am bleeding to death.

Implicitly, this [viewpoint] has tried to show that one has to choose between the two pictures of rights given above. That done, one must also distinguish between the rights and duties which bind us all and those rights and duties which spring from professions, i.e., from special contexts. None of this can be abstracted from the fact that the context of "the right to die" is an exceedingly personal one. Its context demands attention to the human relations which make up the doctor-patient relationship.

None of this is satisfying if one sought a clear and easy answer. But to seek a clear and easy answer is only to ensure a dissatisfaction which is more likely to lead one astray than is the tortuous path to legitimate understanding.

Arthur Zucker is a professor of philosophy at Ohio University in Athens, Ohio.

"I absolutely believe that physicians must be willing, on occasion, to take an active role in the process of death."

viewpoint 4

Physicians Should Practice Active Euthanasia

Phillip J. Miller

Those of us who are products of Western intellectual history and the Judaeo-Christian ethic have been nurtured on the idea that the unity-in-duality of human experience is a result of our animal/angelic natures; we are inseparably body and spirit. In addition, we have come to believe that a celebration of either half of our dual natures is a simultaneous celebration of the other half, that the essence of our humanity is an ecstasy that bridges the gap between the carnal and the ethereal.

In recognising our dual natures, we have also recognised that those ecstasy-producing experiences, those sublime and lofty moments of humanity, are themselves dual in nature; they are personal and private at the same time that they are vehicles for sharing. Thus sexual, spiritual, and intellectual consummations are private activities which provide fruits to be shared by the community. Such events as births, marriages, church services, art shows, concerts, and book publications all allow the community to have some share in the private experiences of its individual members, and at the same time serve as catalysts to inspire and encourage other individuals to engage in those private experiences.

The idea that our lives are both private and public has a strong foundation in Western literature. Every time I pick up one of the ten or so volumes of John Donne's sermons and meditations, I am struck by the incredible sense of community that he sees in his life as a Christian. In one of his most famous meditations, the one on the ringing of the church bells when a parishioner dies, he says that we should not inquire after the specific identity of the deceased when a death-knell is tolled. When death occurs, it is community and not individuality that should be celebrated because 'no man is an island'; each of us is 'a piece of the continent, a part of the main', and we are all diminished when part of our mainland is washed away. Therefore, 'ask not for whom the bell tolls; it tolls for thee'. By implication, of course, we are likewise increased when a new grain of sand washes ashore in the form of a birth.

The Effects of Technology

Western literature from Geoffrey Chaucer to Ken Kesey is full of examples of the importance of community in the celebrations of life. But the attitudes towards, and definitions of, community are far different for Chaucer and his contemporaries than for Kesey and his. Chaucer's pilgrims are, collectively and individually, microcosmic reflections of the larger community, England. They may be from different social and economic classes, but they share an established and fixed view of the important spiritual and moral ends of life. They may violate the precepts imposed by their heritage, but they do so, for the most part, fully aware of what they are doing and willing to accept the consequences of their actions.

In *One Flew Over the Cuckoo's Nest*, the ward group may also be a microcosm of the larger community, but here it is a community turned topsy-turvy. Life on the ward is a barren and carefully controlled chaos whose hallmark is stratification. Rules have become ends in themselves, existing only to preserve a sterile environment in which patients can talk but never communicate, can smile but never laugh, can feel sadness and fear but never weep. In short, the ward is a well-oiled machine that does nothing even when it runs well; that functions simply for the sake of functioning. Not so Chaucer's world, where there is life, vitality, and purpose, where meaning is more important than ritual, where breakdowns are repaired by a laugh, a handshake, a kiss, or a shared drink.

Phillip J. Miller, "Death with Dignity and the Right to Die: Sometimes Doctors Have a Duty to Hasten Death," *Journal of Medical Ethics*, June 1987. Reprinted with permission.

As I see it, a sense of community as Chaucer and Donne envisioned it is no longer possible in modern industrial societies. Technology has created a kind of mobility, both physical and intellectual, that renders the traditional associations of community both meaningless and inappropriate. Indeed, it seems to me nearly absurd for urban newspapers to provide (or impose upon) their thousands of readers announcements of such things as weddings, births, and deaths, items which could not possibly interest people who feel no kinship to the names catalogued before them, people who commonly travel electronic airways worldwide for their news and entertainment. Such newspaper 'services' are an anachronistic attempt to convince us (or to reinforce our conviction) that we live in traditional communities.

However, there are people who touch our lives in profound ways, small communities if you will, that still can and should function in the traditional way. It is on one of these groups, health care professionals, and its response to the process and event of death, that I want to focus.

Death Is a Part of Life

One of the problems of discussing death today is the variety of associations, nearly all of which are negative, that people make with it. Let me use as a modern touchstone of this negative view the comments by Professor Paul Ramsey in *The Indignity of 'Death with Dignity'.* Ramsey argues that the very phrase 'Death with dignity' is a contradiction in terms because death is the ultimate human indignity.

"One of the duties of the medical professional is to aid patients in the achievement of that important, positive, end-beginning of human experience called death."

For theistic substantiation of this view, Professor Ramsey goes to the preacher in Ecclesiastes, from whom he quotes extensively in order to conclude that 'to deny the indignity of death requires that the dignity of man be refused also. The more acceptable in itself death is, the less the worth or uniqueness ascribed to the dying life'. For humanistic substantiation Ramsey again goes primarily to the scriptures in order to illustrate the traditional link between sin and death. The idea, of course, is that since death is punishment for sin, it is evil. No one, after all, could be expected to view punishment for sin or any other evil as anything but an indignity. Indeed, the whole purpose of punishment is to diminish dignity, to deny the punished some degree of autonomy accorded those not being punished. To those who would argue that death is simply a part of life, and therefore no more undignified than other parts of life, Ramsey responds by saying that we do not ennoble such common life experiences as disease, injury, congenital defects, murder, pillage, and rapine.

Ramsey is certainly accurate; no one would talk about murder or disease or any of the others as worthy human aims. But what he fails to note is that these experiences are 'part of life' only in a communal sense. Robert S. Morison and Leon Kass have taken issue with Ramsey's conclusion. Many, indeed most, individuals are able to avoid them, even though no society can do so. However, what I intend by 'part of life' is this essay consists only of those things which may not be avoided by any individual—not those things which are collectively and publicly experienced.

In short, it is my contention that death is a good, as are all other aspects of human life that cannot be avoided by individuals: our births, our appetites, our instincts, our biological functions. This is not to say that these features of life cannot be, and often are, vitiated, corrupted, diverted, in all sorts of ways by all sorts of people. It is to say, however, that one of the duties of the medical professional is to aid patients in the achievement of the important, positive, end-beginning of human experience called death.

Death and the Community

In "The Counsels of Finitude," a perceptive and insightful essay on the sociological and individual importance of death, H. Tristram Engelhardt, Jr. discusses the relationship between the individual and the community concerning death. In his brief synthesis of the Platonic, Christian, and Hegelian attitudes towards human finitude, Engelhardt concludes that we humans should:

> act always to ensure that the general achievement of cultural values by humans is not precluded by the investment of resources and energies in postponing death. The ways in which health and disease can effect such achievement of value is a question properly and best addressed by medicine, but yet it is always addressed in terms of finite goals: the elimination of painful or premature deaths, never death itself.

This comment was occasioned, at least in part, by Engelhardt's feeling that we do, in fact, invest too much of ourselves and our resources in postponing death. Why we do that is a difficult question; partly, I'm sure, for the science of it, for information about the dying process, medications, geriatrics, new technologies. But mostly, I suspect, out of a view that death is an unkind assault on poor old humanity, and something really should be done about it.

Again, Engelhardt's comment is perceptive. He

notes that in Hegel's philosophical system individual finitude was 'not to be transcended in the person of the individual, but was to be resolved through the values of the community ... which outlives the individual'. Thus:

> the attempt to secure physical immortality is likely to obscure the legitimate goal of humanity, the pursuit of a rich but finite life. Considering the large amount of energy expended in medical research and treatment, the issue of balance is unavoidable. One must remember that one prolongs the length of life so that certain values can be realised, not for the mere prolongation itself.

Now, if these assertions about the prolongation of life and the importance of quality in life are valid at all, then it is clearly possible to find instances in which death should be hastened for the sake of quality, quality for both the individual and society.

Eric Cassell points in this direction of balance in an essay in which he argues that physicians have an obligation to urge patients to accept death rather than treatment. Dr. Cassell uses one of his own patients, a woman near 80 whose final hospital stay and death took only nine days (the last three in a coma), to illustrate his position. Interestingly, he spends a good deal of time explaining that it is very hard for physicians to help patients accept death. 'The process strikes deep within and finds painful resonance in the doctor. It is difficult to find the proper words and yet absolute honesty is required—not honesty of words, like "cancer" or "death", which in any case mean more than they mean, but honesty of feelings'.

"There is a qualitative difference between being a dispenser of death and being a physician who will help a patient in the difficult process of dying."

Certainly Dr. Cassell is a sensitive and caring member of the health care profession, and certainly he is leaning in the right direction, but his comment strikes me as missing the mark because it fails to recognise the physician's duty, in some cases, to aid in hastening death rather than simply to urge the avoidance of treatment.

The Right To Die

Another serious problem in the philosophical and practical discussion of death is the 'right to die' issue. As I see it, the difficulty is that the phrase 'right to die' is at best problematic because of the associations that *right* suggests with duties and obligations. Let me give an example. Americans have decided that in America there is a right to food. But since food is traded on the free market, and since the free-market system imposes poverty on some citizens, the government was faced with a duty to devise a way to allow poor people to get their rightful food. Hence the creation of food stamps.

But there are numerous duties, obligations, and rights inherent in both sides of this complex of activities called feeding the country. Individuals have an obligation to both self and society (and I know some will disagree with me here) to eat foods that will promote health and abstain from foods that will decrease health. However, the government has a duty to protect its citizens from coercion in their choices of food. I have an obligation not to eat junk foods, but I certainly have a right to eat them, and the government has a duty to protect my right, even if it is at the same time providing me with the means to purchase my food.

But suppose I am in a hospital, unable to eat normally, and must be nourished by some sort of intravenous line or nasogastric tube. As long as I am not mortally ill, the people responsible for my care have a duty (not just an obligation) to provide me with the best nutrition that technology allows, given my condition. If I say to them, 'feed me a blended mixture of Twinkies, sugar-coated cereal, and a soft-drink', they have a duty not to do so because those foods are not nourishing.

The point is that eating is something that I must do to remain alive, and if I am unable to eat on my own, society has a series of duties and obligations to help me eat. In like manner, when it is time for me to die, the medical profession has a series of duties and obligations to aid me in achieving that end as an autonomous and dignified individual.

A Helping Physician

As Bernard Towers and others have argued, however, many physicians must feel that their only available means of fulfilling those duties and obligations is through the manipulation of technology. Their direct involvement with death seems bound by and limited to the occasional unplugging of some nasogastric tube or other device. Surely one reason for this perceived limitation is the long tradition in medicine that the physician not be cast, as Hans Jonas has said, in 'the role of a dispenser of death'.

Professor Jonas is surely right. I would certainly avoid any physician who had the reputation of being a dispenser of death. But the connotative value of Jonas's phrase is unfortunate. There is a qualitative difference between being a dispenser of death and being a physician who will help a patient in the difficult process of dying.

Leon Kass is also profoundly aware of the problem, and he is afraid that doctors might find themselves essentially removed from dying patients and forced to respond to the process of death 'under some form of external and uniform guidelines'. He feels that physicians have a duty 'to desist from useless procedures' for sustaining life, but his approach to the problem of death and dying is ambiguous. He is very much against the proliferation of rules which alter and diminish the traditional trust-based doctor-patient relationship. But he absolutely wants to retain those rules which prohibit direct intervention in order to hasten death.

Let me say categorically and with sincerest respect for human dignity that, while I am not for killing, I absolutely believe that physicians must be willing, on occasion, to take an active role in the process of death. They must do this to stop suffering (and I am untroubled by such breezy and flippant comments as: 'Oh, yes, eliminate suffering by eliminating the sufferer'), to protect autonomy, and to replace technology by real people in dying situations—in the belief that when I am breathing my last breath, it is better to be touched by a hand than violated by a tube. I want the process of death to be taken out of the control of machines and returned to people. We should, most assuredly, all be able to die, as we evacuate, ingest, respire, and procreate, with a sense of contentment and a feeling that what we are doing is in some small measure an affirmation of our humanity.

Hidden Intentions

Certainly no care-provider or surrogate would philosophically hope to do harm to a patient or to diminish autonomy or dignity by mechanical intervention. But there is often a distinction between what one will pay philosophical lip service to, and what one intends on a practical level. Often, instead of patient benefits, care-givers in fact intend one or more of the following when they begin mechanical interventions.

1. To buy time until a decison can be reached about what to do.
2. To genuflect (almost reflexively) in the direction of established and time-honoured methods—this is simply what one does in this situation.
3. To avoid possible malpractice suits.
4. To try some new material or method—to gain knowledge.

Surrogates, too, often intend practical outcomes that are not articulated in the decision-making process. The following are reasons I have heard (sometimes almost confessionally) from people who acted as spokespersons for others, and it should be noticed that not one of them focuses directly on benefits to the patient.

1. I would have felt guilty if I had not urged the doctors to do everything possible.
2. I could not stand the thought that X might have known that we did not do everything possible.
3. I would not want that done to me, but I did not know for sure that X didn't want it done.
4. It just seemed awful not to do anything, and that was all they could do.

Thus, while it is seldom the intention of health care professionals or surrogates to harm incompetent patients, it is also seldom that the decision to use available technology is made solely for the benefit of the patient. In saying this I do not intend to suggest that, therefore, such decisions should be reversed—more than likely they should not be. What I do intend is to urge both parties in the decision to examine motives, to talk freely about those motives, and to ask, finally, whether this intervention serves the autonomy, the comfort, and the dignity of the individual.

The point is that here, as in the case of competent patients, rights, duties, and obligations need to be considered carefully, with focus on the right of the patient to die without undue efforts to forestall death, and the duties and obligations of the health care professional to aid, when necessary, the process of death.

"We must be willing and prepared to take an active role in the dying process of certain people."

When precisely the doctor has a duty or obligation to hasten death (to kill, if you prefer), I do not know. I can only generalise by saying that patients have a right to die as dignified, thinking human beings and that most people would prefer that to dying as vegetables. Knowing when to act will be difficult for doctors, but surely they can handle the pressure, especially when the result will return some small measure of human dignity to the person participating in the event of his or her own death.

Phillip J. Miller is director of faculty research at the University of Tennessee at Martin.

"It is unnecessary to kill these people in order to provide them with comfort and compassion; much less should physicians be the ones to kill them."

viewpoint 5

Physicians Should Never Practice Active Euthanasia

D. Alan Shewmon

"Whatever proportions these crimes finally assumed... the beginnings at first were merely a subtle shift in emphasis in the basic attitude of the physicians... toward the nonrehabilitable sick."
Leo Alexander, M.D., the U.S. medical consultant at the Nuremberg Trials.

Many physicians remain unaware of the growing general interest in active euthanasia. It was approved by the Rotterdam Criminal Court in 1981, and there is heavy lobbying for its statutory legalization across Europe. Various U.S. "right-to-die" societies have been doing everything possible to create popularity for the issue, and their efforts have not gone entirely unrewarded. A California appellate court, in its *Bouvia* decision, not only asserted the right of an adult with severe disabilities to starve herself to death in a hospital, but went so far as to require the medical staff to assist her against their own consciences. Justice Compton's separate concurring opinion explicitly endorsed active euthanasia on general principles. In January 1987, lawyers for the American Civil Liberties Union petitioned a Colorado court for a lethal injection for Hector Rodas, claiming that he had a "constitutional right... to be provided with medicine and medicinal agents that would cause his death."

The reasons advanced in favor of euthanasia vary according to the audience. On TV talk shows and in newspaper articles, advocates usually emphasize extreme cases of terminally ill patients in great pain, who are kept alive against their wills by means of oppressive and invasive tubes and other technology. The President's Commission for the Study of Ethical Problems in Medicine and Biomedical and Behavioral Research (hereinafter President's Commission), however, emphasized that excessive pain, discomfort and anxiety are nearly always examples of inadequate treatment, not inadequate ethics. The experience of hospices also bears this out. In fact, even the euthanasia advocates themselves admit elsewhere that terminal pain is not the real reason for their efforts. In the words of Derek Humphry, cofounder of the Hemlock Society, "pain is by no means the only reason, if at all, why people contemplate self-deliverance, with or without assistance. Control and choice of when, where and how, plus personal dignity and a wish to avoid distress, physical and emotional, during the dying process are the key considerations."

A Meaningless Phrase

Self-determination is indeed the only issue of any real substance in the controversy over euthanasia. But the legal and medical professions have always recognized the right of competent patients to refuse any and all medical treatment, or to discharge themselves from a hospital at any time (an option Bouvia refused), even if so doing would hasten or directly cause death. What they then do with their lives is their own responsibility.

Taken literally, the catch phrase "right to die" is meaningless. There can be no such thing as a right to something inevitable and unavoidable. But in common parlance, it is an unfortunate ambiguity, meaning sometimes the "right to be allowed to die" from one's terminal illness and other times a supposed "right to be killed." The former has always been recognized by traditional medical ethics.

But can there be a "right to be killed"? The cumulative wisdom of centuries has consistently answered in the negative. Although self-determination is an important right, like all other rights it is not absolute; it can be qualified if it conflicts with the rights of others (e.g., no one has a right to self-determine to be a thief or a murderer). If put into practice consistently, the principle that

D. Alan Shewmon, "Active Voluntary Euthanasia: A Needless Pandora's Box." Reprinted by permission of the publisher, *Issues in Law & Medicine*, Vol. 3, No. 3, Winter, 1987. Copyright © 1987 by the National Legal Center for the Medically Dependent & Disabled, Inc.

death is an acceptable solution to human problems would ultimately destroy the very fabric of society, and with it all individual rights. Therefore, a "right to be killed" cannot derive from the right of self-determination.

Against the Law

This is why legal sanctions against aiding and abetting suicide remain, even though suicide and attempted suicide have been decriminalized in most states. The reason for the latter is not any implicit recognition of a "right to suicide," as is often claimed by euthanasia advocates, but rather "that there is no form of criminal punishment that is acceptable for a completed suicide and that criminal punishment is singularly inefficacious to deter attempts to commit suicide." Furthermore, the drafters of the Model Penal Code stated explicitly that "the interests in the sanctity of life that are represented by the criminal homicide laws are threatened by one who expresses a willingness to participate in taking the life of another, even though the act may be accomplished with the consent, or at the request, of the suicide victim."

The President's Commission reiterated this: "An individual who seeks death at the hands of another, regardless of the reason, does not confer immunity from prosecution on the one who takes the life, because the taking of innocent human life is seen as a wrong to the entire society, not just to the dead person.... Policies prohibiting direct killing may also conflict with the important value of patient self-determination.... The Commission finds this limitation on individual self-determination to be an acceptable cost of securing the general protection of human life afforded by the prohibition of direct killing." Such statements represent a nearly unanimous consensus based on the combined experience, reflection, and wisdom of a great number of people over many centuries. They should not be lightly disregarded.

"Legalized euthanasia would . . . infringe on the rights and consciences of many physicians."

Legalized euthanasia would also infringe on the rights and consciences of many physicians. Proponents argue that, to ensure patients' "right" to euthanasia, the law should establish a corresponding duty on the part of physicians either to comply or to refer the patient to a willing physician. But even a duty of referral would infringe upon a physician's conscience just as much as a duty to provide poison. No patient, in the name of self-determination, can oblige a physician to render treatment that he or she considers inappropriate or unethical, or to find a replacement who will necessarily fulfill such wishes.

One of the main reasons why the legal and medical professions have always opposed active euthanasia is that such societal issues are never static; they necessarily evolve according to the dynamics of their underlying philosophy, with the laws being forever revised to accommodate it. Because the logical endpoint of that evolution is considered undesirable, so is its initiation.

Euthanasia advocates dismiss the "slippery-slope" argument by reference to other societies in which the practice of suicide for specific indications has not evolved into a horror of abuses—for example, the voluntary freezing to death of elderly Eskimos. But such societies are not valid testing grounds for voluntary euthanasia in our own society, because of the differences in basic philosophy and the radically different levels of social complexity. The Netherlands would serve this purpose well, except for the fact that insufficient time has passed, since acceptance of active euthanasia, to observe any long-term effects. Our similarities with pre-Nazi Germany, however, are compelling.... Thus, the President's Commission stated: "Obviously, slippery slope arguments must be very carefully employed lest they serve merely as an unthinking defense of the status quo.... Nevertheless, the Commission has found that in [this] area ... valid concerns warrant being especially cautious before adopting any policy that weakens the protections against taking human life...."

This particular "slippery slope" is not merely a theoretical possibility; it is a present reality. The practice of euthanasia will necessarily facilitate this ongoing evolution along at least two dimensions simultaneously: the scope of indications (beginning with terminal illnesses and ending with euthanasia "on demand") and the degree of voluntariness (beginning with voluntary euthanasia and ending with involuntary "euthanasia" for the benefit of others)....

Defining "Terminal"

According to the *Hemlock Manifesto*, formulated in 1982, one of the guiding principles for the practice of active voluntary euthanasia ought to be that the recipient have a "terminal illness," meaning that "the person is likely, in the judgment of two examining physicians, to die of that condition within six months." But prognoses for survival are never that accurate; about 10% of patients admitted to hospices to die end up being discharged home because of either remission or inappropriate diagnosis....

Moreover, the six month cut-off is arbitrary. Proponents argue that arbitrary line-drawing is unavoidable in many areas that are nonetheless beneficial (e.g., highway speed limits), but statutory arbitrariness in this area will certainly encourage judicial discretion far beyond the literal interpretation of any such requirement. If one receives a speeding ticket and defends oneself in court on the basis that speed limits are inherently arbitrary, one will most likely end up paying the fine. But if a doctor were to administer euthanasia to someone projected to die within seven months who kept pleading for "deliverance," it is not likely that he would be charged with murder, or even for aiding and abetting suicide, if active euthanasia at six months were recognized not only as legal but as good. This is especially true given that the present cut-off of zero months is already not enforced (most defendants in mercy killings or assisted suicides are acquitted). Regardless of where the time limit is placed, there will be patients just beyond it who will demand their "right" to euthanasia; then the advocacy groups will seek to abolish the manifest hypocrisy of the already liberalized law. Once set in motion, this positive feedback cannot halt until its logical culmination in euthanasia on demand....

"Even if the acceptance of euthanasia ... were desirable for society, there would still be no reason to involve physicians in it, and many reasons not to."

We now turn to that other dimension of evolution of legalized euthanasia—the degree of voluntariness. The Hemlock Society believes that active euthanasia should be available, in the context of a terminal illness, to requesting adults "of sound mind," and that it is not "evidence of mental instability or incompetence ... for anyone to plan to or attempt to terminate his/her own life." But how is mental competence for such a momentous decision to be determined in practice? The proponents of euthanasia do not provide criteria for distinguishing between a rationally suicidal patient, whom the doctor will have the supposed "duty" to kill, and a pathologically suicidal patient whom the doctor has the duty to restrain. Even psychiatric experts cannot provide clear criteria here, because the conditions obviously represent but two ends of a continuum. The distinction is particularly fuzzy in patients with chronic illness or disabilities, or borderline mental retardation.

In clinical settings, it is often difficult to determine the true wishes of supposedly competent patients. They sometimes say one thing but communicate the opposite nonverbally. Their desire to live or die may fluctuate, the *Bouvia* case being a prime example. The fact that Bouvia had obtained a college degree and managed to get married indicated that she must have habitually found life meaningful and worth living in spite of her quadriplegia and arthritis. Her decision to die came after her divorce, which must have been a cause of despondency, even though the appellate court considered her decision to be rational and competently made. Nevertheless, by the time Bouvia finally won her legal battle to receive hospital assistance in starving to death, she had changed her mind and opted to go on with life after all. Had euthanasia already been acceptable, she would never have survived to discover the transience of her death wish.

Similarly, cancer patients admitted to hospices sometimes gain a new lease on life once their pain has been appropriately treated, and discharge themselves in order to seek more aggressive medical therapy. When a patient is depressed about a chronic or terminal illness, it is really quite impossible to determine whether he or she is mentally competent to make such a monumental, irreversible, once-in-a-life-time decision as suicide. This is why the law has traditionally erred on the side of regarding attempted suicide as an intrinsically irrational decision, constituting *prima facie* evidence of psychiatric incompetence....

Don't Involve Physicians

Even if the acceptance of euthanasia did not entail all the above problems and were desirable for society, there would still be no reason to involve physicians in it, and many reasons not to. To kill someone (even gently) does not require any medical knowledge. The main reason that physicians are supposedly needed is that the "best" drugs are all prescription drugs. But what about the case of Dr. Julius Hackethal, a German oncologist and contemporary hero of the euthanasia movement, who provided one of his terminal patients with an appropriately lethal amount of potassium cyanide? Cyanide is hardly a prescription drug, even in Germany, and anyone can look up its lethal dose in a toxicology book. The Hemlock Society discourages this method, however, because a cyanide death, though quick, is somewhat unpleasant. It therefore recommends sedative drugs as first choice. Still, it could just as well argue that these drugs be made nonprescription, or that specially certified euthanasists be allowed to establish their own clinics, without having to involve the medical profession at all. Any patient would then have the right to transfer himself from a hospital to the nearest euthanasia center.

It would seem, therefore, that the real reason for Hemlock's insistence on *physician*-assisted suicide is to lend an air of respectability and credibility to its cause. [Robert Jay] Lifton, in his book on the Nazi doctors, emphasizes that the maintenance of a facade of respectability was precisely the reason that the

Nazi regime insisted so much on having *doctors* "select" the recipients for "special treatment," operate the gas chambers, falsify death certificates to resemble natural causes, and in general maintain an aura of medicalization in every aspect of the genocide program.

The advocates of euthanasia attempt to use the medical profession for their own purposes, without regard to the irreparable harm that would be done to society by transforming the public image of physician from healer to killer, which could only undermine the covenant of trust at the very heart of the doctor-patient relationship. If this were not the case, there would be no need for the existing strong policies against physician participation in other legal forms of killing, such as capital punishment. As one article stated "this new method of capital punishment [lethal drug injection by physicians] . . . presents the most serious and intimate challenge in modern American history to active medical participation in state-ordered killing of human beings. . . . [T]his procedure requires the direct application of biomedical knowledge and skills in a corruption and exploitation of the healing profession's role in society."

Learning To Comfort, Not Kill

For all these reasons, efforts to promote death with dignity would be more appropriately channeled in the direction of physician education with regard to care of the dying, research to improve methods of symptomatic relief, and provision by society of improved resources for the persons who are disabled, chronically ill, or dying—particularly the establishment of hospices. It is unnecessary to kill these people in order to provide them with comfort and compassion; much less should physicians be the ones to kill them.

"The advocates of euthanasia attempt to use the medical profession for their own purposes, without regard to the irreparable harm that would be done to society by transforming the public image of physician from healer to killer."

Most proponents of euthanasia are well intentioned, but all are short-sighted. The slippery slope of euthanasia is no mere pro-life bogeyman; it is a present reality. Dr. Leo Alexander, U.S. medical consultant to the Nuremberg trials, was concerned as far back as 1949 about the direction American medicine was heading: "To be sure, American physicians are still far from the point of thinking of killing centers, but they have arrived at a danger point in thinking, at which likelihood of full rehabilitation is considered a factor that should determine the amount of time, effort and cost to be devoted to a particular type of patient. . . . Americans should remember that the enormity of a euthanasia movement is present in their own midst." Thirty-six years later, upon reading in the above-cited *New England Journal of Medicine* article about the policy of selective starvation of certain "hopelessly ill" patients, the same Alexander sadly remarked: "It is much like Germany in the Twenties and Thirties. The barriers against killing are coming down."

They need not. History does not have to repeat itself. Those few terminal patients who may desire to be "helped to die" must rather be helped to realize that their acceptance of the natural process is "an acceptable cost of securing the general protection of human life afforded by the prohibition of direct killing." [President's Commission].

D. Alan Shewmon is assistant professor in the department of pediatrics at the University of California at Los Angeles.

"The withdrawal of nutrition and hydration from other than imminently dying patients... is contrary to law and canons of ethics."

viewpoint 6

Withdrawing Treatment Violates Professional Ethics

Edward R. Grant and Clarke D. Forsythe

For many patients who are profoundly impaired and/or terminally ill, the physicians and, perhaps to a greater degree, the nurses are the "last friends" the patient may ever know. In many cases, this is so because family and other friends have died, moved away, or have otherwise abandoned the patient. In cases involving relatively young persons who are chronically and profoundly disabled, the process of detachment is more subtle. As the cases of Nancy Jobes and Paul Brophy illustrate, the families of these unfortunate patients have undergone a grieving process and have reconciled themselves to the fact that their loved one will never recover. However, they do not always reach a position of unconditional acceptance of the patient in his or her current condition. Their memories of the individual were formed when he or she was healthy. Because the patient in his or her current condition is so unlike the loved one they remember, they may form the opinion, as Patricia Brophy did, that "the patient's life is over." Thus, their treatment choice is to remove all forms of life support, even to the extent of removing feeding tubes that function to provide the patient with nutrition and hydration.

Without judging the behavior of any family, it is important to contrast their perspective with that of the health professional whose duty it is to provide care and treatment to the patient. In most cases, the physician or nurse probably did not know the patient prior to the onset of chronic illness or impairment. Professionally, these caregivers must accept the patient in the condition which has befallen him. Unlike the family member or friend who may be unable to see the patient without experiencing over and over the tragedy which brought about his or her condition, the nurse or doctor will, often unconditionally, accept the patient in his or her current state. Thus, the health care professional becomes, in an important way, the "last friend" of the chronically impaired patient.

As the use of the word "plight" indicates, the position of the "last friend" is often an uneasy one from a legal standpoint. The legal responsibility of individual physicians and nurses in these difficult situations is a gravely neglected area, not only on the issue of nutrition and hydration, but also on the general question of removing life-sustaining medical treatment. An explanation for this neglect may be that very few of the prominent legal cases in this area have involved the legal responsibility or liability of individual physicians and nurses....

The health care professions are somewhat divided on this issue, but there is a substantial and reputable body of opinion holding that the withdrawal of nutrition and hydration from other than imminently dying patients is a form of euthanasia or mercy-killing, and thus, is contrary to law and canons of ethics. Accordingly, the author proposes that the developing law in this area should recognize and give heightened protection to the rights of individual physicians and nurses to refrain from participating in a course of conduct that they consider harmful to the patient and a violation of the ethical, if not legal, obligations of their profession.

The Barber Case

Prior to 1983, no physician had ever been prosecuted for a death resulting from the removal of life-supporting treatment. This fact was often used as an argument against judicial and legislative activism in this area and to demonstrate that the risk of liability to individual health care practitioners was nil.

This argument was tarnished somewhat in the case of *People of California v. Barber*. In that case, fifty-five year old Clarence Herbert "coded" in the recovery

Edward R. Grant and Clarke D. Forsythe, "The Plight of the Last Friend: Legal Issues for Physicians and Nurses in Providing Nutrition and Hydration." Reprinted by permission of the publisher, *Issues in Law & Medicine*, Vol. 3, No. 3, Winter, 1987. Copyright © 1987 by the National Legal Center for the Medically Dependent & Disabled, Inc.

room following intestinal surgery. Brain damage resulted, and Mr. Herbert never regained consciousness. Two days after the incident, physicians, with the apparent approval of the family, removed Mr. Herbert's ventilator support. Surprisingly, he was able to breathe on his own. Two days later, the defendant physicians ordered the removal of Mr. Herbert's intravenous feeding lines, which resulted in the death of the patient in less than a week.

The Los Angeles County District Attorney issued a criminal complaint for first-degree homicide against Dr. Nejdl and Dr. Barber. Analysis of the ensuing preliminary hearing provides a good introduction to the issues of criminal law that are relevant to such cases, and one method by which the issue of criminal liability may be analyzed. The decision of the appeals court, which eventually dismissed all criminal charges against Dr. Barber and Dr. Nejdl, provides a somewhat different mode of analysis. Both of these approaches will be investigated.

The magistrate who conducted the hearing dismissed the criminal complaint on three grounds: first, that the defendant physicians did not "kill" Mr. Herbert, because the *proximate* cause of his death was not attributable to the removal of the intravenous feeding, or any other act of the physicians; second, that the conduct of the physicians was not *unlawful* because the decision to remove the tube was justified by a sound medical judgment that the patient's condition was irreversible; and third, that the physicians had not acted with *malice* in removing the feeding tube....

"The law should recognize and give greater protection to the right of conscientious objection . . . where a nurse, physician, or institution objects to the removal of nourishment."

The proceedings before the magistrate in *Barber* provides one form of analysis for criminal liability in the removal of nutrition and hydration. The appellate court in *Barber*, however, chose a different form of analysis. The appellate court did not disturb the lower court's findings on the issues of causation, justification, and malice. Instead, it held that the fundamental issue in the case was whether there was a *duty* to provide treatment to this patient. The court concluded that there was no such duty and extended this holding to include maintenance of intravenous feeding.

The appellate court relied upon the ethical analysis provided in the testimony of Fr. Paris to conclude that, due to the impaired state of the patient and the alleged dim hope for recovery, there was no medical, ethical, or legal duty to continue any form of treatment, including intravenous feeding. The court provided a curious analysis of the facts of the case to support this conclusion. According to the court, each individual drip of intravenous fluid through a catheter is a separate instance of providing treatment; thus, the interruption of intravenous therapy is comparable to foregoing a manually administered regimen of medication. The court also found that the provision of feeding was useless because it did not improve the prognosis for recovery. However, even though nourishment is not itself a neurological treatment, adequate nutrition is clearly necessary in order for the long process of neurological recovery to take place. In this case, where nourishment was removed five days after the onset of a coma, there was probably insufficient time for a reliable prognosis to be made. In approaching this case from the perspective of the physicians' duty, therefore, the appeals court dealt in generalities and assumptions about comatose patients and failed to come to grips with the duties that were presented by the unique circumstances of the case.

Unsettled Legal Issues

The appellate court in *Barber* was correct in stating that the criminal law rarely places criminal sanctions upon a failure to act. What is questionable, however, is the court's application of the doctrine. Many would argue that a physician has already assumed the duty to act by his original placement of the feeding tube. No matter how that issue is resolved, *Barber* demonstrates that before a criminal prosecution can go forward, there are a number of elements which must be established with each of these elements presenting different opportunities for defense against criminal charges. In addition to these doctrinal problems, the question of evidence and proof remains. A recent case in Texas illustrates the evidentiary problems confronted in the trial process. After a trial lasting several months, a jury was unable to reach a verdict in a criminal case against a nursing home and several nurses and administrators arising out of the death of a patient, allegedly from starvation. Part of the difficulty of proof concerned the cause of death. The prosecution's experts testified that the woman had died from malnutrition, but the defense witnesses testified that the cause of death was cancer. The evidence showed that the woman had been placed on a very reduced diet of several hundred calories per day. The fact that the case reached the jury stage indicates that criminal liability is still a very real possibility in a case where nutrition and hydration are inappropriately withdrawn....

This brief review . . . demonstrates that the legal issues confronting physicians and nurses are great in number and largely unsettled. Individual practitioners are likely to be confused by the current state of law, particularly as it weakens the obligation to provide life-sustaining treatment and care to an ill-defined and potentially large category of patients. The confusion is compounded if one looks beyond the legal cases to examine the proposals for patient care that are advanced by particular schools of thought in medical ethics. One such proposal, formulated at a conference sponsored by the Society for the Right to Die, and published in a prestigious medical journal, equates the provision of nutrition and hydration with invasive therapies such as surgery and chemotherapy. The authors also propose that tube feeding may be withheld not only from patients in a persistent vegetative state (a stance endorsed by the Council on Ethical and Judicial Affairs of the American Medical Association), but also from patients who are terminally ill or severely and irreversibly demented. It is uncertain whether the courts will accept such positions as the new medico-legal standard for the care of such patients, but the potential for their doing so is great.

"Those who oppose and refuse to cooperate in a removal of nourishment are acting from a sound and fundamental principle of conscience."

The resolution of these issues will thus take place on a case-by-case basis, against the backdrop of change and controversy in medical ethics. Individual practitioners should be encouraged to consider, articulate and defend carefully their own ethical position, particularly in cases where the right of the patient to receive basic care, such as nourishment, is jeopardized. The care of terminally ill and chronically ill patients has become a major issue of public policy, as the cost of health care encourages government and private insurers to adopt a philosophy of "cost-containment." For many aspects of the health care system, this philosophy will be beneficial. For those patients who have been abandoned, in whole or in part, and for whom the health care practitioner is truly the "last friend," cost-containment may pose a serious threat. It is evident that the current trend of law which has reduced the obligation to care for these patients has resulted from the courts' conclusion that the removal of care is justified by the patient's right of autonomy. However, if cases concerning the provision of basic care and nourishment were to reach courts in different postures, with physicians and nurses being seen as advocates for the patient's right to receive basic care as against a societal interest in lowering costs, the outcome would probably be different. In the end, therefore, it is individual physicians and nurses, and not merely their professional associations and academic spokespersons, who will establish the legal standards governing the provision of nourishment.

The Right To Object

Given the important role that individual practitioners will play in resolving these legal issues and the controversy that surrounds these issues, the law should recognize and give greater protection to the right of conscientious objection, particularly in cases where a nurse, physician, or institution objects to the removal of nourishment as inappropriate. Where nourishment is removed, death will follow— this much has been clearly recognized, even by courts . . . which have authorized such actions. Accordingly there should be a *prima-facie* assumption that those who oppose and refuse to cooperate in a removal of nourishment are acting from a sound and fundamental principle of conscience. No burden of justifying their objection on specific religious or philosophical principles ought to be imposed. The public, as well as the medical and nursing professions, clearly benefit from the ethic of *primum non nocere* [first do no harm] which is at the heart of the conscientious objection to the withdrawal of nourishment. Those who have either advocated a different ethic, or have argued that removal of nourishment does not actually violate the traditional ethic, have issued assurances, such as that contained in the recent AMA statement, that no practitioner is required to carry out a removal of nourishment. These assurances deserve prompt and effective legal protection.

The plight of the "last friend," of course, is not limited to decisions to remove or provide nourishment. However, by protecting the right of nurses or physicians to object to actions which will bring about the death of the patient, the law would be affirming the practitioners' important role as advocate for the life of the patient. Too easily, our society is accepting the notion that hastening death is the ultimate act of kindness toward our most vulnerable and dependent patients. Physicians and nurses should be encouraged to resist this trend and to take seriously their role as "last friend." If this initiative is successful, society will hopefully also recognize that this role is not one which our physicians and nurses should be expected to bear on their own.

Edward R. Grant is executive director of Americans United for Life and a general counsel for the AUL Legal Defense Fund. Clarke D. Forsythe is a staff counsel for the AUL League Defense Fund.

"It can be morally permissible to withhold or withdraw treatment. It can be legally permissible to withhold or withdraw treatment."

viewpoint 7

Withdrawing Treatment Does Not Violate Professional Ethics

Marsha D. Fowler

Rabbi Judah the Prince, the redactor of the *Mishnah*, lay dying, oppressively afflicted by a debilitating, incurable, and untreatable gastrointestinal disease. His female servant, a woman of unquestioned piety and moral character, prayed for his death while the rabbis surrounding him prayed for life. The prayers of the rabbis were efficacious in prolonging the agonizing dying of Rabbi. Distressed by the action of the rabbis the woman dropped a clay pot from above, shattering it in their midst. Startled from their prayers, the rabbis ceased praying and the soul of Rabbi Judah departed.

Gemara, Ketubbot 104a (paraphrase)

It is both natural and necessary that health professionals seek to conserve and preserve life. It is natural in the sense that both medicine and nursing affirm the value of human biologic life, seek to restore it to health when possible, and care for it when cure is not possible; life and health are valued ends for both professions. It is essential that this be generally understood, because it is necessary that persons who are or would be patients (or guardians of patients) be able to rest in the confidence that health professionals will not cease treatment prematurely. Sometimes, however, whether from pain, pride, pressure, or a misinterpretation of either ethics or the law, the clay pot must shatter in our midst to jolt us into withdrawing treatment from an irretrievably dying and suffering patient.

There are several reasons for this necessity. It is difficult to lose a patient to death. By nature, health care entails a valiant struggle against the slings and arrows of bodily misfortune. The majority of our efforts are directed toward measures, even heroic measures, that will cure illness and delay death. In an era when the lives of patients who unquestionably would formerly have died can be prolonged by simple treatment measures such as an insulin injection, or by complex ones such as a renal transplant, we are loathe to either withhold or withdraw treatment. Death becomes both a failure and an affront.

Other pressures also impinge on clinicians. One is the pressure of the technologic means of intervention that surround us; if the technology is present, it will be used. The seeming "technologic imperative" is hard to resist, particularly when what was once regarded as "high tech" is now considered "routine."

A False Perception

Yet another pressure to which clinicians are susceptible is the perception that it is easier and safer to withhold treatment than to attempt to withdraw it once it has begun. For although it is perceived to be legal to withhold treatment, it is often thought that once treatment is started, it must continue—that withdrawal of life-sustaining treatment is tantamount to murder. If treatment is then discontinued, ethics will swing the sword of St. Michael to wreak vengeance on our wrongdoing, and the law, which hangs by a hair above our heads like the sword of Damocles, will fall on us. Fortunately, the bioethical literature has given substantial attention to the question of withdrawal of life-sustaining treatment and can allay some of these misperceptions. In addition, emerging case law continues to move ahead in this area.

Documents of particular importance to the issue of withdrawing treatment include the *Code for Nurses*, the *Current Opinions of the Judicial Council of the American Medical Association—1984*, and the report of the President's Commission for the Study of Ethical Problems in Medicine and Biomedical and Biobehavioral Research, entitled *Deciding to Forego Life-Sustaining Treatment*. These documents form an ethical "core" for decision making in practice and for the development of professional position

---

Marsha D. Fowler, "And the Rabbi Judah the Prince Died: On the Withdrawal of Treatment," *Heart and Lung*, September 1987. Reprinted from HEART AND LUNG: THE JOURNAL OF CRITICAL CARE, with permission from the C.V. MOSBY COMPANY.

statements and institutional policies or guidelines.

The *Code for Nurses* affirms the moral right of the patient to decide to forego or withdraw from treatment, whether life-sustaining or not. It reads, "Clients have the moral right to determine what will be done with their own person; . . . to accept, refuse or terminate treatment without coercion." The morally autonomous patient need not undergo treatment he or she does not wish. More specifically, for patients who are dying, the nurse must uphold the value system of the patient, even if it leads to the rejection of treatment. The nurse must "enable the client to live with as much physical, emotional, and spiritual comfort as possible, and . . . *maximize the values the client has treasured in life*" [italics added].

Relieve Suffering

The American Medical Association (AMA) Judicial Council asserts a similar position. It states:

> The social commitment of the physician is to prolong life and to relieve suffering. Where the observance of one conflicts with the other, the physician, patient, and/or family of the patient have the discretion to resolve the conflict. For humane reasons, with informed consent a physician may do what is medically necessary to alleviate severe pain, or cease or omit treatment to let a terminally ill patient die, but he [or she] should not intentionally cause death.

Both the American Nurses' Association (ANA) and the AMA maintain that treatment may be withheld or removed, provided that normal care continues to be given to the patient. The AMA Judicial Council further states:

> The consideration of the physician should be what is the best for the individual patient and not the avoidance of a burden to the family or society. Quality of life is a factor to be considered in determining what is best for the individual. . . . Withholding or removing life support means is ethical provided that the normal care given an individual who is ill is not discontinued.

Simply to say, however, that the ANA and the AMA find that not treating in instances where suffering would be prolonged, or where it is against the patient's wishes, is acceptable within the ethics of the profession still does not address the question of withholding versus withdrawing treatment or the question of the legal permissibility of either act.

The President's Commission report addresses both of these questions and establishes guidelines for situations involving life-sustaining treatment and its removal. It states:

> The distinction between failing to initiate and stopping therapy—that is, withholding versus withdrawing treatment—is not itself of moral importance. A justification that is adequate for not commencing a treatment is also sufficient for ceasing it.

The justifications morally sufficient for withholding treatment in the first place include (1) that the patient does not wish the treatment, (2) that the treatment will not medically benefit the patient, and (3) that the treatment is burdensome to the patient, even when it holds out some hope for the prolongation of life or even for recovery. These same reasons are sufficient for withdrawing treatment once it has begun. The distinction between withholding and withdrawing treatment, no matter how much harder the latter seems than the former, is not a moral distinction; it is an emotional or psychologic one.

Legal and Moral

Even so, will the law "hang us" if we withdraw or withhold treatment? No. The President's Commision notes:

> Nothing in current law precludes ethically sound decision making. Neither criminal law nor civil law— if properly interpreted and applied . . . forces patients to undergo procedures that will increase their suffering when they wish to avoid this by foregoing life-sustaining treatment.

If it can be both legally and morally permissible to withdraw or withhold treatment, what, then, are appropriate guidelines for doing so? The President's Commission has made several general recommendations, including the following: First, we ought to respect patient choices, even to forego life-sustaining treatment. Second, institutions should provide guidelines for decision making for patients who cannot decide for themselves. Third, institutions should establish procedures for decision making available for all patients. Fourth, when we cannot know how to decide, presume in favor of life. Finally, patients should receive respectful, responsive, supportive care, even when no further medical care is available or chosen.

"Will the law 'hang us' if we withdraw or withhold treatment? No."

It can be *morally* permissible to withhold or withdraw treatment. It can be *legally* permissible to withhold or withdraw treatment. The distinction between the withholding and the withdrawing of treatment is of neither moral nor legal significance. The need in these sorts of situations is to refuse to allow hubris, or the pressure of technology, or a misunderstanding of either law or ethics to lead us to treat a patient for whom treatment is futile or undesired. Treatment should cease before the pot is ever broken.

Marsha D. Fowler is consulting ethicist and associate professor at California State University in Los Angeles.

"It may well be humane and sound to permit rejection of nutrition."

viewpoint 8

Nutrition May Be Withheld from Dying Patients

Norman L. Cantor

Both medical practice and judicial response indicate that a wide range of medical procedures can be withdrawn in order to ease the dying process for a terminally ill individual. The reported cases have most commonly dealt with measures that are indisputably "medical" in nature—such as blood transfusions, respirators, chemotherapy, or dialysis. An emerging issue is whether nutrition—through intravenous tubes (I.V.), naso-gastric tubes, or even basic oral administration—can sometimes be withdrawn from the terminally ill.

A common instinctive reaction to the issue is to regard nutrition as natural "sustenance" rather than medical treatment. Many religious commentators, whether of Catholic or orthodox Jewish persuasion, adopt this approach. The implication is that nutrition is outside the area of "medical" procedures which might conceivably be withheld from a terminally ill patient. An alternative view—one that I'm inclined to endorse—regards nutrition as a medical procedure where it is part of a program sustaining the existence of a patient threatened by pathology. A third view is that "artificial nutrition"—nourishment administered by medical personnel through injections or implantation of tubes as opposed to oral ingestion of food—can be regarded as a medical procedure.

Normally, feeding is considered part of the palliative care administered by hospital staff to a dying patient in order to promote that patient's comfort. This category of care would include, besides feeding, administration of analgesics and/or sedation, easing of body position, and provision of a clean and warm environment. But at least where associated with underlying pathology which irrevocably fixes the demise of the patient, nutrition might arguably be classified as part of the medical framework potentially removable according to customary criteria—adherence to the patient's desires or to the humane easing of the dying process. This classification is most natural in reference to nutritive processes which are obviously medical in nature—for example, surgical removal of blockages to food passages or surgical implantation of nutrition tubes where natural alimentation processes aren't functioning. Yet even routinely inserted naso-gastric tubes, or intravenous lines, or even hand-feeding might be deemed terminable in order to ease the dying process for a patient who is afflicted with a terminal illness and has made a determination that the potential suffering from further treatment and/or associated effects of the dying process are so distasteful that he or she prefers to expire without further medical intervention. Palliative care of the dying patient, including nutrition, bathing, etc., should be handled according to the competent patient's preferences, just as more complex medical procedures such as chemotherapy or a respirator would be handled.

Unpersuasive Arguments

The arguments against treating nutrition and hydration as part of the medical framework surrounding patients are generally unpersuasive. One claim is that withdrawal of nutrition hastens death, and thus is incompatible with the physician's customary role of striving to preserve life. But the tension between withdrawal of nutrition and the medical role would appear to be little different from the similar tension when machinery is stopped, chemotherapy is foregone, or resuscitation procedures are omitted—all with the object of easing the dying process or adhering to the patient's instructions.

A second claim is that feeding has a special symbolic significance which differentiates it from

Norman L. Cantor, *Legal Frontiers of Death and Dying*. Bloomington, IN: Indiana University Press, 1987. Reprinted with permission.

other aspects of handling dying patients. Feeding a helpless individual normally connotes sharing and compassion. According to Daniel Callahan, it is "the perfect symbol of the fact that human life is inescapably social and communal."

The altruism embodied in feeding seems little different from the altruism normally involved in furnishing antibiotics, blood transfusions, medicines, or chest massage—all of them simplistic, relatively nonintrusive procedures which may be foregone pursuant to the instructions of a terminally ill patient. On occasion, feeding or nutrition may carry with it no benefit to the patient, or may even prolong a torturous dying process, and thus lose its usual symbolic cast. The question becomes not whether nutrition can ever be omitted, but under what circumstances such omissions are ethically and legally permissible.

The Cause of Death

A third objection to viewing the withholding of nutrition as equivalent to the withholding of other medical treatment is that the cause of death becomes starvation (or dehydration) rather than simply allowing a fatal disease process to run its course. The charge is that a patient is "dehydrated" to death, rather than death occurring from natural causes. This charge has no force where the nutrition withheld is "artificial nutrition" (I.V., naso-gastric tube, etc.) necessitated by pathology (such as a blockage in the esophagus or intestines). In those instances, if artificial nutrition is withdrawn or withheld pathological conditions will simply be allowed to run their natural course. Similarly, for the terminally ill patient who is so deteriorated that the swallowing reflex has been lost, as for the patient whose medical pathology prevents oral taking of nourishment, artificial nutrition represents interference with a "natural" decline—just as a respirator does for a patient who can no longer breathe independently. Yet no one argues that a patient is improperly being "choked" to death if a respirator is removed pursuant to a terminal patient's request to be allowed to die. The question in each case is the scope of a patient's prerogative to determine the course of the dying process, and the corresponding obligations of medical personnel.

The independent causation argument (death is caused by dehydration rather than disease) has more force where oral feeding is physically possible. Even there, nutrition might be viewed as simply part of the palliative care being administered to a patient otherwise being treated during a fatal disease process. If the patient is entitled to reject a variety of purely medical treatments and thus provoke death, it may well be humane and sound to permit rejection of nutrition. A terminally ill patient's refusal to eat would not seem very different from a terminally ill patient rejecting antibiotics with the knowledge that an infection will soon set in and the patient will die from the infection. Permitting death by starvation or dehydration may well be humane in the sense that any associated discomfort may well be less than the pain accompanying the dying process if that process is allowed to run its course. Moreover, forced feeding of a dying patient who chooses to resist nutrition might well be viewed as a disturbing affront to that patient's dignity. Legal permissibility of withholding nutrition should hinge not on the precise cause of death on the medical certificate (whether dehydration or cancer), but on the scope of the affirmative obligations owed to a dying patient by surrounding medical personnel.

Legal Support

The question remains how much support the view of feeding as medical therapy can garner in the legal arena.... [There is] widespread and growing medical and judicial recognition that individual autonomy and self-determination entitle a competent patient to shape the dying process, even if that means rejection of procedures which could forestall death. This principle, which allows the patient to determine when the burdens of the dying process outweigh the benefits of life-preserving measures, seems fully applicable to the matter of nutrition and hydration. A [1983] Presidential Commission report, in accepting this principle, specifically noted its applicability to such simplistic procedures as blood transfusions, administration of antibiotics, and "parenteral nutrition and hydration." A 1984 article by medical figures from several eminent teaching centers also acknowledged that hydration and nutrition may be withheld from patients in the terminal phase of an irreversible illness, at least where consistent with a patient's comfort and wishes.

"The question becomes not whether nutrition can ever be omitted, but under what circumstances such omissions are ethically and legally permissible."

Judicial authority is likely to accept and endorse this medical recognition of a terminally ill patient's prerogative to resist nutrition. For the courts will be guided in this area, in the absence of legislative direction, by sensitive and humane medical practices. That is, if medical authorities widely adopt the view that nutrition is part of the array of medical interventions surrounding terminal care, the chances of judicial acceptance of the position will be enhanced.

There has been very little judicial treatment of the precise issue.... A lower court in New York refused to intervene when an eighty-five-year-old former college president, suffering from the effects of a disabling stroke, resisted nutrition and starved himself to death. And one court has even allowed hunger-striking prisoners to resist feeding—an extension of self-determination well beyond the context of the terminally ill medical patient. Such a court would presumably endorse patients' resistance to nutrition in the context of a patient's shaping of an inexorable dying process.

A Favorable Ruling

The bulk of the judicial discussion of nutrition as part of medical therapy has come in the context of several cases involving incompetent patients. One clear expression of judicial willingness to regard nutrition as part of the medical framework surrounding the dying patient came in a 1983 California case, *Barber v. Superior Court*. In *Barber*, an intermediate appellate court rejected efforts to prosecute physicians who, pursuant to a family's request, had removed intravenous tubes providing nutrition and hydration to a permanently comatose patient. The patient had previously lapsed into "an indefinite vegetative existence" without any higher cognitive brain function. At first, the family requested removal of all machines sustaining life, including a respirator. When the patient continued to breathe, the family asked that he not be disturbed at all. After two days of deliberation, the responsible physicians complied and ordered removal of the tubes providing hydration and nourishment, thus precipitating death. When local authorities initiated criminal prosecution, the physicians sought a judicial declaration that their conduct had been lawful. A lower court initially ruled that their conduct did ostensibly involve homicide, but an appellate court reversed the decision.

The appellate court ruled that despite "the emotional symbolism" of feeding, artificial nutrition could, in the context of a permanently comatose patient, be addressed like other medically administered life support procedures. That is, the benefits and burdens of each procedure could be assessed, and any process could be withdrawn where it was of no net benefit to the patient. The court observed:

> Medical procedures to provide nutrition and hydration are more similar to other medical procedures than to typical human ways of providing nutrition and hydration. Their benefits and burdens ought to be evaluated in the same manner as any other medical procedure.

The basis for this conclusion—that nutrition could legitimately be withdrawn from a permanently comatose patient—was laid in the classic *Quinlan* case. There, the New Jersey Supreme Court authorized removal of a respirator from a twenty-two-year-old in a "persistent vegetative state," with the expectation that the comatose woman would soon die. In *Quinlan*, removal of the naso-gastric feeding tube and of antibiotic administration were not specifically addressed; the patient's guardian was guided by a religious precept that such simple measures were "ordinary" and therefore not expendable under any circumstances. But the guiding principles set down by the court with respect to the respirator would seem to permit withdrawal of such measures as antibiotic and nutrition administration. As to both a respirator and a naso-gastric tube, the permanently comatose patient would not be deemed to benefit from continuation of the procedures and, the patient being insensate, could not suffer from their removal. Humane medical practice—a consideration valued by the court—would then permit removal of all artificial interventions sustaining such a marginal and dismal existence.

"A terminally ill patient's refusal to eat would not seem very different from a terminally ill patient rejecting antibiotics."

In January 1985, in the *Conroy* case, the New Jersey Supreme Court followed up on the groundwork laid in *Quinlan*. That court ruled that "artificial feedings" such as naso-gastric tubes, gastrostomies, and intravenous infusions are "medical procedures" potentially withdrawable from a dying patient according to standards applied to other forms of medical treatment. That ruling came in the context of an effort to remove a naso-gastric tube sustaining an eighty-four-year-old woman, bedridden, virtually insensate, and afflicted with a variety of fatal conditions including heart disease and diabetes. Her nephew, as guardian, sought judicial authorization to have the naso-gastric tube removed so that Ms. Conroy could be allowed to die from starvation within a few days. Otherwise, the projection was that she could languish for months or even a year. In response to the hospital's contention that provision of basic nutrition is categorically different from medical treatment such as a respirator, the court commented:

> Analytically, artificial feeding by means of a nasogastric tube or intravenous infusion can be seen as equivalent to artificial breathing by means of a respirator. Both prolong life through mechanical means when the body is no longer able to perform a vital bodily function on its own....

While I would go further and include manual feeding as a procedure potentially withholdable at the patient's request (even though the patient is still physically capable of normal ingestion and digestion), the *Conroy* opinion is a major step forward. Presumably, it will greatly influence subsequent judicial decisions as did the *Quinlan* case before it. *Conroy*, an expression by New Jersey's highest state court, reinforces the conclusion previously reached by intermediate appellate courts in California and Massachusetts, that artificial feeding can be regarded as part of the medical procedures potentially terminable in the context of a dying patient.

Conroy also raises, in stark terms, the difficult issue of how to handle incompetent patients in chronic, degenerative states who are not facing immediately life-threatening conditions. (The patient there was projected to live for as long as a year if nutrition were maintained.) The question is not just nourishment. Nonresuscitation orders will inevitably be an issue, and continuation of antibiotics and other measures to forestall life-threatening conditions must be addressed. These questions are part of the larger problem of how to handle the incompetent, terminally ill patient.... At the very least where the moribund patient is competent to make his or her own decisions surrounding the dying process, artificial nutrition can be regarded as part of the general range of medical decisions and handled according to the same criteria as other medical interventions (as to which patient autonomy plays a predominant role).

Easing the Dying Process

Death sometimes comes to a geriatric patient after a slow and gentle decline, ending with a few hours of terminal bronchopneumonia with the patient in coma. But in other instances, the dying process can be extremely distressful. This may be so for end stage renal disease, respiratory failure, or cancer, as examples. The end may come hard for a chronic emphysema sufferer, unable to speak because of a tracheotomy and tortured by breathing difficulty or paroxysms of cough. For these latter classes of patient, the prospect of rejecting further nutrition (as well as other life-preserving measures) would seem to offer welcome relief.

Up to this point, discussion has focussed on nutrition as a form of medical intervention during the last stages of a terminal illness. The naso-gastric tube or intravenous line, it is suggested, is then just part of the variety of medical paraphernalia potentially removable from the patient. For some patients suffering from chronic degenerative diseases, such as Alzheimer's disease, death may come after a torturous process of deterioration, loss of faculties, and agonizing suffering. I respectfully suggest that for these chronic disease sufferers, as well, nutrition can be regarded as an essentially medical process terminable at the request of the competent patient. That is, even before a terminal stage at which death is imminent, the patient facing a torturous and inexorable decline ought to be able to repudiate nutrition just as he or she might repudiate further chemotherapy or a respirator. In short, imminence of death should not be a prerequisite to a terminally ill patient's prerogative to reject nutrition any more than it would be a precondition to the rejection of more complex therapy. This is consistent with the position ... that the autonomy accorded a dying medical patient includes the prerogative to decide when the projected existence is so dismal that further intervention may be rejected.

The reported cases in which patients were in effect allowed to accelerate a nonimminent death usually entailed rejection of physically invasive procedures—amputations, or dialysis treatments. But I submit that less invasive procedures—such as blood transfusions, or cardiopulmonary resuscitation, or antibiotics—can also be foregone by the dying patient.

As to nutrition, if the patient can find medical personnel who, in good conscience, will cooperate with the patient's decision to forego feeding even though death is not yet imminent, that rejection too should be permissible. Thus, as noted, the evolving attitudes of physicians will play a large role in shaping ultimate judicial approaches.

The Patient's Prerogative

As mentioned above, I would go even further than the *Conroy* case and support rejection of manual feeding (not just artificial nutrition) by a competent medical patient. That is, even when the terminally ill patient's physical condition doesn't necessitate artificial nourishment and the patient has been receiving oral feeding, the patient should have the prerogative to reject all nutrition including oral feeding—at least where the patient's condition is such that a request to forego further medical treatment would be honored.

"The basis for this conclusion—that nutrition could legitimately be withdrawn from a permanently comatose patient—was laid in the classic Quinlan *case."*

A poignant example of the kind of case in which a competent, chronically ill person should be permitted to resist nutrition arose in 1984 in New York. The individual in question was a fifty-four-year-old woman who, until a tragic fall in 1982, had been a vigorous and active person. She was the devoted mother of five children, three of them married, a fourth in college, and the fifth a fifteen-year-old living at home. The tragic fall in 1982 fractured vertebrae and left the woman a total quadriplegic. She was unable to move her hands, feet, arms, or legs. She was incontinent, and unable to breathe on her own. A mechanical ventilator pumped air into her lungs via an opening made in the trachea.

The woman petitioned a court for a declaratory judgment that, in the event she were again hospitalized (as was frequently the case), she could take only such nourishment as she wished, and that palliative care (pain killers or sedatives) would be administered pursuant to her request. In effect, she wanted confirmation that she would be permitted to starve to death. (For reasons not made clear in the court's opinion, the petitioner was not asking that the ventilator be withdrawn, though she had resisted it in the past.)

"The patient facing a torturous and inexorable decline ought to be able to repudiate nutrition just as he or she might repudiate further chemotherapy."

The New York court ducked the basic question regarding feeding. The decision was that the legal controversy was not yet ripe for judicial intervention because the woman was not yet hospitalized. But the judge hinted that the woman's petition would be granted, and her self-determination honored, if a controversy arose after she was hospitalized.

This anonymous woman's situation illustrates why I would classify feeding as a medical procedure—potentially withdrawable at the instigation of a patient—where nutrition is part of an overall medical program sustaining the life of a patient whose life is threatened by independent pathology. Otherwise, a patient may be needlessly condemned to linger in a protracted, distasteful dying process.

Norman L. Cantor is a senior faculty member at Rutgers University School of Law in Newark, New Jersey, and the author of Legal Frontiers of Death and Dying.

"It is misplaced paternalism for the courts to assume that incompetent persons would choose the indignity of death by starvation and dehydration."

viewpoint 9

Nutrition Should Not Be Withheld from Dying Patients

Jacqueline M. Nolan-Haley and Joseph R. Stanton

Rapid advances in medical technology over the last twenty-five years permit human life to be sustained for indefinite periods of time. Lives which once might have ended quickly forty years ago can be prolonged through the application of assorted medical technologies and apparatus. For a variety of reasons including economics and the "quality of life" ethic, current medical and ethical thinking no longer wishes to sustain life. Since it is not prepared to actively "kill," it advocates withdrawal of nutrition and water from patients, a notion which would have been considered outrageous as recently as five years ago. The appealing rhetoric of the "death with dignity" movement, which began as an attempt to ameliorate the depersonalization of the dying patient inherent in modern technology (which, paradoxically, has produced medical miracles), is now used to justify death by cessation of fluids and nourishment.

While some medical articles oppose this trend, the emerging stream flows in the other direction. The starting point for rationalizing starvation and dehydration deaths was in 1983 when the President's Commission for the Study of Ethical Problems in Medicine and Biomedical and Behavioral Research stated that nutrition and hydration were not "universally warranted" for dying patients. The American Medical Association went further. In 1986 its seven-member Judicial Council determined that it would be ethical for physicians to withhold "all means of life prolonging medical treatment" including food and water from patients in irreversible comas *even if death were not imminent.* A report in the New York *Times* said that at least 10,000 Americans in irreversible comas could be affected by the AMA opinion.

Jacqueline M. Nolan-Haley and Joseph R. Stanton, "On Rationalizing Death." Reprinted with permission from the *Human Life Review*, Spring, 1987 (© 1987 by the Human Life Foundation, Inc., 150 E. 35th St., New York, NY 10016).

It is not surprising then that the reported appellate-court decisions which have ruled on the legality of death by dehydration and starvation have all sanctioned it as a "right" possessed by the person for whose alleged benefit it is sought. The terminology used by the courts rarely describes what is in fact being sanctioned: certain death from starvation and dehydration. Rather, the courts speak of "withdrawal of nutrition and fluids," and "termination of treatment." The process of rationalizing death by dehydration and starvation involves semantic juggling: the courts deny that it is suicide, euthanasia, or homicide; it is simply letting "nature take its course." But surely the rationalizations can be used to justify death for ever-widening segments of the population?

Legally Withdrawing Treatment

Court decisions on the withholding or withdrawing of medical treatment begin with a recognition of the common-law rule that a competent adult has the right to determine what will be done with his or her body. Thirty-five states and the District of Columbia have enacted statutes which codify this common-law right. These statutes, known as "living will" or "natural death" laws, typically provide that a competent adult may decline life-prolonging treatment. Eighteen of these state statutes expressly exclude nutrition and hydration from the life-prolonging procedures which may be withdrawn under a "living will."

The right to refuse medical treatment has never been considered absolute. It is usually balanced against the state's interest in preserving human life, preventing suicide, protecting third persons such as minor children, and protecting the integrity of the medical profession. A well-known example of the courts limiting the exercise of the common-law right of patient autonomy is in the case of a pregnant woman who refuses blood transfusions for reasons

death / dying 37

of religious conviction.

Incompetent persons obviously pose difficulty for the courts because someone else has to decide for them. In these cases the courts use two doctrines to support withdrawal of medical treatment. Under the doctrine of "substituted judgment," if the incompetent person expressed wishes regarding his or her future course of medical treatment while competent, then the court will honor those wishes. If the incompetent person made no such express wishes while competent, a surrogate decision-maker is empowered to determine what the patient would want. The doctrine of substituted judgment was applied in the New York case of Brother Joseph Fox who suffered cardiac arrest during surgery and entered into what doctors refer to as a "vegetative state." His superior, Father Philip Eichner, requested that Brother Fox be removed from the respirator in accordance with Brother Fox's wishes that he not be kept alive by any "extraordinary business" if his condition were hopeless. Brother Fox died before the court acknowledged his right to be removed from the respirator.

An alternative approach with incompetent persons, known as the "best interests" doctrine, would make treatment or non-treatment decisions based upon a surrogate decision-maker's perception of the patient's best interests. What the patient wants is not necessarily determinative. In the New York case of *In re Storar* the New York Court of Appeals refused to allow blood transfusions to be discontinued for a fifty-two-year-old retarded man with bladder cancer. Staff physicians testified that without the transfusions, he would eventually bleed to death. Despite his mother's request that they be discontinued the court stated that ". . . a court should not in the circumstances of this case allow an incompetent patient to bleed to death because someone, even someone as close as a parent or sibling, feels that this is best for one with an incurable disease."

Within the contours of these two doctrines the courts have grappled with deciding what kinds of treatment could be stopped: chemotherapy? dialysis? respirators? The decisions often turned on the distinction between ordinary and extraordinary care or between proportionate and disproportionate care with the courts weighing the benefits and burdens of treatment to the patient.

The Starvation Cases

In 1983 the courts confronted for the first time the question of whether feeding a person through a tube constitutes "medical treatment." The question was a critical one because of the already-existing legal doctrine which permits competent adults to reject medical treatment, and allows surrogate decision-makers to do the same for incompetent persons. All of the cases—most of which frequently cited the President's Commission Report—held that feeding a person through a tube was "medical treatment" and thus not required.

The first case to consider the food-and-water issue involved Clarence Herbert, a fifty-five-year-old security guard who suffered cardiorespiratory arrest and became comatose following surgery. He was immediately placed on life-support equipment. But his wife decided to allow withdrawal of medical treatment *and* nutrition and hydration when informed that her husband had suffered "brain death." In fact, he had not. Clarence Herbert continued to breathe spontaneously long after the respirator was discontinued. The two physicians who ordered the removal of the respirator and intravenous tubes which provided nourishment and water were eventually charged with murder.

The Court's Ruling

In *Barber v. Superior Court* the California Court of Appeals held that the physicians who acted knowingly and with full knowledge that Clarence Herbert would die, were not criminally responsible for his death since they had breached no legal duty. Relying on the President's Commission Report, the court decided that intravenous feedings of nourishment and fluid are equivalent to respirators and other forms of life support. They are essentially treatment decisions and should be evaluated on a benefit/burden scale. If treatment results in a "complete cure or significant improvement in the patient's condition," it is beneficial. On the other hand, "if the prognosis is virtually hopeless for any significant improvement in condition," treatment is disproportionate in terms of benefits and not warranted. Since no one could say with certainty whether Clarence Herbert would ever recover from a persistent vegetative state to full recovery, the court held that there was no legal obligation to "treat" him by feeding.

"The Mary Hier story which is not frequently told in legal circles is that Mary Hier had never expressed a preference not to eat. Indeed, she would steal food from other patients' trays."

Relying on the precedent established in *Barber* and on the President's Commission Report, the Massachusetts Appeals Court decided in 1984 that surgery to provide nutrition to a ninety-two-year-old woman was substantially more burdensome than it would be for a "younger, healthier" person, and thus inappropriate. The case, *In re Hier*, involved a woman who had suffered from mental and physical illness for many years. Since 1974 she had received nourishment through a gastronomy feeding tube. After she pulled the gastronomy tube from her abdomen several times the nursing home brought a legal action to obtain permission for surgery to re-insert the gastronomy tube. Applying a "substituted judgment" analysis, the court determined that Mary Hier would not want to undergo the surgery necessary for tube feeding and refused to order surgery.

> "One of the more troublesome aspects of the starvation cases is that only the sick are implicated."

The Mary Hier story which is *not* frequently told in legal circles is that Mary Hier had never expressed a preference not to eat. Indeed, she would steal food from other patients' trays. Her guardian *ad litem* returned to court with seven additional medical witnesses and persuaded the original judge to authorize the performance of surgery to re-insert the gastronomy tube....

Claire Conroy

In 1985 the New Jersey Supreme Court issued a lengthy opinion on the "rights" of incompetent, seriously ill nursing home patients to have feeding discontinued. The case, *In re Conroy*, arose when the nephew of eighty-four-year-old Claire Conroy sought legal permission to have his aunt's feeding tube removed. Before the court decided upon his request, Claire Conroy died with the feeding tube in place.

The court offered three ways which life-sustaining feeding treatment including feeding tubes could be withheld or withdrawn from patients: first, if it were clear that the patient would have refused "treatment" if competent; second, if there were no evidence of a patient's wishes, a substitute decision-maker could have "treatment" withdrawn if there were some trustworthy evidence that the patient would have refused treatment and the decision-maker was satisfied that the burdens of the patient's life with the treatment outweighed the benefits of that life; third, even if there were *no* evidence that a patient would have declined "treatment," it may still be withdrawn if the burden of life with "treatment" outweighs the benefit the patient derives from life.

Conroy is limited to nursing home patients with less than one year to live who never expressed "unequivocal" wishes to receive life-sustaining treatment while they were competent....

In Florida, Helen Corbett, 75, had been in a vegetative state since March 1982 receiving nutrition through a nasogastric feeding tube. Her husband requested a court order to permit withdrawal of the tube. Helen Corbett died before the court decided in *Corbett v. D'Alessandro* that she had a constitutional right to have the tube removed.

One of the most disturbing aspects of *Corbett* is the court's disregard of Florida's "living will" statute which specifically excluded nourishment from the life-prolonging procedures which a person could decline. Somehow the court thought that this should not affect the constitutional rights of someone in a permanent, vegetative state.

Elizabeth Bouvia

Bouvia v. Superior Court is the only appellate starvation case involving a competent adult. Elizabeth Bouvia, 28, had suffered from severe cerebral palsy since birth, and sought to have her nasogastric feeding tube removed. Although Bouvia had announced her intent to starve herself, the California Court of Appeals held that her motives were immaterial because she had a constitutional right to refuse "treatment." A concurring opinion called it a "right to die" and stated that this should ". . . include the ability to enlist assistance from others including the medical profession, making death as painless and quick as possible." Bouvia has apparently chosen not to exercise her constitutional right to refuse "treatment"—she now eats voluntarily.

Brophy v. New England Sinai Hospital, Inc. is the only reported appellate court decision where a court actually authorized death in advance of the person's death. In the other starvation cases the patients either died before the court rendered a decision (*Barber, Conroy, Corbett*) or the patient, once given the right to starve, declined to exercise that right (*Bouvia*).

In March 1983, forty-seven-year-old Paul Brophy suffered a ruptured aneurysm which left him in a "persistent vegetative state." Nine months later a gastronomy tube was inserted in his stomach to provide him with nutrition and hydration. There was expert testimony that Brophy could live for several years, that he was not terminally ill, nor was he in danger of death from any underlying illness. His wife requested that his feedings be discontinued. The trial court said "no." The Supreme Judicial Court, in a 4-3 decision, said "yes." Applying the doctrine of substituted judgment, the court decided that Brophy would have wanted it that way. The court's analysis, which relied heavily on the President's Commission Report, is by now a familiar syllogism: there is a common-law right to refuse treatment; nutrition and hydration by means of a feeding tube is "treatment"; therefore, Paul Brophy had the right to refuse feeding through the gastronomy tube.

Brophy was decided on September 11, 1986. Several weeks later he was transferred to Emerson Hospital in Concord, Massachusetts where he died on October 23, after eight days without food. The cause of death was listed as pneumonia. According to the chief of neurology at that hospital, "Not providing food may have weakened him to some degree but it was not starvation like Dachau. What killed him was the decision not to do a bronchoscopy to suck out infection in his lungs."

To its credit, the Massachusetts Supreme Judicial Court did not require the hospital which cared for Paul Brophy to participate in his death. A later court has not been so considerate. On January 22, 1987 a Colorado court required a hospital to "terminate medicinal, feeding and hydration treatment" for a mentally alert Hector Rodas, 34, who wanted to starve to death after becoming paralyzed from drug abuse. In response to the hospital's objection that its staff was being required to participate in suicide, the court engaged in what has now become a familiar denial syndrome: "... suicide does not occur where the natural consequence of a person's illness is death."

Starving the Sick

One of the more troublesome aspects of the starvation cases is that only the sick are implicated. Courts typically reject requests by healthy persons such as prisoners to starve themselves, relying on the principle that the state's interest in preserving life outweighs a person's death wish.

The courts' willingness to let only sick persons be starved has an uncomfortable similarity to the Third Reich's program for the mentally ill. Professor Robert Lifton writes (in ... *Nazi Doctors: Medical Killing and the Psychology of Genocide*): "Starvation as a method of killing was a logical extension of the frequent imagery of mental patients as 'useless eaters.'" The terminology used was never "starvation." Instead, special diets with inadequate calories to sustain life were given to patients. This ensured a slow death in about three months.

"The starvation and dehydration process is imposed and is irreversible. Can anyone feel complacent about that?"

Until 1983 there was no precedent in American jurisprudence for permitting the starvation and dehydration of human beings. The notion that withdrawing food and water from individuals would be elevated to a constitutional right was unthinkable. The courts, assisted by the President's Commission Report and the American Medical Association, have accomplished this result in a three-part process which began with labeling food and water received through a tube as "medical treatment." Starvation and dehydration were then distinguished from killing. Finally, the courts formulated a tenuous rights-based analysis to show that competent and incompetent individuals are exercising a common-law and constitutional right while being starved or dehydrated.

Practicing Denial

In order to separate the ideas of killing, euthanasia, and suicide from the idea of deliberate starvation and dehydration, the courts had to engage in conscious denial. Consider some of the statements:

> Euthanasia, of course, is neither justifiable nor excusable in California. (*Barber*)
>
> Her decision to allow nature to take its course is not equivalent to an election to commit suicide with real parties aiding and abetting therein. (*Bouvia*)
>
> Nor do we consider his [Brophy's] death to be against the State's interest in the prevention of suicide. He suffers an "affliction," ... which makes him incapable of swallowing. The discontinuance of the G-tube feedings will not be the death-producing agent set in motion with the intent of causing his death. A death which occurs after the removal of life-sustaining systems is from natural causes, neither set in motion nor intended by the patient. (*Brophy*)
>
> Declining life-sustaining medical treatment may not properly be viewed as an attempt to commit suicide. Refusing medical intervention merely allows the disease to take its natural course; if death were to eventually occur, it would be the result, primarily, of the underlying disease, and not the result of self-inflicted injury. (*Conroy*)

Distinguishing suicide from dying of natural causes is not only artificial line-drawing ... it is deceptive. A cerebral palsy victim such as Elizabeth Bouvia who does not eat and drink, dies as a direct result of not eating and drinking. She does not die from "natural causes." The New York Court of Appeals illustrated this point quite simply when it refused a request to discontinue blood transfusions for a cancer victim, John Storar: "... the transfusions were analogous to food—they would not cure the cancer, but they could eliminate the risk of death from another treatable cause."

Despite the courts' protestations, suicide *is* an issue when a competent patient asks to starve. At the 1986 meeting of the American Academy of Psychiatry and the Law, Dr. Robert Simon stated that without realizing it the courts may be accomplices to "silent suicide" in emphasizing the right of competent patients to forego medical treatment. He defines this as "the masked intention, usually by depressed people, to kill themselves by not complying with essential medical treatment or by starvation."

The common law and constitutional right which the courts have conferred so gratuitously on incompetent patients is not without its downside.

Two physicians who observed Claire Conroy testified that her death from dehydration would be painful. The trial judge who refused to allow Paul

Brophy to be starved made the following findings:

> If food and water are withheld from Brophy pursuant to the guardian's request, his prognosis will be certain death from starvation, or more probably from dehydration, which would occur within a period of time ranging from a minimum of five days to a maximum of three weeks.
>
> During this time, Brophy's body would be likely to experience the following effects from the lack of hydration and nutrition:
>
> a) His mouth would dry out and become caked or coated with thick material.
>
> b) His lips would become parched and cracked or fissured.
>
> c) His tongue would become swollen and might crack.
>
> d) His eyes would sink back into their orbits.
>
> e) His cheeks would become hollow.
>
> f) The mucosa (lining) of his nose might crack and cause his nose to bleed.
>
> g) His skin would hang loose on his body and become dry and scaly.
>
> h) His urine would become highly concentrated, causing burning of the bladder.
>
> i) The lining of his stomach would dry out causing dry heaves and vomiting.
>
> j) He would develop hyperthermia, a very high body temperature.
>
> k) His brain cells would begin drying out, causing convulsions.
>
> l) His respiratory tract would dry out, giving rise to very thick secretions, which could plug his lungs and cause death.
>
> m) Eventually his major organs would fail, including his lungs, heart and brain.
>
> The above-described process is extremely painful for a human being. Brophy's attending physician was unable to imagine a more cruel and violent death than thirsting to death.

It is difficult to imagine any person choosing starvation and dehydration. In fact there are few recorded instances in history where individuals have chosen this type of death voluntarily.

The denial syndrome is dangerous and not easily controlled. How will the courts contain the population at risk? Already, a question has arisen in the medical literature on the acceptability of withholding food and liquids from persons with Alzheimer's disease. What about bottle-fed infants? The most vulnerable group right now are incompetent sick persons. Unlike Elizabeth Bouvia, they are not able to change their minds and choose not to starve. For the incompetent, the starvation and dehydration process is *imposed* and is *irreversible*. Can anyone feel complacent about that?

The Right *Not* To Die

It is misplaced paternalism for the courts to assume that incompetent persons would choose the indignity of death by starvation and dehydration. The fact that the incompetent person, while competent, never expressed a desire to receive life-sustaining treatment is beside the point. How many Americans know that food and water is life-sustaining "treatment"?

The logic that supports this gratuitous right for incompetents equally supports a right *not* to be starved and dehydrated. This is the direction in which the courts must move *now*.

Jacqueline M. Nolan-Haley teaches law at Fordham University School of Law. Joseph R. Stanton is a retired associate clinical professor of medicine at Tufts University School of Medicine.

"The right to die is as integral a part of our human freedoms as the right to live."

viewpoint 10

Critically Ill Patients Have a Right to Die

Howard Moody

Elizabeth Bouvia, a 28-year-old California woman, suffers from severe cerebral palsy; she is quadriplegic—physically helpless and wholly unable to care for herself, totally dependent on others for all her needs. She can only lie flat on her back for the rest of her life, for she also suffers from degenerative arthritis and is in continuous pain.

Our society, using the medical establishment as our surrogate, has condemned Elizabeth Bouvia to life even though this intelligent, if despairing, young woman wants to die. The hospital in which she is a patient, practicing defensive medicine out of fear of liability, denies her the right to refuse treatment on the grounds that it will result in her death.

Elizabeth Bouvia exposes the underside of the miracle of modern medical technology. Her predicament threatens our "happy ending" culture which wants to believe that every problem has a solution, every question an answer, and that the admission of complexity and ambiguity are ways of avoiding progress. She makes it impossible to ignore the fact that the same technologies that make human life more bearable and bodily suffering less formidable can also keep alive severely brain-damaged children, the comatose, and others like Bouvia who endure extreme degrees of pain. Her decision to die and her inability to have that decision honored lay bare our society's attitudes and values about not only modern medical technology but also our most fundamental beliefs about death and life.

Who Shall Say?

The petitioner for Elizabeth Bouvia in the Court of Appeals in the State of California stated what I believe to be the only morally defensible position:

Howard Moody, "Life Sentence: Individual Autonomy, Medical Technology, and the 'Common Good';" *Christianity and Crisis*, October 12, 1987. Reprinted with permission. Copyright 1987 Christianity & Crisis, 537 West 121st Street, New York, New York 10027.

Who shall say what the minimum amount of available life must be? Does it matter if it be 15 to 20 years, 15 to 20 months or 15 to 20 days, if such life has been physically destroyed and its quality, dignity and purpose gone? As in all matters, lines must be drawn at some point, somewhere, but the decision must ultimately belong to the one whose life is at issue.

Here Elizabeth Bouvia's decision to forego medical treatment or life support through mechanical means belongs to her. It is not a medical decision for physicians to make. Neither is it a legal question whose soundness is to be resolved by lawyers and judges. It is not a conditional right subject to approval by ethics committees or courts of law. It is a moral and philosophical decision that, being a competent adult, is hers alone.

But Elizabeth Bouvia does not have the right to make that decision. The medical experts and attendants testify that if she is force-fed, she could live 15 or 20 more years in that demoralizing and debilitating condition. The "right-to-lifers" believe she has a duty to endure. The concern about there being no foul play or breaching of medical ethics is legitimate. So too is resistance to the unending pain inflicted on her body and mind until death comes to end her artificially prolonged life. Bouvia's passive acceptance of death is no longer sufficient. Our technology has negated that alternative and forced her to endure a highly invasive therapeutic prolongation of her life against her will. In other words, society is protecting her from the death she prefers to her interminable pain.

The person in our society best protected from death is the one that society has condemned to die. Death row inmates are under meticulous surveillance lest they take their own lives before the appointed hour—namely that time when the state has decided they shall die. Ironically, Bouvia also has no right to end her wretched existence until the state is ready. Only when her body finally revolts against all the new technologies of medicine will the

death / dying 43

state allow her to die.

If you are a hospital chaplain or Bouvia's pastor, what do you say to her or do for her in her utterly helpless and powerless position? How will you honor her integrity in the face of this massive resistance pitted against her weak will? The only theology germane to her case will be that which is born in and of her pain.

Ancient Beliefs

Many, of course, believe that it is wrong for an individual to commit suicide or at least that the individual decision to terminate life cannot be aided or abetted by the larger community (the public). Such beliefs are as old as the ancient Greeks and continue to influence contemporary medical ethics.

"... [W]e must not participate or assist in taking life, for that would violate what we as a civic community stand for," says Francis I. Kane in a Hastings Center Report ("Keeping Elizabeth Bouvia Alive for the Public Good," December 1985). "Ironically in demanding her individual autonomy, Elizabeth Bouvia has forced us to reaffirm the common good. In demanding that we help destroy her life, she has led us to profess, not just abstractly, the value of this individual life."

But what is the value of this individual life, and who shall make that determination? Society's harsh moralism against the right of a person to terminate his or her own life makes it difficult to draw any distinctions concerning the reason for such decisions. So of course does the medical professional's (society's surrogate) inordinate preoccupation with prolonging life no matter the quality or the circumstances.

If the Constitution of this nation defends any freedom, it is the fundamental "right to privacy." And in a number of Superior Court cases, a person of adult years and in sound mind has the right to determine whether or not to submit to lawful medical treatment. It follows that such a patient has the right to refuse any medical treatment, even that which may prolong or save her life. This basic right to privacy informed the Presidential Commission for the Study of Ethical Problems in Medicine in its conclusion:

> The voluntary choice of a competent and informed patient should determine whether or not life sustaining therapy will be undertaken, just as such choices provide the basis for other decisions about medical treatment... Health care professionals serve patients best by maintaining a presumption in favor of sustaining life while recognizing that competent patients are entitled to choose to forego any treatments including those that sustain life (*Deciding to Forego Life Sustaining Treatment,* U.S. Govt. Printing Office).

This right to privacy might enhance an individual's ability to choose life or death. Clearly this has not been the case for Bouvia. Why this is so is related to our society's view of death. Death is thoroughly institutionalized and medicalized. The Enemy or the Grim Reaper, not a welcome Friend, death is deemed unnatural, and its delay, however briefly, seen as the triumph of human achievement over the limitations of nature.

"A patient has the right to refuse any medical treatment, even that which may prolong or save her life."

This medical warfare against death is highly dramatized in media events of artificial organ transplants and the heart of a baboon in the body of a newborn baby. A medical and scientific hubris promises a seemingly unending and miraculous control of the life process, foretelling the time when death is a curable disease and immortality a medical commodity.

A "few setbacks" occur. The plague of AIDS is killing off our young people at alarming rates. But this is but a momentary setback to inevitable progress; AIDS will be conquered like all the diseases before it. Listen to the language of "right-to-lifers." In their fanatical semantics God is no longer ultimate but life is the ultimate. And if life becomes God, then the death of a life is deicide. A fetus must not be allowed to die no matter what pain, sorrow, or suffering may result from the consequence of its birth. Likewise, a brain-dead 80-year-old must be kept alive no matter the pain and expense to family and society.

The same logic leads to the refusal to let Elizabeth Bouvia die. That decree does not come from overzealous fundamentalists but from a secular court of law deciding on the values that this society stands for. The absolutizing of life can occur whether one is religious or not.

But surely, the absolute deification of life is an idolatry for the followers of a Master who said "Greater love hath no man than he who lays down his life for a friend" or "she who loses life will find it." For people of faith, life is meaningful and precious (sometimes), but not the only value in this world. Something more important can cause us to lay it on the line. Or we may lay it down when it becomes unbearably painful and meaningless.

In our faith, death and life go together. Death may be irrational to the mind's grasp and irreconcilable to the spirit's longing, but it is natural to the body's functioning. When we say death and life go together, we mean that death is written into our bodies—these bodies are the timekeepers of our lives. A symbol of our finitude and creatureliness, death is also an integral part of our human existence.

In Stanley Keleman's book *Living Your Dying*, he writes, "Our bodies know about dying and at some point in our lives are irrefutably, absolutely and totally committed to it with the lived experience of the genetic code." Death is inscribed into the birth of our bodies. We die to uterine life when we are born into the world, and our dying begins with that birth. But very quickly our minds deny what our bodies know, and in that repression or denial of the idea of our death grows fear, dread, and anxiety. For a society which values eternal youth and deifies life, thinking and talking about death—not as a morbid distraction from the joy of living, but as part of that living, just like illness and disease—is hard but necessary.

Death Not an End

Death with its mystery and unknown quality sometimes repels us, or scares us with its foreboding. Yet we still affirm that some part of us is unafraid of death; something sometimes is elevated and confirmed by death, something we cherish in the face of death, something we sometimes choose even though it means our death. I find it very hard to name, but I know that only in the presence of death are some things made believable.

Those of us believers, conservative and liberal, who loudly proclaim in our faith that life not death has the last word ought to be able to affirm the wish of an Elizabeth Bouvia. We ought to question seriously the use of a technology that, at incredible cost, might prolong life for a few more weeks or months, when the pain is intolerable or existence is a drugged semiconsciousness. Furthermore, people of faith who declare their belief in the resurrection and another reality that is the promise of God ought, more than most, to know that death is not the last word. Therefore, to grasp one more week or month or year even at unbearable pain and often excessive cost is a kind of act of ultimate distrust in God. The cynic in me conjectures that if Christians really believed in life after death, we could save the billions of dollars in health care spent in the last six months of life, trying to rob death of a few more days, weeks, or months.

"Control is meaningless if finally the state, through its medical surrogates, decides the time of death."

We need to resist the very real temptation to idolize life while at the same time we value and affirm life as a precious gift of creation. Not life as some kind of intellectual abstraction but life as a contextual reality where body, mind, and spirit are functioning so as to make it desirable, even with its disabilities and suffering.

The sole determiner of that life's quality and meaning is the one whose life it is. In an earlier time when death gave us no options and came earlier, individuals had no choice. With the advance of medical technology and the institutionalization of death, that choice is as valuable as life itself. That choice in modern society may be the ultimate test of our freedom, and to be able to say *no* to life is only possible if we have control of our lives. That control is meaningless if finally the state, through its medical surrogates, decides the time of death.

The right to die is as integral a part of our human freedoms as the right to live, and that right should not be hampered by the state's threat to impose penal sanctions on those medical personnel who might be disposed to lend assistance in ending an unbearable life. The medical profession freed from the threat of governmental or legal reprisal would, very likely, have no difficulty in accommodating an individual in Elizabeth Bouvia's situation.

Editor's note: Elizabeth Bouvia has been transferred to a nursing home and has accepted life-sustaining treatment. She dropped her suit against the hospital which denied her request to withdraw treatment.

Howard Moody is a contributing editor to Christianity and Crisis, *a bimonthly religious magazine.*

"If we are really autonomous to the point of having a right to choose death, then life . . . is absurd."

viewpoint 11

Critically Ill Patients Do Not Have a Right To Die

Robert Barry and Frank Morriss

Editor's note: The following viewpoint consists of two articles. Part I is by Robert Barry. Part II is by Frank Morriss.

I

The CBS television program "60 Minutes" reported in January 1985 that during the previous year, one out of every six terminally ill patients in Holland died from lethal injections administered upon request. During the summer of 1986, three bills were introduced in the Dutch legislature that would have legalized physician-administered lethal injections upon the request of terminally ill patients, and many Dutch courts have refused to convict physicians who have given injections at the request of terminally ill patients or quadriplegics (*The Right to Die*, by Derek Humphry and Ann Wickett, 1985).

Earlier this year when Christian Democrats gained a majority in the Dutch legislature, they were able to prevent these bills from being enacted. The vast majority of the Dutch people seem to support legalized mercy killing for the terminally ill, however, and it appears that only the Dutch pro-life movement and the Dutch Roman Catholic hierarchy are raising any objections to voluntary euthanasia. It is not at all clear that they will be able to withstand the contemporary tide favoring mercy killing.

Will America legalize mercy killing? The legal foundation for it is quietly being laid.

The Bouvia Case

In the Elizabeth Bouvia case, the California Supreme Court upheld an appellate court decision which permitted her to reject a feeding tube she judged to be too burdensome, but which physicians judged to be life sustaining. The court denied that the medical profession had any duties to preserve life against the wish of patients:

"It is incongruous, if not monstrous, for medical practitioners to assert . . . that someone else must live, or more accurately, endure, for '15 to 20 years.' We cannot conceive it to be the policy of this State to inflict such an ordeal upon anyone."

This decision caused dismay among pro-lifers. Causing even greater dismay was the concurring opinion of Judge Lynn Compton of the California Second District Appellate Court:

"Elizabeth has apparently made a conscious and informed choice that she prefers death to continued existence in her helpless and, to her, intolerable condition. I believe she has an absolute right to effectuate that decision. The state and the medical profession, instead of frustrating her desire, should be attempting to relieve her suffering by permitting and in fact assisting her to die with ease and dignity. The fact that she is forced to suffer the ordeal of self-starvation to achieve her objective is in itself inhumane.

"The right to die is an integral part of our right to control our own destinies so long as the rights of others are not affected. That right should, in my opinion, include the ability to enlist assistance from others, including the medical profession, in making death as painless and quick as possible. That ability should not be hampered by the state's threat to impose legal sanctions on those who might be disposed to lend assistance.

"The medical profession, freed of the threat of government or legal reprisal, would, I am sure, have no difficulty in accommodating an individual in Elizabeth's situation."

An "Absolute" Right

Judge Compton's decision makes it clear that Ms. Bouvia's aim was not merely to reject a "burdensome medical treatment," but to starve

---

Robert Barry, "A Step Closer to 'Mercy Killing'?" *Medical Moral Newsletter*, February 1987. Reprinted with permission.
Frank Morriss, "Court's Hideous Decision Makes Life the Ultimate Absurdity," *The Wanderer*, February 5, 1987. Reprinted with permission.

herself to death with the cooperation of the medical profession and the approval of the state. Those who recall the early days of the abortion controversy will remember that the right to an abortion also was called "absolute," and it was argued that abortion should be tolerated when it did not affect the rights of others. Judge Compton's decision makes clear that there is a movement to make the "right" to commit suicide as broad as the "fundamental" right to abortion.

Legalizing suicide for those who are medically stable and who are not imminently, certainly and irreversibly dying is morally objectionable not only because it is direct killing, but because of the "educational" value it has for others. When the law against killing is breached so that a certain class of citizens can be allowed to deliberately kill themselves or others, then a "whirlpool" is created which drags others into that breach who do not want to go.

> *"People have certain moral obligations to preserve their life, even when they are terminally ill or imminently dying."*

We have seen this happen with pornography. For the most part, those who actually appear in the films and photos are not the wealthy and powerful, but the desperate and impoverished. Just as pornography exploits the weak, so also legalized suicide will exploit the immature, despairing and lonely. They will be the ones who will be dragged into that "whirlpool" because they are most threatened by suicide. They will be the ones who could readily justify their suicide attempts by arguing that their pain, suffering and despair is greater than that of the terminal or hopelessly ill. Suicide is not a threat to people whose lives proceed without trouble, strife or tragedy. But to the sick, lonely, despairing or immature, suicide is a real and present danger, and sometimes it is the prohibitions of the law alone that prevent these unfortunates from ending their lives.

Mercy Killing

Mercy killing by omission is being actively promoted in the United States by the Society for the Right to Die. This organization believes we should have the right to have absolute control over all medical judgments in all circumstances, including the right to reject even food and water when the diagnosis is a "hopeless" condition. A "hopeless" condition is so vaguely defined by this organization that it could include myopia or diabetes.

Positive acts of mercy killing are being promoted by the Hemlock Society of California. This organization is promoting legislation that would permit physicians to assist "terminally ill" patients in their suicides by giving them lethal injections on request. In addition, Hemlock will introduce an amendment to the California state constitution that would permit voluntary suicide for the terminally ill.

One should not underestimate the seductiveness of these organizations' proposals. A person in severe pain or whose family faces large medical expenses could find very attractive a quick and painless death from a lethal injection. America's fixation with autonomy and self-determination makes us vulnerable to claims that a patient can reject any and all treatments. Such claims, however, obscure the fact that people have certain moral obligations to preserve their life, even when they are terminally ill or imminently dying.

Permitting those who decide that their medical condition is "hopeless" or "terminal" to end their lives establishes an elastic criterion that cannot prohibit others from ending their lives. There is no reason to say the sufferings of the terminally ill or dying are more intolerable than those of a lovelorn teenager or a perfectly healthy man who has just seen his family killed. If the terminally ill are allowed to kill themselves because of their pain, then all who suffer worse pains should have the same "privilege."

Suicide is not a felony in our country, but those who attempt it can have their freedom extensively restricted by the law to prevent them from harming themselves.

Although America may not legalize mercy killing in the near future, the chances of its happening are very strong now. The American pro-life movement and the nation's Roman Catholic bishops have voiced the only substantial opposition to the removal of life-sustaining, readily-providable food and water from medically stable but not terminally ill patients. Few moral theologians have raised objections to the court decisions in the past three or four years that have allowed feeding to be withdrawn from comatose patients. But the pro-life movement and the bishops have begun to take effective measures to prevent the legalization of mercy killing.

If suicide for the "terminal" or "hopelessly ill" should become legalized, we will probably see a sharp increase in teenage suicide, for when adolescents see that it is permissible for the sick or dying to kill themselves, they will judge it to be permissible for themselves. If America legalizes suicide in some circumstances, it might put our young people in serious danger.

II

A Colorado district judge has ruled that a person has a "right to die," and that no one may interfere with that choice. The implications of Judge Charles Buss' ruling are frightening and hideous, and since in the case at hand there was no appeal, the ruling will stand as precedent law until and if it is overruled.

Hector Rodas, 35, has been paralyzed for many months as a result of drug abuse. He cannot speak or swallow, but it is claimed he can communicate by eye or finger movement. A message he began delivering many months ago, it is said, asked that injected nutrition via tubes being given at Hilltop Rehabilitation Hospital, Grand Junction, be discontinued so he could die. The hospital refused this request, claiming it would be liable under suicide or homicide statutes, and questioned Rodas' competence owing to his condition.

In defending his decision on television, Judge Buss insisted that life belongs to the individual and may be terminated at choice. In his opinion, the judge wrote that unwanted treatment such as was being given to Rodas amounted to "an on-going battery" imposed on him. Thus, forced feeding becomes a "battery."

If this is the case, then certainly seizing a person about to jump from a bridge or a building ledge becomes a "battery" if the jumper chooses to discontinue living. Doctors, who are pledged to do all possible to sustain life and prevent death, become guilty of battery if they act to revive someone who has overdosed on drugs in order to kill themselves.

A Small Step

Society is ordered by Judge Buss to become the abetter of self-chosen death, even if by being prohibited from interfering. It is only a small step to demanding that society become the active cooperator in suicide, even though in the Rodas case, Judge Buss by fiat declared the action neither suicide nor murder. Judges, however, do not have the miraculous power to change the nature of an act by renaming it.

Since I have only media reports on this case, I don't know if the judge was able to cite just from where the "right to die" is derived. Of course, the U.S. Supreme Court gave him the example of fabricating a deadly "right" when it held in *Roe v. Wade* that a woman has the "right" to kill her unborn child, and by fiat declared such action by her and her physician not homicide or murder.

Rodas' physician, Larry Cobb, was reported to have refused to take part in the discontinuation of the nutritional sustenance via tubes of his patient's life. The hospital's attorney said that another physician had agreed to step in and act as Rodas' "physician" in the process of neglect that will lead to his death.

It may be that God's right over life—now subordinated to the individual's—is not defensible in our present judicial climate. That divine right was, however, in effect, recognized all through the history of English law by recognition of the natural law, which, as Hamlet said, sets its canon against self-slaughter. We are now seeing the evil fruits of the abandonment of the natural law.

A Wave of Teen Suicides

Just how far will the "right to die" be carried? There is a veritable wave of teenage suicides at present. Will parents be denied the right to interfere with their children's "right to die," as they are denied the right to interfere with their children's sexual "choices" and even the "choice" for abortion?

How determined and prolonged must the desire to die be to earn recognition by the judicial system of this country?

By putting the choice to die on the level of a "right," all such questions become irrelevant. The mere choice becomes constitutionally enshrined along with all the other rights of citizens. Death now takes its place by judicial decision in the opening words of the Declaration of Independence, which spoke of the "unalienable" right to life, liberty, and the pursuit of happiness. That must read, if Judge Buss' decision prevails, the right to life *or* death.

"If there is indeed a right to die based on the autonomy of the individual, then no individual really owes anything to God, much less to society."

The Rodas decision was reinforced by Dr. Frederick R. Abrams, said to be "a nationally recognized medical ethicist," principally I suppose by his association with the Center for Applied Biomedical Ethics at Rose Medical Center, Denver.

Dr. Abrams called the "right to die" a "legitimate upholding of personal autonomy." But if the natural law prohibition of suicide can be nullified by "personal autonomy," why should not every other evil a person can commit be justified? Bestiality, Devil worship, the Black Mass, become a "right." I cite those because they are so-called victimless acts, done by personal choice. Of course, we know society is a victim of those evils, just as society shall surely be the victim of legalized suicide, even if judges do not wish to consider the subject of the suicide—the individual choosing death—a victim.

Limits to Autonomy

Were we really given life as an absolute possession, which we may discard as we may throw away any gift? This speaks of the existential idea that life is absurd. But only if life is an absolute possession, to be honored or trashed, can the "right to die" be recognized, as Dr. Abrams' logic recognizes.

The very purpose of life then becomes subject to

individual opinion. Autonomy installs each individual as the master of his own life and for his own purposes.

If the autonomous individual sees happiness as his purpose in living, then unhappiness becomes the excuse for the "right to die." If he sees success as his purpose in living, then failure becomes such an excuse. If education and advancement are his purposes, then failure in school or in career becomes an excuse to exercise the "right to die."

> "There is little to live for in a culture and society that talks about death and dying as a 'right.'"

If there is indeed a right to die based on the autonomy of the individual, then no individual really owes anything to God, much less to society. Why should tobacco, cocaine, the taking of poison, refusing to obey protective laws such as wearing helmets or using seatbelts be a problem for society in the face of the individual's autonomy?

If a person has a true right to die, and is truly autonomous, which is the basis of that right, then what can society insist he do in regard to lesser obligations? I mean if the right to live is no obligation at all, what of the duty to support one's children, or to pay one's debts, or to serve one's country? All of those duties fade away in a civilization that recognizes the choice to die as a right. Let society try to enforce such duties in the face of the autonomous individual's right to say "I won't do them" by taking his life.

The next time you see someone drowning, don't attempt a rescue until you determine whether or not it is an exercise of the right to die. You may be charged with assault and battery!

What Will We Tell Our Youth?

What are we going to tell our youth in the face of the Judge Buss decision and the reasoning of Dr. Abrams? We can only say, we think there are things to live for, but if you prefer to die we can't interfere. Quite frankly, the most compelling argument they might offer in reply is that there is little to live for in a culture and society that talks about death and dying as a "right." What can Dr. Abrams have to say to a young person who might say, "If death is a right and if that right is based upon my autonomy, what indeed outside of myself is there to live for?" If, as Dr. Abrams says, Rodas was trapped in a paralyzed body, I might say in his ethic of the autonomous individual we are all trapped in a paralyzed vision of humanity. We are trapped in the evil idea that man is supreme—his own end and purpose, his own measure of the value of any and all things.

It is a terrible situation, as indeed the history of modern society shows, particularly the history of the effect of the philosophy of atheistic existentialism.

If we aren't the property of God, then we are the playthings of chance, or worse, of the Devil. If we are really autonomous to the point of having a right to choose death, then life as a gift we did not ask to be given and did not have the chance to refuse indeed is absurd—as the radical existentialists have said all along.

Hell is the proper home of the fully autonomous individual. It is the place where those who choose to be "on their own" have that wish fulfilled. Heaven is the place for those who concluded life was given to them not by blind fortune, but by a living God. Heaven is the reason *for* life and the end *of* life. You don't get there by concluding that life is given you for your own purposes, rather than God's. Heaven is the reward for accepting life on God's terms and using it on those terms. If that insults your individual autonomy and your "right to die," don't blame God for your missing that reward.

Robert Barry is a Dominican priest and an assistant professor of religious studies at the University of Illinois. Frank Morriss is a contributing editor to The Wanderer, *a national Catholic weekly.*

"Sound moral principles support the view that it is sometimes permissible to forgo life-sustaining treatments."

viewpoint 12

Critically Ill Patients' Right To Die Is Limited

Ruth Macklin

Few would argue against the proposition that modern medicine has brought untold benefits to millions of people. Most would agree that cures for diseases, relief from pain and suffering, and the ability to prolong life are advances for which we can be grateful. But for some patients the burdens of modern medical treatment outweigh the benefits, with the result that an increasing number are now claiming the "right to die."

If the "right to die" seems like an odd sort of right, it is easy to see why. Our society not only opposes suicide, but it spends a considerable amount of money and effort on prevention. It appears to be inconsistent, then, to denounce suicide on the one hand, and yet to proclaim that there exists a "right to die." But the inconsistency is only apparent, as can be shown by first identifying clear, undisputed cases of suicidal behavior, and then comparing these cases with the circumstances in which patients and their families seek to exercise the newly recognized "right to die."

Ann B., a seventy-year-old woman, was admitted against her wishes to the psychiatric ward at City Hospital. She was found by a housekeeper in her apartment, playing with a knife at her wrists. The housekeeper called the emergency medical service, and Ann B. was whisked by ambulance to the psychiatric emergency room, where a psychiatrist evaluated her and found her to be "dangerous to self," meaning "suicidal." The psychiatrist also made a diagnosis of depression. Once she was admitted, Ann B. revealed that she had made a suicide pact with her sister, who had recently fallen ill and was a patient in another unit at City Hospital. The two sisters had had little contact with the outside world and, it appears, had led a somewhat eccentric life in isolation from anyone but each other. Ann B.'s actions with the knife, along with her disclosure of the pact with her sister, make this a clear, undisputed case of genuinely suicidal behavior.

A Change in Condition

Soon after her admission Ann B. developed a fever and was found to have pneumonia. She said she wanted to die and had to be restrained to keep her in the hospital bed. From that point on, her medical condition deteriorated: a catheter, or thin tube, had to be inserted into her bladder because she was retaining her urine; her respiratory status declined, and a breathing tube was placed; she developed skin infections over her whole body, as well as localized bedsores; and she became incontinent, unable to control her bowel functions. Although the patient had been mentally alert and oriented when she was admitted to the hospital, by this time her mental status had changed. She became lethargic and unresponsive. She lay in bed all day staring at the ceiling. Caregivers rarely found her in any other position. They wondered: Is this patient mentally capable of making decisions on her own behalf? Does her suicidal behavior suggest that she suffers from diminished autonomy, thus opening the way for justified paternalism on the part of her caregivers? Or, on the other hand, does the onset of multiple medical problems change the picture, so that now Ann B. has a rational reason to refuse life-prolonging medical treatments?

Psychiatrists consider depression to be both a life-threatening condition and a "treatable illness." The incidence of suicide attempts among depressed persons is high, and so clinicians in psychiatry and other medical specialties consider it their obligation to treat depression. They tend to dismiss refusals of treatment made by such patients. By definition, it is claimed, a diagnosis of depression means the patient has a bleak outlook on life, decision-making is

From *Mortal Choices* by Ruth Macklin. Copyright © 1987 by Ruth Macklin. Reprinted by permission of Pantheon Books, a division of Random House, Inc.

death / dying 51

impaired, and paternalistic behavior toward the patient is warranted. If the depression can be cured, the patient's outlook will improve and he will most likely cease to refuse life-prolonging medical therapies. This reasoning demonstrates the need to distinguish between refusals of medical treatment that stem from suicidal wishes and those that emanate from patients' rational judgments about their own quality of life.

> *"[There is] a distinction, one that has ethical implications, between . . . attempts to end one's life that are a consequence of mental illness or emotional disorder and those that arise from a miserable quality of life."*

Patients can be kept alive hooked up to respirators, dialysis machines, and other devices that keep their vital organs functioning; terminally ill cancer patients suffering intractable pain are given chemotherapy, blood transfusions, radiation, and other treatments to prolong their lives by a few weeks or months; severely demented elderly patients must often have a tube inserted through the nose and esophagas to the stomach, in order to receive medicines and food. To equate the right to die with suicide would be to fail to recognize that such treatments can sometimes make continued life an excessive burden. Many patients on life supports, who are not depressed, judge the quality of their own life to be so poor that they do not want it prolonged further by artificial means. And those patients whose depression results from learning their diagnosis of terminal illness may wish to die sooner rather than later. Such a wish might then be entirely rational.

"Rational" Suicide

Suicidologists have devised the category of "rational" or "logical" suicide to apply to such cases. This approach recognizes a distinction, one that has ethical implications, between suicidal wishes or actual attempts to end one's life that are a consequence of mental illness or emotional disorder and those that arise from a miserable quality of life or a hopeless prognosis. To mark these distinctions, better than the simple phrase "the right to die" are two alternative descriptions: "the right to die a natural death" and "the right to die with dignity."

Hospitalized patients have come up against two formidable barriers in seeking to have treatments withdrawn or withheld. The first is the unwillingness of physicians to allow their patients to forgo therapies that could preserve their lives.

Doctors are dedicated to curing disease and to prolonging life. They have traditionally seen it as their duty to pursue these goals, even in the face of refusals by patients who are fully competent to decide about their own treatments. The second barrier has been the law, which until quite recently stood behind physicians in their reluctance to allow patients to refuse treatments when the likely result would be death.

Now, however, much has changed, because of some leading court decisions as well as more assertive actions by patients and their families. Physicians are acknowledging, alongside their obligation to preserve and prolong life, another equally valid goal of medical practice: to relieve suffering. As in any practice having multiple goals, these two noble aims of medicine may sometimes conflict. Even when a life could be prolonged, a physician might question the wisdom of continuing treatment. . . .

Legal and Moral Problems

The legal developments surrounding patients' rights to refuse life-sustaining treatments are not without their moral problems. Although the trend in living-will statutes suggests that formerly competent patients can now have their wishes honored once they are no longer able to decide for themselves, what about individuals who have never stated what they would want done medically when they are no longer capable of making decisions? Is it morally acceptable for others to make decisions for them? And if so, who should those others be: Doctors? Family members? Judges? Hospital ethics committees? Is there an objective basis for making such decisions? And is there a danger in allowing any person to decide for another based on "quality-of-life" considerations?

These now-familiar questions have no simple answers. But they can be approached in order of decreasing certainty about what is the morally right thing to do. The greatest certainty lies in cases involving mentally competent adult patients. There is little or no difference between the general situation regarding decisions about how aggressive treatments should be and specific decisions to forgo life-sustaining treatments. Neither a moral nor a legal justification exists for ignoring patients' clearly stated wishes to withdraw or withhold those treatments, even if the family begs the doctor to "do everything possible." As in the case of Ann B., exceptions to this rule arise when patients are depressed and therefore lack proper judgment to decide about forgoing life-prolonging treatment. But in nondepressed patients, and especially when the patient suffers from a fatal illness, even the traditional reluctance of the courts to go against physicians' recommendations has all but disappeared. . . .

Somewhat less certainty surrounds the situation of patients who are no longer mentally competent at the time a decision must be made but who had given indications about desired medical treatment while still competent. Although evidence of patients' wishes need not be in the form of a written living will, such a document probably offers the most solid evidence. However, a statement made orally to family members might be equally valid....

A factor of considerable moral importance is the mode of dying. The process of dying can be peaceful and easy for the patient, or it can be painful and frightening. For many patients, prolonging their lives amounts to prolonging an agonizing dying process, one fraught with discomfort, nausea, shortness of breath, or mental confusion. In deciding which treatments may be withheld or withdrawn, physicians should consider the manner of death and, if possible, choose a plan of selective therapy that will result in the "least worst death."

The Conroy Case

In the years since courts were first brought into cases involving termination of life supports, there has been a gradual progression from greater to lesser moral certainty. Early cases dealt with removal of respirators from patients in permanent coma, or withdrawing treatment from patients who had clearly stated their wishes about life prolongation. The final court case to consider here is one in which these features were absent, and in which several important precedents were set. In January 1985, nine years after the [Karen Ann] Quinlan case was decided, the New Jersey Supreme Court permitted the withdrawal of life supports from a nursing-home patient who was not comatose. The patient had no written living will, the "treatment" in question was food and fluids rather than a respirator or other high-technology device, and the life-sustaining measures had to be withdrawn rather than simply withheld.

Claire Conroy was an eighty-four-year-old nursing-home resident who suffered from serious and irreversible physical and mental impairments, including arteriosclerotic heart disease, hypertension, and diabetes. Her condition eventually reached a point where she could not speak and could not swallow enough food and water to sustain herself. She was fed and medicated through a nasogastric tube inserted through her nose and extending down into her stomach. She was incontinent. She could, though, move to a minor extent, and occasionally smiled and moaned in response to stimuli. The patient's nephew, her guardian, sought court permission to remove his incompetent aunt's feeding tube. This request was opposed by the patient's court-appointed guardian, known as guardian *ad litem* (a guardian appointed solely for the purpose of making specific decisions during a limited time period). The patient's own physician stated that he did not think it would be acceptable medical practice to remove the tube and that he was in favor of keeping it in place. Ms. Conroy's nephew, based on his knowledge of his aunt's attitudes, said that if she had been competent, she would never have permitted the nasogastric tube to be inserted in the first place.

"Physicians should consider the manner of death and, if possible, choose a plan of selective therapy that will result in the 'least worst death.'"

Ms. Conroy was a Roman Catholic. A Catholic priest testified in the case that acceptable church teaching could be found in a document entitled "Declaration of Euthanasia" published by the Vatican Congregation for the Doctrine of the Faith, dated June 26, 1980. The test that this document used required a weighing of the burdens and benefits to the patient of remaining alive with the aid of extraordinary life-sustaining medical treatment. The priest said that life-sustaining procedures could be withdrawn if they were extraordinary, which he defined to embrace "all procedures, operations or other interventions which are excessively expensive, burdensome or inconvenient or which offer no hope of benefit to a patient." The priest concluded that the use of the nasogastric tube was extraordinary, and that removal of the tube would be ethical and moral, even though the ensuing period until Ms. Conroy's death would be painful....

Ethical Uncertainty

Situations involving great ethical and legal uncertainty are those in which a patient is no longer competent, had never clearly stated any preferences while still competent about what sorts of medical treatment should be administered or withheld, but had provided some bit of evidence through attitudes or behavior during prior illnesses. Even more troubling are situations in which no evidence whatsoever is available about what the patient would have wanted. The standard in such cases should be the "best interest" of the patient. But that is precisely the problem: Is there any objective way of determining what is in the best interest of someone lacking the mental capacity to decide about continued life?

The court in the Conroy case tackled this problem head-on. It did not want to rule out the possibility of terminating life-sustaining treatment for persons who had never clearly expressed any desires but who are now suffering a prolonged and painful death. Judge

Schreiber, who wrote the opinion in the Conroy case, articulated two best-interest tests for determining when life-sustaining treatment may be withheld, tests that supplement the "subjective test" (what the patient would have wanted).

> *"A morally acceptable reason to withdraw or withhold life supports exists when continued life would not be a benefit to the patient."*

The two standards are a "limited-objective" test and a "pure-objective" test.

> Under the "limited-objective" test, life-sustaining treatment may be withheld or withdrawn from a patient in Claire Conroy's situation when there is some trustworthy evidence that the patient would have refused treatment, and the decision-maker is satisfied that it is clear that the burdens of the patient's continued life with the treatment outweigh the benefits of that life for him. By this we mean that the patient is suffering, and will continue to suffer throughout the expected duration of his life, unavoidable pain, and that the net burdens of his prolonged life (the pain and suffering of his life with the treatment less the amount and duration of pain that the patient would likely experience if the treatment were withdrawn) markedly outweigh any physical pleasure, emotional enjoyment, or intellectual satisfaction that the patient may still be able to derive from life.

The pure-objective test is similar to the limited-objective test but omits the element requiring evidence of the patient's prior wishes. Thus,

> the net burdens of the patient's life with the treatment should clearly and markedly outweigh the benefits that the patient derives from life. Further, the recurring, unavoidable and severe pain of the patient's life with the treatment should be such that the effect of administering life-sustaining treatment would be inhumane.

These two tests—limited-objective and pure-objective—constitute a bold step in interpreting the vague notion of "best interest," and the Conroy decision sets an important legal precedent. This is not to say that it will always be an easy matter to apply the tests. The court's wording makes it appear that determining a patient's objective best interest is a matter of arithmetic calculation: the net burdens of his prolonged life (the pain and suffering of his life with the treatment less the amount and duration of pain that the patient would likely experience if the treatment were withdrawn) markedly outweigh any physical pleasure, emotional enjoyment, or intellectual satisfaction that the patient may still be able to derive from life. Yet even if this cannot be accomplished by means of simple calculations, it is a step forward in trying to explicate the notion of "best interest" as it applies to incompetent patients.

As important as the court's positive attempt to give meaning to the best-interest doctrine is, what it explicitly ruled out was when such determinations must be made. The opinion stated quite clearly that it would not be appropriate for a decision-maker to determine that someone else's life is not worth living simply because, to the decision-maker, the patient's "quality of life" or value to society seems negligible.

Sound Moral Principles

It is widely agreed—but with objections voiced by some—that decisions to forgo life-sustaining treatment should not be based on assessments of the personal worth or social utility of another's life, or the value of that life to others. A morally acceptable reason to withdraw or withhold life supports exists when continued life would not be a benefit to the patient. This description clearly fits patients who are irreversibly comatose. With perhaps less certainty it also applies to patients on life supports who have deteriorated mentally to the point where they can no longer recognize their loved ones, cannot experience any pleasure, and can engage in no human relationships. Although safeguards should always be in place for the protection of patients, sound moral principles support the view that it is sometimes permissible to forgo life-sustaining treatments.

Ruth Macklin is professor of bioethics in the department of epidemiology and social medicine at Albert Einstein College of Medicine in New York.

"At all costs avoid doctors who don't believe there's at least some hope for a person with AIDS."

viewpoint 13

AIDS Should Be Faced with Hope

Tom O'Connor

Few things in AIDS are as tragic as the hopelessness the disease can bring. Most people see no outcome to AIDS but death. Yet AIDS is not a hopeless disease. Neither hopelessness nor helplessness has to be a part of any disease at all. In fact, these attitudes often precede and hasten a number of fatal diseases. None of us can live long without hope, yet finding it can be difficult when we face AIDS.

Where should we seek hope for AIDS? Not in the six o'clock news. Television's message is one of endless hopelessness: no hope for treatment, no hope for cure, and no hope for an end to the deaths. Television presents what people like, and people like to be scared. The news draws on AIDS hysteria and feeds it back to already hyped viewers. For TV, AIDS is just another docudrama. Unless you believe they will contribute to your mental health, avoid the news and the so-called AIDS specials, and seek your information elsewhere.

Unfortunately, TV and the other news media are not our only sources of hopelessness. They take their cue from medical authorities whose well-intentioned but grim opinions can squelch hope in even the strongest optimist. Many doctors believe no hope is better than false hope, one that is later cruelly shattered by reality. But how can hope be false? By its very nature, false hope, like false truth, false beauty, or false good, cannot exist.

Malpractice suits, however, do exist, and offering no hope is often a doctor's surest way to avoid them. "According to the malpractice law," physician Robert F. Cathcart III states, "if you predict the worst, you're covered; if you're optimistic and you fail, you get sued." A healthy amount of caution need not result in the bleak, untherapeutic attitude so common in medical circles today. Instead of saying, "This disease is serious. Most people don't live past eighteen months," a physician could say, "We don't really know how the disease will progress. There are several treatment avenues to explore, and we will certainly do our best to help you deal with the disease and keep a good quality of life." What your physician says often tells more about his or her attitude toward life than about the disease itself. At all costs avoid doctors who don't believe there's at least some hope for a person with AIDS.

Pessimism and AIDS

Remaining staunchly pessimistic is like hiding your head in the sand. No matter how devastating, almost no disease in the world has proven 100 percent fatal, and AIDS is no exception. A small but growing number of people with AIDS have lived—and are still living—much longer than the predictions of their doctors. There are those who say these PWAs (persons with AIDS) are *yet* to die of the disease. But when you find yourself living and enjoying life three or four years beyond your predicted time of death, that *yet* objection becomes a matter of mere words. Any of us might die in that period of time, and no one can foretell whether death is as close as an accident tomorrow or as far away as an old person's bed. This uncertainty allows us to look at the future any way we please. You can expect life just as easily as you can expect death.

Hope and a positive attitude are matters of choice, of seeing the glass half full rather than half empty. I do not for a moment suggest that you cheerlead yourself into an illusion of wellness, which is the kind of denial found in many participants in the San Francisco biopsychosocial AIDS pilot study. A positive attitude calls for a realistic, hard look at what is as well as the most optimistic assessment of what can be. Such an attitude toward AIDS begins

Tom O'Connor, *Living With AIDS*. San Francisco, CA: Corwin Publishers, 1987. Reprinted with permission.

only when you realize the disease is likely to be fatal. But you must go beyond this realization and recognize that although life will give you no guarantees, it will constantly offer you new possibilities. Failing to take this step toward hope, many people lie down and wait for death. Their tragedy rests not in dying (for there are those for whom death is a new opportunity) but in failing to live while alive. Surrendering your will to live by giving up and waiting passively for the end can be a last-ditch attempt to control and deny death by trying to have the last say about its time: "I will die now, when I want, and not later, when death wants."

"You can expect life just as easily as you can expect death."

Hopelessness can be alluring and comforting for some of us. Since life with AIDS can be so uncertain, we often grab on to the reassuring guarantee of death after AIDS. That's why so many gay men feel an initial relief when diagnosed. Immune deterioration spurs many people to make changes early on. But some of us interpret this signal to mean only that the disease is near and unavoidable. Our emotional life is thrown into chaos. The certainty of death can end one's emotional turmoil, so the idea of hope—the possibility that death might not happen after all—could raise a disquieting specter.

Why do some people cling adamantly to hope while others do not? Several studies suggest that hopelessness and lack of self-worth go together. One study found that 76 percent of subjects who felt hopeless about their cancer suffered from low self-esteem, usually a result of a stressful childhood occasioned by a broken home, abuse, or lack of closeness to their parents. "Why should I hope?" was a frequent theme. "The last time I did and opened myself up, I was let down. I will never go through that pain again." Deep inside, these people were waiting to die because they could not live with themselves.

The message that "gay is no good," drummed into us as we grew up and still lurking in our minds, makes this kind of self-hatred too frequent among gays. Loving ourselves as gay people—let alone just as people—is often no easy task.

Beating the Odds

Learning self-love and forgiveness is the first step toward strengthening hope and nurturing your health. "You have to forgive yourself first," says Los Angeles bodybuilding contestant and AIDS veteran Louie Nassaney, "then forgive the rest of the world, including your family. A lot of people have a lot of parental guidance they just don't agree with. They blame their parents for what happened in their life, and that's no way to get anywhere in this world. *You've got to do the work."*

When Louie was diagnosed with Kaposi's sarcoma in 1982, he expected his doctors to save him immediately. Seven months of interferon treatment gave him very unpleasant side effects. Then the doctors wanted to try chemotherapy and radiation. Louie said no; friends who had undergone radiation and chemotherapy had died. Instead, he changed his diet, engaged in exercise and body-work methods, and turned to the self-affirmation, meditation, and guided imagery techniques of Louise Hay, the director of the Love Yourself, Heal Yourself Center in Santa Monica, California. Louie also sought, and got, the support of family and friends.

"I cleaned up all the garbage," Louie says. "I talked a lot about death and about my personal friends who were dying. [Louise] said that was okay, that's part of what's going on." Louie's particular visualization consisted in "erasing" the purple lesion of his sarcoma as if it had been just pencil marks on his skin. Six months later, the doctors confirmed that his sarcoma had disappeared. Louie became a participant in the Los Angeles Superman Contest, a bodybuilding pageant in which he was runner-up. When I saw him at a San Francisco healing service last August [1986], I would not have known he had AIDS. Those who had set their eyes on this beautifully muscular thirty-year-old man were also surprised when he told them about his disease. "My personal view is that the AIDS virus doesn't like people with AIDS to go and put energy into themselves and work out. When I go to the gym and do aerobics, I'm not being lazy and letting it grow. The virus might still exist in my body. But it's been three years now, and see how I look."

Success Stories

San Francisco playwright and composer Dan Turner refused to crumple when he was diagnosed with Kaposi's sarcoma in February 1982. Dan remembered how depression and a belief that he would not get well had prolonged an earlier bout with hepatitis. "When I was told I had cancer," Dan says, "I reflected on that experience. I knew I could win. And I knew if I got into the same negative head trip again, it would kill me."

Believing that emotional expression through music, his lifelong avocation, would help lower stress, Dan started writing a musical after giving up his word-processing job and going on disability. To bolster his immunity Dan now works in his garden, practices transcendental meditation, has used acupuncture and Chinese herbal medicine, and employs the visualization techniques developed by well-known cancer therapists O. Carl Simonton and Stephanie

Matthews Simonton.

Dan is a Catholic, so he uses the image of the doubting Thomas in his visualization. "I put my hands on the wounds of Christ," he says, "and feel the blood of Christ go through my hands, into my body, and eliminate all my toxins. The blood of Christ is such a powerful image if it's part of your faith." The week-long course of interferon shots Dan gives himself every third week does not seem to have produced serious side effects. He hasn't had any new sarcoma lesions since April 1982.

Although Dan became an activist and spokesman early in the fight against AIDS, he rose to national fame when a photograph in an AIDS article in the June 1986 issue of the *National Geographic* magazine showed him working out on a Nautilus machine. "People have to know they have an option," says Dan. "You can focus on living in the present moment, or you can get wrapped up in the horrors of the future and let those burden you. If you blame everything on AIDS and become obsessed with it, you can create a powerful monster within."

Because stories about AIDS successes do not usually make the news (understandably, quite a few long-term survivors avoid publicity), the idea that one can survive the disease despite lack of a medical cure or effective treatment fails to reach many with AIDS. . . .

Death

Many people with AIDS or ARC [AIDS-related complex] show no progress despite their perseverance. Sometimes the disease cannot be reversed, and death then becomes an acceptable alternative. There comes a time in our lives when we feel we either have attained our goals or shouldn't struggle any longer to do so, when our desire for peace is greater than the happiness we derive from survival. At such times, death liberates.

"Learning self-love and forgiveness is the first step toward strengthening hope and nurturing your health."

Death is a natural process in which all of us sooner or later must participate, and we shouldn't feel guilty or defeated when we switch from fighting the disease to accepting death. But in accepting death we should approach it without anger or bitterness. It is sad that many people have died from AIDS hating and blaming themselves for having gotten the disease, bitterly accusing their gay brothers and sisters of abandoning them, and resenting the medical community for not curing them. What a terrible burden to bear as you leave this world! Freeing yourself from obligations has little to do with material matters such as debts, wills, and the disposition of your possessions (although these could be attended to, if the time and desire exist). But it has everything to do with *trying* to leave this world loving yourself and loving others. To die this way is never a failure. It is to die in a state of hope and grace.

Recurring symptoms or deterioration might be asking you to investigate two alternatives: dying or living. Even taking an honest approach to this question, you might find it difficult to choose between preparing yourself for death or working back towards health. This ambivalence and confusion is natural. If death haunts you, go inside, be introspective. Perhaps exploring and even visualizing the possibility of your death will bring you a measure of comfort. It is perfectly normal to wonder what your death will be like, how it will come about, if you will feel pain, and whether you want to be conscious. Do not shun such questions. Facing things is the essence of living.

The Will To Live

After exploring your death, you might find yourself reaffirming life all the more. You have rekindled your will to live by being imaginative and creative about your death.

The will to live is a powerful biological and psychological force that operates unconsciously. It is perceived as a sense of connection with the rest of the universe and as being part of a higher order, often referred to as spirit. It is also a vital force that enhances your body's ability to fight disease. Some societies, such as some native American, Australian aborigine, and African tribes, believe that a person succumbs to disease because his or her spirit has been taken away. Many doctors today would agree with this observation. "[The will to live] is not a theoretical abstraction," says Norman Cousins, "but a physiologic reality with therapeutic characteristics."

To be human is to engage in a struggle between the will to live and the will to die, a pull between our own creative and destructive forces, with love, hope, and freedom on one side and self-hate, hopelessness, and despair on the other. We can express our will to act, our will to propel ourselves forward, either creatively or destructively. When we express our creative energies fully, no room is left for destructive forces to operate. But when our creative forces are blocked by emotional entanglement or suppression, the destructive forces become unleashed and endanger our health.

The Existential Vacuum

Unlike animals, we possess few instincts that tell us what to do. We live mostly by choice, and during the twentieth century many of the traditions that once guided these choices have been lost. As a consequence, we often don't know what to do with our lives and live in what psychiatrist and concentration-camp survivor Victor E. Frankl calls the "existential vacuum." Our lives seem empty.

To ease this unbearable boredom, we resort to satisfying obsessions for money, possessions, and power. We turn to alcohol and addictive drugs and mindlessly pursue sexual pleasures. Self-destruction seems preferable to ennui. (How many have committed suicide out of excruciating boredom?) When all these material pursuits lose their appeal—as they must at one point or another—we're back to the initial emptiness. Without meaning in our lives we become hopeless, and not knowing what to do we feel helpless. We give up on living.

Existential despair in gay men often results from the fear of aging. Many of us therefore fill our existential vacuum with an exclusive concern for physical beauty that we believe is at its best during our twenties and thirties. The forties signal the end of this beauty for many of us. Hair starts to thin out or gray, wrinkles appear, the body goes to pot, and life loses its meaning. How many times have you heard "I shall never live to be 40"? "AIDS is the perfect answer to check out at that age," says Louie Nassaney.

"After exploring your death, you might find yourself reaffirming life all the more."

The existential vacuum need not exist. We *can* get back in touch with our will to live by trying to be a part of the rest of creation and seeing ourselves as part of a greater scheme of things. For some people this greater order might be God—the higher power personified. For others it might be the realization that things in the universe are interrelated in a way that defies explanation—a conceptual higher power.

When you wake up in the morning, try to feel grateful for your participation in the scheme of things. Give thanks for your food, for the rain and the sun, for the cold and the warmth, for your life. Whether or not you believe in a higher order doesn't matter. What does matter is the beneficial effect of giving thanks, which every once in a while reminds you that life is worth living. If you don't remind yourself of this or if you habitually start your day thinking how miserable it will be, you might eventually forget why life is worth living and decide to leave it.

Meaning and Purpose in Life

It is natural to ask why your disease happened to you because in doing so you are trying see how it is woven into the fabric of your life. You are trying to assign meaning to your disease. But in asking this question you risk falling into the trap of blaming rather than coping.

You might blame your parents for the inevitable mistakes they made, your friends for abandoning or failing to understand you, or the medical community for not coming up with a cure or treatment. If you are religious, you might even blame God for allowing your illness to exist. But most likely you will blame yourself and find many things in your past to feel guilty about. Your past is over, however; you cannot go back and do it again. Laying blame is often an unwillingness to live in the present. As long as you ask, "Why me?" to blame someone or something, you are avoiding your current reality.

Another way to avoid the present is to hold fate responsible for the way things turn out. Such a fatalistic view of life comes swathed in pseudoscientific argument nowadays, as when people say that surviving AIDS depends solely on whether you're infected by a "weak" or "strong" HIV virus or got "good" or "bad" genes from your parents, on whether you had your tonsils removed when you were a child, or on any such happenstance. Whether or not these events have any bearing on survival is beside the point. What matters is that by proclaiming yourself the innocent victim of circumstance, you are abandoning your free will. People—especially those with AIDS or ARC—who claim that surviving the disease is a question of a lucky draw are usually saying, between words, that they will eventually pick a losing number.

Responsibility

A productive inquiry into the past should first ask, "What did I do?" and then focus on "What can I do about it now?" "What can I do?" implies responsibility, the recognition that you are the one who can best solve your problems. You must also recognize your limitations, however, and know when to seek support from others. Responsibility means admitting that problems do not go away unless they are worked through, sometimes painfully. By facing your pain, you make freedom and healing possible. Blame makes you feel guilty and depressed, but responsibility brings control back into your life and strengthens your will to live. Its benefits can also compensate for the pain.

To acquire meaning, our lives may need restructuring. We often suppress or reject our creative selves. Have you ever found yourself wishing for a freer life or wanting to abandon a nine-to-five routine so you could really do what you wanted? If you have, you may have once suppressed a vital part of your identity. Somewhere in life's journey, you forgot what you wanted to be when you grew up. Go back and rescue this forgotten self from that old toy chest. Dust it, oil it, wind it up, and listen again to its tune. You might be prompted to turn your life around, as Dan Turner did when he turned to music. And you might also turn back to health by revitalizing your creative self.

"What reason do I have for living now that I have AIDS? Why should I plan things I will never live to do?" I realize these are tough questions. Life can seem rather short after an AIDS diagnosis. Then again, we have no crystal ball with which to foretell the future. Life can be equally short for everyone. The future exists only in our minds, and seeing it as meaningless or purposeless will only make life more difficult. The question "What reason do I have for living?" can be turned to your advantage. Use it to find out what you really want from life so you can reorder your priorities. Your distress about life might mean you have been living for the wrong reason, not that you have no reason for living.

Visualizing Death

Death visualization can serve as an aid to reorganizing your life. Start by finding a quiet, comfortable place where you can relax your body and quiet your mind. Then visualize a peaceful and painless death. See yourself leaving your body and observe those you have left behind. Review your life, both its good and its bad moments. Now that you can no longer speak, what would you want to say to those who were close to you? Now that life is over, what would you do differently if you could do it over again? Now that there is no way to turn things around, what do you regret not doing or saying? Live your death in all its intensity. Get in touch with your feelings, and tune in to your emotions as you answer these questions.

Not all is past; you have been given a reprieve and can come back again. What are the things you must do this time around? Reestablishing priorities may become easier after you do this several times.

"As long as you ask, 'Why me?' to blame someone or something, you are avoiding your current reality."

Meaning and purpose in life are reinforced by concrete goals. Purpose is a fixed horizon that we never reach but that gives us a general sense of direction in life. Goals are the passing landmarks that tell us we are indeed moving. The excitement of achieving positive goals can help spark the will to live and mobilize our healing energies. Setting goals can make us aware of our needs, clarify priorities, and reinforce meaning in our lives. Moreover, goals are excellent tools for change and often can provide very powerful reasons for staying around. Goals commit us to life.

It takes practice to determine which goals are proper for you. You should write down your goals, because unwritten goals remain vague and are usually ineffective. Written goals can be analyzed, refined, and changed. This doesn't mean you should keep laundry lists of goals (unless you are indeed the laundry list kind). Goals might be written as part of a journal or diary. For starters, write down what your death exercise taught you about making changes in your behavior. Ask yourself, "If I die in one week, how do I want to live until then? What are the things I want to do that I am not doing now?" Ask the same question giving yourself a month, three months, a year, and three years to live. Whether or not you will, in fact, live this long doesn't matter. Just come up with the goals.

Weekly and monthly goals should be quickly accomplished and provide immediate benefits. Long-term goals basically say we are willing to work to be here in the future. Goals should be concrete, preferably things you can observe or experience—learning to draw, increasing the size of your chest, or visiting the Parthenon. Be realistic. Don't commit yourself to more than you can do, or you might be setting yourself up for failure. ("See, I told you I couldn't do it.") Be sure that by being realistic, however, you do not limit yourself. Realism can be an excuse for no growth, and then it defeats the purpose of goals. Remember your childhood dreams. These visions turn goals into plans worth living for. Above all, your goals should be challenging and balanced. They should meet all your physical, emotional, and spiritual needs.

While writing down your goals, include what you will gain or lose by achieving them. This is the time to analyze the enjoyment you get out of harmful habits and to decide which beneficial activities could replace them. Review your goals and revise them as needed. Abandon any that do not turn out to be realistic. Remember, you should always plan plans and never plan exact results. Things rarely turn out the way you envision them, but they can come close.

We achieve goals through actions. Only activities, not goals, are doable, so figuring out the specific actions that will take us to our goals—especially the long-term ones—can be helpful: breaking down a large task into smaller actions makes it less formidable. Rewards can also help you accomplish things. Make sure you reward yourself each time you attain a goal.

Using the Subconscious

Visualization, creative imagery, or directed imagination can also help you accomplish goals. You visualize every day but are probably not aware of it. There are many ways to do creative visualization. The gist of it, however, consists in finding a quiet place, relaxing your body through deep breathing, and trying to live in your mind the goal you want to accomplish. Let's say you want better health. Affirm your goal with something like "I have a healthy body that is strong, energetic, and well defined" while you picture yourself with a muscular body, running up a hillside. Your vision might not reflect the truth about your current physical condition, but it reflects the truth of what you want to be. Try to include as much detail and emotion as possible in your visualization. Smell the grass, hear the birds singing and your heart beating, taste the sweat running down your face, see the bright blue sky and the puffy white clouds. You could even have your friends cheering you on to the summit. Your visualizations don't have to be as vivid as dreams, but they should involve as many of your senses as possible.

The subconscious cannot distinguish between real or imaginary experiences; it will say "yes" to either an actual or a visualized uphill run. Visualization will not only help your body's relaxation mechanisms to mobilize your immunity but will also help dissolve the blocks to your creative energy and reprogram the deep processes of your mind.

Changing the Balance of Your Life

Health is optimum communication between the physical, emotional, and spiritual parts of your self. In this ideal state all your different parts constantly balance each other. To bring the balance of health back to your life, you should consider all the various techniques I have described . . . accepting death, dealing with the possibility of survival, nurturing your hope and your will to live, loving yourself and others, finding a new meaning and purpose for your life, and setting goals to accomplish your newly found priorities. These things represent a good amount of work and might require support from others or professional help. Once this balance is re-established, it will feed back into and enhance the things that helped bring it about. You will find goals easier to accomplish, your life will acquire an exciting purpose, and you will love yourself and life more and more. . . .

"Death visualization can serve as an aid to reorganizing your life."

Without health you will not be able to deal with stress and will have little room for hope, love, and the will to live. And without hope, love, and positive expectations you won't be able to handle stress, and your health will be impaired. Changes in one area of ourselves will bring about changes in other areas. That's why we need to look at the totality of ourselves. No single approach can be effective in AIDS or ARC. We must combine spiritual awakening, self-knowledge, meditation, exercise, nutrition, vitamins, and conventional and alternative therapies in a comprehensive program that will lead us back to health.

Tom O'Connor is an activist on behalf of AIDS patients. He has had AIDS-related-complex (ARC) for several years.

"AIDS is an incurable disease. The advice I would give those who are suffering with AIDS is to accept that eventuality and to live fully to the extent that they can."

viewpoint 14

AIDS Should Be Faced with Acceptance

Elisabeth Kübler-Ross

Although this is rapidly changing, the largest group of AIDS patients is still homosexual men. They have carried the stigma of this disease for six years and have buried hundreds of their friends. At the same time, they have educated themselves and have organized extraordinary support systems that now serve as examples to other cities and other countries.

If there is ever a vaccine for AIDS, it will not in the least be the result of their strength and their efforts. For more than half a decade they have been isolated by most communities, have allowed doctors to experiment with them, suffered incredible side effects from experimental drugs, ruined the lives of their families, and participated in anything that promised a cure. In the end, they have succeeded in forcing people to see that AIDS is not just a "gay disease," but affects everyone.

The best known and most successful of the support systems is in San Francisco. My first patient there was Chuck, forty-two, whom I visited at his house shortly after I saw him on the East Coast.

Receiving the Diagnosis

Q: *You were diagnosed in December?...*

A: Yes, December 7, Pearl Harbor Day. Yes, however, I knew that I had K.S. [Kaposi's sarcoma] long before that. However, my doctor never knew that I had K.S., even though he saw lesions, he didn't recognize them. And even though a dermatologist saw them, he didn't recognize what they were.

Q: *What was the first thing you felt when you were told?*

A: Relief. On December 7, I had a bronchoscopy which determined it, and I received the results of that bronchoscopy right away, within twenty-five or thirty minutes, something like that, that I had a mild case of pneumocystis, and the first thing I felt was "I'm glad," in a way, because it relieved all of that stress that I had been worrying about whether or not I had AIDS. So my first feeling was one of relief, knowing that I had AIDS. The enormity of the situation has been something that I've been trying to deal with since then, but my first feeling was intellectual, and it was relief from the stress and anxiety that I was suffering....

Q: *When did you first come to an understanding that you would die?*

A: A realistic understanding that I would die? Only relatively recently. I think I had an actual awareness that I would die because I had AIDS from the moment of diagnosis, but feeling something and philosophizing are two different things, and I never felt that I would die although I could intellectually say, "Well, yes, I am going to die. I have AIDS." And I was very brave. It was only recently that I felt the real fear that comes with facing eternity, whatever that is.

Anger

Q: *What are you feeling today?*

A: Today I am feeling anger. I am angry that I'm going to die. Anger is a strong motivator, and I became angry another time and was motivated to start living again, and today I feel the same way. I feel positive and stronger as the result of my anger. So anger is something I feel today. I'm pissed off because I'm going to die, while others aren't.

Q: *When you get angry, what do you usually do about it?*

A: What I have done in the past is that I have cleaned house.

Q: *Do you mean "physically" cleaned house?*

A: I do those things that need to be done. When I become angry—it is a motivator and I do those things that need to be done that I haven't done in the past due to depression, self-pity, or whatever

Reprinted with permission of Macmillan Publishing Company from *AIDS: The Ultimate Challenge* by Elisabeth Kübler Ross, MD. Copyright © 1987 by Elisabeth Kübler Ross, MD.

other feelings I may have. So when I get angry, it is generally an anger that I'm going to die and I am pissed off at others because they're going to live, and I feel stronger as a result. The anger, I don't know, produces adrenaline, or whatever it produces, but it does something—I get pissed. I don't want to be dependent on people, and so I do things. I accomplish tasks, which seems pretty reasonable. It's better than going around bashing people, I suppose.

"Letting go of anything is hard, especially the most personal parts of you."

Q: *What worries you most about your present situation?*

A: I think the thing that worries me most is that I will become disfigured and dependent. And that's the thing that I haven't yet come to terms with. Being incontinent, being disfigured—those are frightening situations for me, and yet I understand that they may occur, and I should allow whatever is to occur, to occur. And it's letting go, that's hard. And letting go of anything is hard, especially the most personal parts of you, which, of course, includes your body, and surrendering in point of fact, my ego, and that's very, very difficult.

Advice for Doctors and Family

Q: *That's a big package, isn't it? A big package for all of us. If you were going to give a word of advice to doctors and nurses about the best way that they can help people with AIDS, [what] would that word of advice be?*

A: I don't know that I could put it into words, but I think it is terribly important to be honest with the patient. The doctor that I had who diagnosed me with AIDS, eventually, was not honest with me. I had a lesion in my mouth and he never told me. He never recognized, or never told me that he recognized, the lesion on my head. He wasn't honest with me, and he also told me I had about a year to a year and a half to live. I don't think that's honest either because I don't think he knows, and I don't think anyone knows. I believe that a doctor should be very honest and if a patient has AIDS, which is a terminal illness, he should tell the patient that he can only treat the symptoms of the illness and he can do nothing else, and that there is a mortality rate that is 100 percent in five years, or whatever it is. I believe that that is being honest with the patient. Moreover, I believe that among the protocols, and I mentioned this to my new doctor just yesterday, I said that I think immediate prescription of therapeutic massage is essential because it will help the patient deal with stress and anxiety, physical symptoms of stress and anxiety.

Q: *What about family and friends? If you were to give them some advice that would help?*

A: I believe family and friends should be supportive and while it's natural, everyone I suppose, goes through a certain amount of denial. They should understand that AIDS is, in fact, a terminal illness, and not console the person who has AIDS with all sorts of "well maybe there will be a cure, etcetera, etcetera." I'm not saying that one should be totally negative. I think that in a very positive sense, the family should realize that AIDS is a terminal illness and they mustn't wish the patient to get well soon, because it is only denial and what that does is make the patient feel that he can't communicate the reality to the family and friends and that can result in loneliness and even self-hatred. Moreover, I think it is very important that the family understand that it is a virus that is suspected to cause AIDS, and that there should be no guilt label put on the person who is sick because he is sick. Family and friends will feel anger. I have found that people feel anger because I'm ill and they take out the anger in subtle ways on me through either rejection or through not wanting to listen to me talk about death. There's denial, there's anger, there's hostility. We change the subject. We don't discuss reality. We don't discuss situations that will occur. The disease is relentless in its course and I believe that family and friends should understand that and not deny it to the person with AIDS. They should be supportive.

Dealing with AIDS

Q: *How do you feel about taking treatments?*

A: Well, I believe that treatments should be—first of all, AIDS cannot be treated. It is symptomatic. Symptoms can be treated and I believe that if there's some impairment to function, palliative measures should be given, but I, personally, don't feel that palliative measures include chemotherapy. If I had a lesion in my throat and had difficulty swallowing, radiation can take care of that. If I had a lesion on the end of my nose that bothered me, radiation can take care of that just as a palliative measure. There's control for pain. There are means of controlling pain. There are means of controlling diarrhea. There are means of controlling all sorts of things, but there is no cure, and no one, at this point, with AIDS will get well, as far as I am told, and so it seems to me that one can cling to hope by having chemotherapy and losing one's hair and having nausea, if that's the type of therapy that is given. To me, I'd rather not spend my time being ill.

Q: *Being well is important to you?*

A: The quality of life is real important and I think that one can die healthy, rather than die sick.

Q: *Depression is a common problem with people with a terminal condition. When you get depressed, or when* *you get a feeling of being hopeless and helpless, how do you know that you're depressed? And then what helps you pull yourself out of the depression?*

A: I know I'm depressed when my house becomes a mess, when I don't care about things or myself, when I can't concentrate on a task that needs to be done. I respond to the depression when I become aware of depression....

Very often I call upon my priest, you, my friend; others that will help me understand feelings, and/or I become angry at myself for not enjoying the days that I have left; sitting around and moping and not doing something will get me angry. There was a time, for example, when I was deeply depressed and I had read somewhere, a couple of places within a few days of each other, I read that the average person diagnosed with AIDS lives approximately nine and a half months. I had, at that time, been diagnosed with AIDS for four and a half months, although, parenthetically, I know that I had AIDS long before I was diagnosed—several months before, in fact. And it made me angry that I was sitting around staring out the window and being depressed with things, and so I cleaned the house, started working in the garden, and started living and enjoying those days that I have left. There is no reason why I can't do many of the things that I did when I was well, except for fatigue or depression, and if depression is the cause, then I only have to get this off of myself—that's the boot in the ass. And then I can start growing again—one day at a time.

Q: *Being alive is nice?*

A: Yes! And while I am alive, I should live, not slowly die. That makes sense.

Q: *Insofar as we are all slowly dying?*

A: Yes.

"While I am alive, I should live, not slowly die."

Q: *Do you pray?*

A: Yes, I do. I have had some spiritual moments and even some religious experiences which scared me because these moments and experiences were very real and very frightening. They occurred during Lent, and during Lent I was identifying with the passion of Christ—more than identifying. I don't want to presume that I was reliving the passion of Christ, but I certainly was empathizing to an extreme degree with death and suffering, and that may have contributed to some extent to the depression that I was in. On the other hand, in a very positive way I realized that I was being shown the way by Jesus....

Q: *Do you ever get afraid?*

A: I have fears and I have felt fear only relatively recently. There is something I've been denying. Fear resides in the solar plexus region and I was talking to my psychologist and he asked me to scan my body and to tell him what I felt. Well, at that point in time, I was feeling very positive and energetic and living one day at a time very well and feeling good, and I was having those religious experiences that were remarkable. I was feeling secure and comfortable and he asked me to scan my body from the tip of my toes to the tip of my nose and I did. I scanned my body and he said, "What do you feel?" I heard myself say, "Fear." I don't know why I said it, but there it was, and he asked me where I felt it, and I pointed and rubbed my solar plexus area and he said that's where fear resides, and I went into a horrible depression after that because I was aware of a new feeling and that feeling was fear. I mentioned that I have always intellectualized situations and here I was having a feeling that I hadn't felt before, or that I had denied myself feeling.

Taking Risks

Q: *Are you afraid of dying? Or are you afraid of death?*

A: Oh, I think it is the getting there that's the hard part. I don't want to be dependent.

Q: *We don't always get what we want. We get what we need.*

A: Yes, I'm a little afraid of dying and I'm not afraid of death. I am probably a lot afraid of dying, but I'm not afraid of death. I do believe in a higher level of existence, whatever it may be. Whatever form Eternity takes, I don't know. There is nothing I can do about it, except to accept it, to allow it to occur. That's the hard part....

Q: *If you were to die today, what would be your parting words that you would like to say?*

A: Good heavens! I would like to say different things to different people. In general, my message to everybody would be to live, to grow each day, to not be afraid of taking risks and to enjoy life and allow things to occur. In my years, I was so frightened to live, I had so little self-confidence that I was unable to really fully explore my potential as a human being. I believe that while we are alive, we are called upon to live and to grow and to take risks. Without risks, there is no growth. No reward, as they say in the investment business. And also, one has to be true to oneself. In my case, I'm an artist, a poet, and a storyteller; a dreamer, a healer; and I became a banker in life because it was expected of me. I allowed myself to be put into situations not consistent with myself, and I feel that I did myself a great disservice. I don't blame myself for it, but my words to everyone would be to live life, not be afraid to grow each day if possible, and to help others do the same.

Q: *What one thing about yourself would you like to be most remembered for?*

A: I would like to be most remembered as being helpful to people. Just helpful.

Q: *What kinds of advice would you give to AIDS patients?*

A: Wow! Even though I have AIDS, I don't know that I can give advice to AIDS patients. I believe that AIDS is an incurable disease. The advice I would give those who are suffering with AIDS is to accept that eventuality and to live fully to the extent that they can. I meet lots of people who have AIDS and lots of those people are concerned with which chemical they can take to cure them of their illness, or having crushed grapefruit seed stuffed up their ass, or whatever they think will cure them of AIDS. They're all looking for the great panacea to cure, and there is none. I think that the advice I would give the patient with AIDS is to consider the quality of the life that they have, rather than the quantity of it, since, as you told me, so correctly, we can control the quality, but we cannot control the quantity of life. People with AIDS have a limited life expectancy and that's a big concept to become aware of. I think that one of the things that I would tell a patient with AIDS, the advice I would give them is to learn as much as they can about their illness and not delude themselves with the dream that they're not going to die. For example, I recall a friend of mine who has K.S. attending a seminar with me and others on K.S.—he is taking chemotherapy for the K.S.—and he was shocked and depressed to find that there was no cure for AIDS. He has had AIDS longer than I have and he assumed that by getting rid of the K.S. he was going to get rid of his immune deficiency and become immune efficient, I suppose, and he was shocked.

"Family and friends should be supportive and . . . should understand that AIDS is, in fact, a terminal illness."

Q: *Do you think it is important that AIDS patients demand straight answers from their medical providers—the doctors, the nurses, and other people concerned with their medical care?*

A: Yes. I think that's essential, but I also feel that a lot of AIDS patients don't want to know that. They won't demand it. They'll say, "Hey, Doc, cure me," or they will assume that the doctor is curing them of their illness. They will simply assume that when the doctor subscribes whatever—my doctor, I am fortunate in that the doctor that I now have, is one who is very straightforward and he offers his suggestions based on his medical knowledge, but I have the ability to say yes or no. The doctor I went to formerly simply prescribed medication and didn't necessarily tell me why, or what the side effects might be, or what the end result might be, any of those things, and if I didn't ask those questions, he wouldn't give me the answers. He wouldn't volunteer, so there was a conspiracy, in effect, of silence. I didn't know what questions to ask and I'm an intelligent, knowledgeable person, more so, perhaps, than many of those who have AIDS. I know more than they do about medicine and about illness, and if I didn't know the questions to ask, I doubt very seriously that a lot of those other patients will. It is a rare doctor, I think, who understands that the patient must be in control. . . .

A Last Testament

Shortly before Chuck died he sent me a tape with his deepest and innermost thoughts.

"Today I'm recovering from an emotional roller coaster. Yesterday was the anniversary of my father's death, and I also externalized a lot of anger and rage and grief with a facilitator known to Elisabeth Kübler-Ross. For two hours I beat apart four West Los Angeles telephone directories with a rubber hose and cried and screamed, heard my voice for the very first time since I was a baby. I was returning to my crib. . . . I was exhausted. And I'm still so emotionally drained from that experience that I don't feel very well physically. I will, for example, cry for no seeming reason or just tears will come. It's grief for me, it's grief and sadness for those I love. It's surrender, me against the ego. These feelings are uncontrollable. . . .

"There's lots of things that go into making or taking a journey or trip. You have to get ready for it. You have to make sure your place is reserved, and you have to get on the train or get on whatever conveyance is appropriate and get there.

"That requires control and that's what's been so frightening to me because I don't know how to get where I'm going, and it's a matter of simply being taken . . . allowing myself to surrender to whatever it is that allows me to get to where I'm going. It's very difficult not knowing where I'm going. It's frightening to me, and it means that I must surrender myself and be content in the knowledge that there is that beautiful eternal part that will never change and never die. It's hard to remember that I have that part in me and that the physical body is nothing more than a shell, a cocoon. That's what I need to remember, to concentrate on the good and the light rather than the dark . . . the trials and tribulations of day-to-day life. . . .

"I'm learning how to live now, ironically, as I die, and what I suppose that means is to give unconditionally . . . to give and not be judgmental . . . to give love. And whatever I give is returned to me. I learn that now in my passion. It escaped me when I was well. I think it's probably because I didn't love myself. I was judgmental or harsh with myself and with others. I didn't experience love. I had been in California for two years or so, and I had written in a journal I kept that my spirit was dead. What did I mean by that? It meant, I suppose, that I was simply not in contact with that essential part of me that is love.... I didn't feel loved and I didn't receive love. I was looking for love, as they say, in all the wrong places. And I was depressed and agonizing over the situation in which I found myself, that is to say the low standard of living I had for years. I didn't know what to do. I was ill-equipped for life and that's partially because emotions were bottled up, partially due to other stresses... guilt, anxiety... all that crap. Not having any friends or an emotional support system. My spirit *was* dead. I lived in a dark, very dreary apartment and that's where I placed myself. I have no doubt that that has contributed to my illness. My own self-destruction was at work. I was destroying myself by not loving myself. I was destroying myself by keeping in anger and not externalizing grief. That evil that was in me, evil in the form of anger that I characterize as evil, negative energy, created the situation that I have to face today. So, in a way, I'm the author of my own destruction. I'm responsible now for living each day as well as I can. I lose sight of that sometimes, and dwell on the self-pity and become mired in depression, suffer physical ills, and as I mentioned earlier, I'm on an emotional roller coaster. So death represents a lot of peace to me, and while I don't look forward to dying because I'm afraid of letting go, I look forward to death, on the other hand, because it represents peace and eternal whatever....

"The advice I would give [people with AIDS] is to learn as much as they can about their illness and not delude themselves with the dream that they're not going to die."

"If I die, then I want to be dead. I believe that there are many people saved by Code Blue, but in the case of someone with AIDS, pneumocystis, Kaposi's sarcoma, God knows what other infectious diseases, Code Blue is like—is very similar to what occurred with my grandmother. At eighty-four years of age, filled with cancer, and she had a seizure and a heart attack, and died, and the doctors rushed in with, I suppose, what is called Code Blue and broke all of her ribs in an attempt to resuscitate the eighty-four-year-old lady who was filled with cancer, and who was dead, clinically dead. What a miserable thing to have happen to a body at death. So I do not want to go through anything like that. I do not think it is appropriate under these circumstances for me to be resuscitated, and then keep going for another day, or a week, or whatever, and not get better. At least at this point there is no chance that people can get better with AIDS. There is nothing that I have seen, anyway, to indicate it. I don't want people to think that I have a hopeless viewpoint, but I do have the knowledge and understanding of all the implications at this point and it may sound hopeless to a lot of people....

Every Day a Test

"My earnest prayer and hope is that I will have been helpful in some way, that my life will be not simply a 'hollow,' as it was. I have had more life and more experiences in the last six months than I've had in my other years, and I have had wonderful experiences and I've done great things, but I've really learned more about myself, more than I ever expected, and I'm able to muddle through all of this stuff, with faith and courage, because there is no other way. And, I guess, I have to have that confidence. As I become more—as I get closer to death, I'm gaining knowledge all the time. I'm learning about me, about my needs, and I hope I'm doing something with myself, with those needs, that I'm just not becoming aware of them and that's that. Although that knowledge is good, it's just like— mind-boggling. And love—I've grown to feel love of me, and others, as I never could have if I did not come down with AIDS. So the terminal illness with AIDS has been my biggest blessing. And it's been a big test. It continues to be a big test every day...."

Elisabeth Kübler-Ross is a psychiatrist who has written extensively on death and dying.

"Accepting the reality of a terminal disease—a reality that is often shrouded and complicated, slow to reveal itself—is a wrenching process."

viewpoint 15

Accepting AIDS As Fatal Helps Victims

George Whitmore

February 15, 1985. At 6:30 a.m., as on every weekday morning, the alarm rings and Dennis rolls out of bed. Soon Jim hears the sound of the shower.

Every morning when Jim wakes up, as soon as he opens his eyes, he asks himself, Am I going to get out of bed today? Am I going to bounce out of bed? Or am I going to lie here? Every morning he wakes up to that....

One night recently, Jim Sharp and Edward Dunn spent a few hours together discussing God, mortality, and eternity. Edward, who has pronounced opinions on most subjects, says he has no answers on this one. Lately, he says, he's been asking more questions. Jim, born and raised in Texas and a regular churchgoer, will tell you tongue in cheek that his idea of heaven "based on my childhood beliefs" is "a canasta game with lots of coffee and cigarettes." But he's been asking more questions, too. He's concluded, he says, that God will not give him more than he can handle.

Officially, Edward is Jim's "crisis intervention worker," a counselor from the Gay Men's Health Crisis, [GMHC], which provides outpatient assistance to New Yorkers with AIDS like Jim. Edward's job is to help Jim and his lover Dennis through the many difficulties—financial, legal, medical—they're certain to encounter due to Jim's condition. Jim has had one of the opportunistic infections that indicate severe immune deficiency but it was a relatively light case. He hasn't yet had anything else major so there have been no repeated, protracted hospital stays. It they come, Edward is ready for them. He knows about AIDS. His own lover died of less than 18 months ago....

On top of a stereo speaker in Jim's apartment is a stuffed piranha. Edward brought it back from Brazil and when he gave it to Jim he said, joking, "This is how you look when you don't get your way."

The fish is mounted as if poised for attack, bristling, jaws agape. Like AIDS, the piranha is at first glance shocking, repulsive. But on closer inspection, it doesn't look real. It looks like something whipped up out of latex and horsehair for some low-budget horror movie. Thus demystified, it can be dismissed—that is, until your eye happens to fall on it again. Then you wish it weren't in the same room with you.

AIDS Panic

AIDS won't go away. Four years into the epidemic, it is now a fact of life for thousands upon thousands of Americans—even if most of them don't yet know it....

AIDS is almost always fatal. Most people with AIDS die within 18 months after diagnosis. The mortality rate for AIDS has been established at 95-100 percent two years after onset.

Initially, the AIDS story was reported vigorously in the gay press and almost not at all in the general media. But public concern over the disease suddenly burgeoned in 1983 and something very close to panic gripped parts of the country.

The piranha thrives on terror. Acts of violence against gay men—or those perceived to be gay men—increased. Funeral homes refused to bury the AIDS dead. Stories already abounded about hospital workers so frightened of the disease that they left food trays outside rooms and refused AIDS patients the most elementary amenities. Now discrimination against people with AIDS or those perceived to have AIDS became relatively common. Some people with AIDS—or suspected of having AIDS, even suspected of associating with people with AIDS—were ostracized on the job or fired outright. They were evicted from their apartments. Often they were abandoned by friends and acquaintances, by loved

From *Someone Was Here: Profiles in the AIDS Epidemic* by George Whitmore. Copyright © 1988 by George Whitmore. Reprinted by arrangement with NAL Penguin Inc., New York, New York.

death / dying 67

ones as well. . . .

There's a roll of film Edward Dunn can't bring himself to develop. On it is a photograph of him and his lover Robert, taken by a nurse at New York Hospital in November 1983. Edward says echoes are forming around memories that used to be crisp. There is a kind of separation happening, he says. But he still has a recollection of what Robert looked like when the photo was taken, a month or so before his death.

Watching Robert die from AIDS was, says Edward, like standing by powerless while a freight train roared through his life. When he called GMHC to volunteer, he did it because "I felt desperately that I had to be doing something. I couldn't just sit by impotently and watch." He wanted to make a difference. He hadn't, he felt, made enough of a difference for Robert. . . .

"He knew what AIDS meant. He knew what happens. Your friends desert you, your lover kicks you out onto the street. . . . You're a leper. You die alone."

In the training sessions, Edward listened to other new volunteers talk about death and AIDS. They talked about AIDS, it occurred to him, as if it were a kind of gentle, Camille-like wasting away. But Edward knew—he'd seen—AIDS is about shit and blood.

In August of last year, Edward received his first assignment. He went to the GMHC offices and read the intake report on Jim Sharp, who had just been diagnosed with a syndrome commonly called AIDS-Related Complex, or ARC.

As scientists have come to understand, AIDS is not a black-and-white illness but a spectrum of immune deficiency. Characterized especially by swollen lymph nodes and persistent fever, ARC is sometimes called "pre-AIDS" by doctors since it falls short of a complete suppression of the immune system.

It's now thought that for every person infected with the AIDS virus who goes on to develop full-blown AIDS, there are ten with ARC. Sometimes ARC turns into AIDS, sometimes it doesn't. Estimates vary on the percentage of cases where it does. Researchers estimate that from 4 to 19 percent of people infected with the virus will eventually develop AIDS.

Since 1985, most AIDS experts have revised this estimate and now believe that from 20 percent to 30 percent of HIV-infected people will develop AIDS symptoms within five years of exposure to the virus. Current medical thinking is that virtually every HIV-infected person will eventually manifest AIDS.

In Jim's case, ARC turned into AIDS in December, when his doctor made an impirical diagnosis of *pneumocystis carinii* pneumonia—"empirical" because he didn't insist on a confirmatory lung biopsy and simply gave Jim medication that seemed to clear up this rare lung infection. *Pneumocystis* is one of the two diseases physicians first noticed in gay men and connected with immune supression in 1981. Since then, the Centers for Disease Control in Atlanta has used *pneumocystis* and Kaposi's sarcoma, a highly unusual skin cancer, to define AIDS. . . .

The Elephant in the Room

Some people fall to pieces when they receive the kind of news Jim had. But, Edward recalls, at their first meeting in Jim's apartment, Jim appeared quite calm.

There had been an attempt at GMHC to match them. Jim learned that Edward was a freelance advertising copywriter. Edward already knew Jim had left a good job in advertising in Houston the year before and took a substantial salary cut to come to New York because he felt he had to challenge the citadel of the business. He'd done well.

Jim asked Edward if he'd like a cup of coffee. Stiffly, formally, they chatted for an hour or so. Edward offered his services but, curiously, they didn't talk directly about AIDS. Edward remembers, it was "as if there were a dead elephant in the middle of the floor and we were both too polite to mention it.". . .

Jim smoked cigarette after cigarette—clearly, he had no intention of quitting smoking—but generally, Edward thought, for a man who was facing a condition most people regarded as a death sentence, Jim seemed almost blasé.

Jim was most assuredly not blasé. He was terrified. He knew what AIDS meant. He knew what happens. Your friends desert you, your lover kicks you out onto the street. You get fired, you get evicted from your apartment. You're a leper. You die alone.

The day the doctor told Jim, he walked out of the office onto Central Park West and down the sidewalk in a daze. It was a beautiful day. All he could think was, This isn't funny. It was as if God had been lounging around up there with the angels and had just decided,

Now, let's give it to—hmmm—Jim Sharp!

This is not funny, Jim thought. After all the other crap that's gone down in my life, this isn't funny.

Things were going great. He'd only been in New York a year and a half and he'd found a job he loved and the lover he'd always dreamed of. Then in one visit to the doctor, everything got turned inside out.

"My life changed. My life changed. You walk into some doctor's office and he tells you you have the beginnings of a disease no one has an answer for, that you've been reading about in the newspaper, that is killing people, that you've just had a friend die of." Jim pauses. "I very much like being in control. The control was taken away. I was relieved because I finally knew what was going on inside of me—but it was sort of like waiting for the Germans to attack at the Battle of the Bulge. You're sick and tired of waiting for the attack to come, but when it does, you're not really relieved because there are bullets whizzing around your head. It's a 'Catch-22' situation."

The doctor encouraged Jim to continue working, not to drop out and go onto disability as some people were.

"I most certainly will continue working."

He walked out onto the street.

Jim called GMHC because he knew he'd need help. Now he was meeting a so-called "crisis intervention worker." But it was like watching someone else go through the motions. Jim knew he was really in this alone.

Jim grew up poor. He put himself through school and forged ahead mainly on the currency of his own considerable native intelligence. A recovered alcoholic, Jim had saved his life once before. If sheer will power meant anything, Jim would save his life again.

Feeling disoriented soon after he moved to New York, Jim had sought out a psychotherapist. Jim's therapist says Jim "has this image of himself as a cowboy, a person who can pull himself together" no matter what. Jim agrees. He says he grew up to believe "that you get up in the morning and you pull your boots on by the straps. You get up and go.

"This disease has taught me," he adds in his soft drawl, "that this is not necessarily so."

"AIDS, it often seems, is as much about denial as it is about death."

Jim's sole request of Edward that first month was that he help him find a dentist, so Edward gave him the name of one registered at GMHC as willing to treat people with AIDS. Jim also allowed Edward to enroll him in a support group at GMHC for people with AIDS, but at the meeting he got into an argument with the group leader, who said he couldn't smoke. Jim smoked anyway. He did not go back. The truth was, Jim identified with the sickest man in the room and it scared him to death. . . .

"Jim can put up a wonderful front," Edward says. "Very breezy. He can be charming and light. Evasive."

Gradually, Edward began to understand. He was on the outside and Jim wasn't going to let him in. Jim had his life strictly compartmentalized—his lover, his therapist, his doctor, his job. It was as if Jim were in a room with four doors. Every once in a while he'd open one of them, but for the most part he remained alone in the center, isolated.

In addition, Edward began to understand the essence of the crisis Jim was enduring. Jim was in crisis precisely to the degree that he needed to deny that any crisis existed.

AIDS Denial

Edward saw he quite literally represented AIDS to Jim. And Jim was determined—maybe AIDS had its foot in the door, but he was damned if he would let it into the house.

He was deluded. AIDS had moved in.

Jim's response to AIDS was far from atypical. AIDS, it often seems, is as much about denial as it is about death.

I don't really have it. I won't let it stop me. I'm going to beat it. Denial is a powerful, often healthy, initial reaction. In the face of an AIDS diagnosis, short-term, even total denial can be the only thing that wards off a nervous breakdown. Being able to say, *I know I have it but who knows what that means?* can be what's called a *mitzvah* in Yiddish, a godsend. Continuing denial of one aspect or another of the disease can be a way of protecting oneself from the unremitting fears that accompany it. *It's not going to happen to me that way* is a means to assert one's individuality in the midst of an ego-leveling calamity. Denial explains why the person who has been diagnosed often seems utterly immune to the consequences of the disease. Family and friends might be devastated, but he or she seems to reside in the calm center of the eye of the storm. And it shouldn't be forgotten that *I'm different* is quite literally true—each case *is* different, bringing with it its own set of circumstances.

Accepting the reality of a terminal disease—a reality that is often shrouded and complicated, slow to reveal itself—is a wrenching process. Some never fully accept. Edward's lover Robert, for instance, wasn't ever able to accept the full implications of having AIDS. At the end, Edward needed to say good-bye to Robert and tell him how much he'd miss him. But Robert, even in the last excruciating months of his illness, couldn't admit he was dying.

Loved ones of the afflicted can promote elaborate denial. Parents often learn simultaneously about AIDS and a son's homosexuality—or his drug abuse. Sometimes they choose not to deal with the existence of either. And although hospice workers are struck by the breadth of support gay men can summon up from friends and lovers, peers sometimes postpone coming to terms with the role AIDS plays in their own lives by avoiding friends who have it.

Dixie Beckham, a psychotherapist in private practice who also runs a support group at GMHC for people with AIDS, notes the severe isolation they experience. "There are so many taboos a gay man who is dying of AIDS has to deal with," she says, "it would be easier to talk about an amputation." And, of course, there is still unwarranted fear of contagion. Most people would not so much as touch an AIDS patient. Even now when so much more is known about its transmission, AIDS continues to carry with it wholly inappropriate associations of a contagious plague, rather than an infectious disease.

There is a particularly cruel dimension to AIDS. The piranha not only churns up terror, it swims in a medium charged with shame and guilt. At its most rudimentary, "AIDS denial" reflects the tacit judgment of society that AIDS happens only to an outcast few—people who somehow deserve the disease. Jim says he and his lover Dennis paid little attention to AIDS until he was diagnosed. It was not something that happened to churchgoing people like them who were in a monogamous relationship. . . .

"I wondered probably what everyone who has ever lost a mate wonders—does anybody really know how much I've lost?"

AIDS denial in sexually active gay and bisexual men can prevent early diagnosis of the condition, hamper treatment of the diseases that accompany AIDS, encourage illusions of immunity. . . .

Denial does not stop with death. Edward found, when Robert died, that society has not "necessarily dictated how you should react when your gay son loses his lover to a horrifying, deadly, possibly disreputable disease." His attempts to discuss his loss with his family were deflected, as if nothing had happened. . . .

Robert's Grave

Last December [1984], three days after what would have been their fifth anniversary, Edward visited his lover Robert's grave for the first time.

Robert died at New York Hospital on December 22, 1983, from *pneumocystis* pneumonia, Kaposi's sarcoma, and a host of other illnesses.

Robert's final hospital stay lasted four months. Edward visited him every afternoon. If Robert's family visited, they came in the evening. Robert was not "out" to his family. He had not told them he was gay. Edward was known as "Robert's friend.". . .

I wondered probably what everyone who has ever lost a mate wonders—does anybody really know how much I've lost? I'm very self-sufficient. Maybe I don't encourage people to be sympathetic. But would anybody ever be able to acknowledge the depth of my loss? Standing there, looking down at the tombstone, it became so real to me, how intense the loss is. The truth may be that nobody else can acknowledge a loss like that. That may be the truth.

Every day when Edward had visited the hospital, he'd taken Robert a red carnation. It was the flower he'd always given Robert. After standing by the grave a while, Edward lay a red carnation at the base of the stone and left.

Several weeks after he visited Robert's grave, Edward called Robert's mother, as he sometimes does. "By the way," he said, "I went to the cemetery."

"I know," she said.

"But how did you know?"

"I saw the carnation."

It had never crossed his mind that she might have known—he was, of course, the one who brought Robert a carnation every day. Now, Edward saw, she'd known that and perhaps more, but could never have said what she knew.

It began with what they thought was a bruise. It was a Kaposi's sarcoma lesion.

When it came to really serious, big things, he wasn't a great communicator. I would have to draw him out. He didn't deny he had AIDS but he denied the fact that it was fatal. Initially he was optimistic. Then, after several trips in and out of the hospital and having to leave work and severe weight loss and the beginning of a series of devastating parasitic infections—he just stopped communicating on an emotional level.

When Robert was diagnosed with AIDS, in the fall of 1982, not much was known about the disease. This encouraged Robert in his optimism. "Don't worry about it," he would tell Edward. "We're going to beat it."

Robert was treated for Kaposi's sarcoma at New York Hospital and the cancer went into remission. He went back to work. Robert was a social worker in a nonprofit agency. A lot of people depended on him.

I saw him go through something I'm seeing Jim go through now—that time when he had to remove himself from the rest of the world. He had a real hard time. He took his work seriously. When he could no longer do it, that bothered him.

We did a lot of lying to each other—I would agree that all he needed was some time off. . . .

On Labor Day weekend, Edward took Robert to the hospital in an ambulance.

He was in intensive care and hooked up to a respirator. I didn't have clearance to visit him in intensive care because I wasn't acknowledged as anything but a friend. . . .

Unable To Talk About Death

When Robert got out of intensive care, Edward visited him every day from one to four in the afternoon, so they could be alone together. The doctor had told Robert's family he had AIDS. Just as

Robert was able to acknowledge that he had AIDS but not that it was fatal, his family knew Robert was dying of AIDS but never were able to acknowledge that he was gay. At one time, Robert had been married and his mother was sure he was going to marry again.

It's hard to say which kind of denial created more pain for Edward, but as it gradually became apparent that Robert would never leave the hospital, Edward needed to say good-bye.

I wanted to talk to him about how much he had meant to me, about how much I would miss him. And I wanted to hear that from him. And yet, talking about someone's death is a place you have to be invited into. He couldn't let anybody in there. . . .

When Robert died, Edward's years with him got canceled out in one stroke. He didn't go to Robert's funeral. He was invited to the funeral but Edward says he couldn't share Robert any longer. He could no longer pretend for Robert's sake in front of Robert's family that they were not lovers.

AIDS isn't like cancer, Edward says. Cancer is frightening but respectable, he says. His gay friends, when Robert died, wanted desperately for Edward to bounce back. They didn't encourage him to talk to them about Robert's death. They didn't want to deal with the fact that Robert had died of AIDS. "AIDS was a dark, terrifying pit they didn't want to look into," says Edward. . . .

About two weeks after Robert died, Edward's friend Bob called and said, "I want to see you, let's get together."

They met for lunch and Edward suddenly found himself feeling very edgy. Bob hadn't yet found the time to sit down with him and talk about Robert's death. He'd always seemed to have too many things to do. Edward was edgy.

"I wanted to talk to him about how much he had meant to me. . . . Yet, talking about someone's death is a place you have to be invited into. He couldn't let anybody in there."

They ordered.

"You're really pissed off at me," Bob said. "Aren't you?"

Edward look at him. "Yeah, I really am." He realized it when Bob said it.

"Why?"

Edward was incredulous. "Because you just disappeared for two weeks."

Bob weighed that. "Edward, what do you want to say to me?"

And Edward screamed—*"Where were you?"*

He held onto the edge of the table and let it out. Bob didn't seem surprised. People turned to look at them. Edward began to shake.

"I got it," Bob said.

Edward began to cry.

The truth was, Robert was all Edward wanted to talk about. He wanted to sit in a room without sleep and babble incoherently every detail he had ever known about Robert. He wanted to talk about Robert and nothing else.

Edward sought out a bereavement counselor through GMHC. Edward's counselor encouraged him to remember Robert before his illness and disintegration. He encouraged Edward to pay attention to his dreams, because Edward's unconscious was helping him to mourn. He encouraged Edward to bring mementos of Robert into their sessions. He encouraged Edward to talk to Robert and say what he hadn't been able to say when Robert was alive. He encouraged Edward to say good-bye. . . .

Frederico Delgado

[February 24, 1987] Noon. On 4-D, in room 219, Albert Schult sits in a chair feeding Frederico Delgado out of a bottle and talking to him. The HIV virus was transmitted to Frederico in the womb by his mother. He has lived in the hospital since last June. He is two and a half years old.

Frederico's father, Hector, died from AIDS last September. His mother, Peggy, died from AIDS two months later. Now Frederico is a so-called boarder baby. He is "on hold," waiting for placement. He is one of about 300 children living in hospitals in New York City this afternoon because accredited foster homes can't be found for them. Frederico happens to be disabled—he was born with cerebral palsy in addition to his HIV infection—but children all over the city who have no handicaps or illnesses are in the same position.

Mr. Schult, Frederico's only visitor from the outside, comes to the hospital each week on Tuesdays and Sundays. Frederico's mother, a niece by marriage, was to Mr. Schult "the daughter I never had." When Peggy died, Mr. Schult was essentially her closest living relative. Her mother had died when Peggy was in her teens. A telegram was sent to her father's address in Florida—it was not returned but it wasn't answered either. . . .

Frederico can't sit up or stand. He can't hold a bottle. It's extra work to feed him and keep him clean. His eyes are severely crossed. When he was brought to the hospital, already bearing the label "HIV-infected," the doctors determined that Frederico was brain damaged. It's hard to know how much. It's possible he'll learn to talk, but since he has so little adult companionship, he hasn't had much of a chance to learn. Children need adults for growth and company. Generally, the hospital

death / dying

personnel do as well as they can but they're busy.

This week there are 471 children under 13 who have been officially diagnosed with AIDS in the U.S. As many as 2,000 have other illnesses related to HIV infection....

Why I Wrote About AIDS

Early in 1985, when I suggested an article to the editors of *The New York Times Magazine* on "the human cost of AIDS," most reporting on the epidemic was scientific in nature and people with AIDS were often portrayed as faceless victims. I wanted to show the devastating impact AIDS was having on individual lives. It had certainly had an impact on mine. I was pretty sure I was carrying the virus and I was terrified....

What I didn't fully appreciate then, however, was the extent to which I was trying to bargain with AIDS: if I wrote about it, maybe I wouldn't get it.

My article on Jim Sharp and Edward Dunn ran in the *Times Magazine* in May 1985. But AIDS didn't keep its part of the bargain. Less than a year later, after discovering a small strawberry-colored spot on my calf, I was diagnosed with Kaposi's sarcoma....

> "This week there are 471 children under 13 who have been officially diagnosed with AIDS in the U.S."

Jim's grief, his despair, his terror—they were mine, too. But Jim's special gift was for anger. Life-affirming anger was the lesson Jim taught me, and anger has enabled me to write about the ocean of pain that engulfs us without drowning in it.

When I met Jim, I have to confess, I could only see a dying man. A chasm separated me from him and all the other men with AIDS I interviewed. Even though they were gay, as I am, even though most of them were my own age, even though after I left those interviews I had to stop on the street to cry, each one of them remained safely "on the other side of the fence" for me. But now, for good or ill, there is no "other side of the fence" and no safety.

When I first met Jim, I could only see a dying man. Last summer in Houston, when Jim came to his front door to greet me, I met myself....

Edward's Gift

Soon after the *Times* article on him and Jim was published, Edward Dunn brought me a gift. It was a little teddy bear—a nice ginger-colored teddy bear with a gingham ribbon tied around its neck. Since I didn't collect toys, I didn't know quite what to make of it. But Edward explained to me that he often gave teddy bears to friends because they represented warmth and gentleness to him. Later, he asked me what I was going to name mine.

"I hadn't thought of naming it."

"Oh, you have to name him," Edward said.

"I don't know, what do you think?"

"I thought you might call him Robert."

Since Robert was the pseudonym we'd chosen for his late lover, I saw Edward's gift in a new light. I realized that after the grueling interviews I'd put him through, Edward was paying me an enormous compliment. He was, in a way, placing a share of Robert's memory in my hands....

One gloomy Saturday afternoon, a month after I began visiting Lincoln Hospital, I interviewed Sr. Fran Whelan at her home in East Harlem. That day she told me about the child I've called Frederico and I asked if I could meet him....

I peered into the crib. I heard a ringing in my ears. I almost bolted out of the room. Somehow, I kept my two feet planted where they were on the floor.

I'd seen eyes unblinking from lesions. I'd spoken to deaf ears. I'd held the hand of the dying man. But nothing had prepared me for this.

I wanted to snatch Frederico out of his crib, snatch him up and run away, run away with him. It was horribly, cruelly clear that I wanted for him what I wanted for myself, and I was powerless....

The day I first saw Frederico, when Sr. Fran was distracted for a moment, I took "Robert" out of the plastic bag I was carrying and set him down among the other stuffed animals in the crib. I knew Edward would approve. What I didn't know was that Edward had AIDS and would die before the year was out.

It's taken me months to write this. I'm afraid to finish this book. I'm afraid of what will happen next.

When I met Jim, all I could see was a dying man. The day he left New York, I was sure I'd never see him alive again. But I did see him again, in Houston last time. He lives in a modest bungalow house on a tree-lined street. He's something of a celebrity. Until recently, he served on the board of the local AIDS foundation and he spends lots of time every day on the phone, dispensing comfort and advice to other people with AIDS. Among his other distinctions, Jim is probably the only man with AIDS in Texas who's lived long enough to collect Medicaid there.

Playing in Heaven

A week after I got back from Texas, Mr. Schult called to tell me Frederico was dead....

I went to the funeral home. Frederico lay in a little coffin lined with swagged white satin. He was dressed in a blue playsuit with speedboats on it.

"You dressed him in a playsuit," I said to Mr. Schult. "And now he's at play," Mr. Schult sobbed, at my side. "He's romping in heaven now with Jesus like he never was able to down here."

I held Mr. Schult's arm tightly until the sobbing passed. The coffin was too small for the top of catafalaque. You could see gouges and scrapes and scars in the wood in the parts the coffin didn't cover. I looked down at the body in the coffin, beyond help. I agreed aloud with Mr. Schult that Frederico was in heaven now because it seemed to make him feel a little better.

I don't know why, but I always thought Frederico would live.

George Whitmore is a novelist and free-lance journalist whose work has been published in The New York Times, The Village Voice, The Washington Post, *and* The Advocate.

"If we could truly believe in the possibility of living with AIDS, I think that survival figures would be higher."

viewpoint 16

Accepting AIDS As Fatal Harms Victims

Michael Callen

"Max just asked if you were dead yet." Max is the precocious 6-year-old son of the piano player in my lover's jazz band. Max hadn't seen me in several months, and so it must have seemed a logical question.

My lover laughed nervously, not knowing what to make of the expression on my face when he told me. I was momentarily paralyzed by the insight that here in America, the essential fact about AIDS—a notion so simple as to be accessible to a six year old—is that everyone who gets it dies.

I did a quick reality check: I have AIDS, but as far as I could tell, I was not dead.

I resolved then to write about the best-kept secret of the epidemic: not everyone dies from AIDS. Some of us are still alive and well, five years or longer after being diagnosed. The uncritical repetition of the myth that everyone with AIDS dies denies the reality of—but perhaps more important, the possibility of—our survival.

I remember asking several researchers, in 1982 and 1983, whether they thought AIDS would prove to be uniformly fatal. Some said yes, others said probably not—that there are very few infectious agents with a mortality of 100 per cent for the simple reason that, from an evolutionary standpoint, any disease that killed all its hosts would die out itself. I learned that survival rates for the various types of cancer are generally based on observing patients for at least five years. Since AIDS was new—or at least newly observed—no one seemed willing to hazard mortality projections.

In the early years of AIDS, it seemed that everyone did die. But by 1987, the odds of surviving had improved dramatically. Doctors have learned to recognize opportunistic complications earlier and they've gotten a better handle on treatment. Almost no one dies from their first bout of pneumocystis pneumonia [PCP] these days. And I suspect that the mortality rate in the early days was higher than it might have been because so many people died from complications of the treatments. (It never made much sense to me that someone who had developed cancer because he was immunosuppressed would be treated with violently immunosuppressive chemotherapy. Often, that cured the cancer but killed the patient, who died of PCP as a complication of having no white blood cells left.)

As doctors watched patient after patient expire despite their best ministrations, it must have *seemed* that everyone who got AIDS died. And this emotional impression of 100 per cent mortality must have been picked up by a press too lazy to seek out evidence to the contrary. Mostly the press got it's information from "experts" in medical centers who probably had an exaggerated sense of the mortality rate because only the sickest patients were referred to them. In a recent issue of *AIDS Treatment News*, Dr. Nathaniel Pier, a New York physician with a large AIDS practice, remarked: "There's a serious bias in the medical literature as to what's being reported, and it's giving people a distorted picture of what is going on with AIDS. They're not seeing the people who are doing well, the people who are surviving long, the people who have good quality of life, because those people don't go to medical centers and therefore they don't get papers written about them."

The Media's Distorted Picture

So, despite the distorted picture of AIDS passed on to journalists by researchers, the reality is that not everyone dies of AIDS. It's become especially clear over time that people whose only opportunistic infection is Kaposi's sarcoma [KS] are often able to lead quite normal lives, and are surviving

---

Michael Callen, "Not Everyone Dies of AIDS: I Will Survive," *The Village Voice*, May 3, 1988. Reprinted with the author's permission.

significantly longer than other people with AIDS. But for whatever reason, these seeds of hope never germinated in the public consciousness.

Now that published reports prove we long term survivors officially exist, it's almost amusing, to watch those who knew, or ought to have known, that we existed race to excuse that silence. City Health Commissioner Stephen Joseph said recently that the proportion of patients surviving five years was "greater than I would have intuitively expected it to be." What the hell does that mean? In New York City, 15 per cent of all people with AIDS have survived five or more years. Shouldn't the Health Commissioner have known that? And is it enough for him and others now to say "Oops! Guess we were wrong about 100 per cent mortality"? Is there no one to hold accountable for the lie and its harmful effect on PWAs [people with AIDS]?

"When I'm a 'good patient,' when I toe the party line and talk about my feelings, no one questions my right to represent myself as a PWA."

Well, more than five years have passed since AIDS was first described, and right on cue come studies on the phenomenon of long-term survival. The first widely publicized report came last October [1987], from an ongoing CDC [Centers for Disease Control] study of long-term survivors directed by Dr. Ann Hardy. This study found a depressing two to five per cent survival rate after three years. Then, a CDC study by a Dr. Richard Rothenberg was published in *The New England Journal of Medicine.* This study found that 15 per cent of PWAs survived five years after diagnosis. (The rates varied by risk group: Female IV drug users, most of whom are black and Hispanic, had the worst prognosis; white gay men, most of whom have KS as their sole opportunistic infection, did much better.)

Which is it—two per cent or 15? How could two CDC researchers have come up with such drastically different survival rates? Pursuing an answer to this troubling question, I realized that, before it is possible to agree on the number of long-term survivors (much less on what contributes to survival), one must define precisely what is meant by "AIDS." An interview with Dr. Hardy revealed startling assumptions about who counts as a long-term survivor and who doesn't. Dr. Hardy explained that blood tests on 20 per cent of her sample produced no evidence at all of HIV infection. Rather than consider what it might mean that the so-called AIDS virus could not be found in some individuals who'd had pneumocystis or Kaposi's sarcoma or cryptococcal meningitis—all diseases which qualify one for an official diagnosis—the decision was made to discount them as genuine long-term survivors. As Dr. Hardy explained, "They met the case definition for AIDS, but really did not have AIDS."

I tried to imagine the CDC contacting these long-term survivors to tell them they hadn't *really* survived AIDS. And what would it feel like to have suffered the stigma and endless propaganda about AIDS, to have struggled with every ounce of energy to beat the odds, to have given blood to countless researchers, only to be informed that your survival doesn't count?

A Silly Definition

There is a tautology built into the CDC's definition of AIDS. When most people use that word, they generally mean the terminal stage of a spectrum of illness. If you're only going to count as AIDS cases those that are terminal, then by definition the mortality rate will be 100 per cent. Death from AIDS will become a self-fulfilling prophecy, and if you're not dead within three years, maybe you never really had AIDS in the first place.

My own case illustrates some of the problems inherent in defining this disease. I was diagnosed with AIDS in 1982 as a result of a parasitic intestinal infection, cryptosporidium. I was the first case of "crypto" (as it's called in PWA slang) my hospital doctor had seen. At the time, crypto was not thought to infect humans; it was a disease of livestock. It was—and remains—on the list of infections that qualify one for a diagnosis of AIDS. Subsequently, it's been discovered that crypto is more common in humans than had been thought. Consequently, some doctors feel it ought to be removed from the list of qualifying infections. Others argue strenuously that crypto in an immuno-compromised patient can and frequently does kill, and that therefore it should remain on the list. So doctors now say that in order to qualify for AIDS, the particular case of crypto must produce a certain number of stools of a certain liquid consistency over a specific period of time. (I like to imagine some CDC mole measuring stool consistency to separate the men from the boys, so to speak.) By these standards, my own case still qualifies as frank AIDS. And yet a whispering campaign continues to follow me: are you now or have you ever been.

The uncertainty about my own right to claim that I have AIDS—and that, therefore, I'm a "genuine," a long-term survivor—has caused me a great deal of pain. When I'm a "good patient" when I toe the party line and talk about my feelings, no one questions my right to represent myself as a PWA. But when I am a "bad patient," when I insist on talking about science or politics, some of my critics claim I have no right to speak as a PWA. Frankly, I can't fathom why anyone would pretend to have

AIDS. There are easier ways to be photographed with Liz Taylor.

One doctor, in an interesting blend of epidemiology and astrology, proposed a new category for me, suggesting that I'm on the "cusp" between AIDS and ARC [AIDS-Related Complex]. All this splitting of hairs seems pointless. But it is interesting to examine the underlying message of those who challenge my right to count myself as a survivor. If I had died from crypto in the summer of '82, no one would have questioned my diagnosis. It is the fact that I refused to die that makes me suspect.

Meanwhile, AIDS-Related Complex, thought to be a "lesser" form of the disease, has killed between 500 and several thousand people. Consider my friend Larry. He's sicker than many PWAs I know and certainly sicker than most PWAs whose only opportunistic infection is KS. Larry is a bisexual, former IV-drug user who's had several types of skin cancer; who was hospitalized with pneumonia that proved not to be PCP; who is suffering neurological symptoms of unknown causation; who, for the past seven years, has endured fevers, night sweats, and fatigue; and whose blood tests are as bad as most PWAs. But since he hasn't had any of the 24 opportunistic infections that would qualify him for an official diagnosis, does he count as a long-term survivor of AIDS? Does he have ARC? And if you can die from ARC as well as AIDS, how useful is the distinction?

"Those of us who've insisted on the possibility of surviving AIDS have been patronized, handed [Elisabeth] Kübler-Ross, sent into therapy, or faced the charge of AIDS dementia."

What does it mean that hope has been so long denied? Max Navarre, who is just shy of my arbitrary three-year cutoff, articulates the bitterness of many PWAs . . . "In the media, everyone's a victim: of fire, of cancer, of mugging, of rape, of AIDS," he writes. "In the world of reportage, no one is doing well. Victims sell newspapers. Does anyone consider the impact of this cult of the victim? Does anyone realize the power of the message 'You are helpless. There is no hope for you?'

"I'm not immune to the reinforcement of hopelessness that surrounds me. That reinforcement causes despair, and I believe that despair kills people with AIDS as much as any of AIDS' physical manifestations. If we could truly believe in the possibility of living with AIDS, I think that survival figures would be higher."

Those of us who've lived with AIDS for more than three years did so against unknown odds and a conspiracy to deny the possibility of survival. Many survivors simply chose to ignore media reports. Some never asked their doctors what the prognosis was. Many clung to the knowledge of others who had survived longer than they. Will we ever be able to measure the damage done by the media's refusal to seek out long-term survivors? How many PWAs have obediently fulfilled the gloom and doom prophecy? And how many physicians have simply given up on AIDS patients because they assume, consciously or otherwise, that there's no point to aggressively diagnosing and treating complications?

"There is absolutely no question that proper patient management can contribute significantly to patient survival," says Dr. Joseph Sonnabend. "And there's been an assumption on the part of the doctors at medical centers, who really are removed from the day-to-day realities of AIDS, that there's nothing you can do. This is a terrible assumption which has cost lives. Of course, there are those who might say, 'So what? If you're adding a few months or adding a year, what does it matter?' But I think it's very important that doctors not lose the sense of what we're doing, which is to maintain life and try to work out a cure to this disease."

Those of us who've insisted on the possibility of surviving AIDS have been patronized, handed [Elisabeth] Kübler-Ross, sent into therapy, or faced the charge of AIDS dementia. Those caring for us could humor our illusions and ration out their emotional strength, certain that, however draining, however horrible it may be to watch the progress of AIDS, the end is inevitable. Admitting the possibility of survival will mean that people around us must suffer the disappointment of our hopes along with us in a new way. If death from AIDS is not inevitable, then each death is uniquely painful. And each struggle to survive is uniquely empowering.

Let the academics haggle with Talmudic exactitude over what they choose to call AIDS. When you're battling immune deficiency, it doesn't much matter what you call it. Answering the question of why some of us have survived life-threatening conditions despite dire predictions is more important. There is the general sense among AIDS researchers that we long-term survivors may hold an important key to beating AIDS. Is it attitude? Is it something in our blood? Like many researchers, the CDC's Dr. Hardy believes it is crucial to study long-term survivors: "The answer's there. It's just a matter of finding it."

Characteristics of Survivors

Dr. George Solomon and his colleagues at the University of California, San Francisco sketched a tentative profile of the long-term AIDS survivor in a recent issue of *The Annals of the New York Academy of Sciences*. Dr. Solomon discovered that survivors:

(1) Accept the reality of an AIDS diagnosis, but

refuse to believe that AIDS is necessarily an automatic death sentence;

(2) Refuse to be helpless or hopeless;

(3) Make lifestyle adjustments;

(4) Actively participate in a healing partnership with their health-care providers and take responsibility for their own healing;

(5) Share a powerful belief that life is worth living;

(6) Often have a previous history of overcoming obstacles;

(7) Value exercise and general fitness;

(8) Find value in peer support groups and in helping others;

(9) Are assertive and able to say "no";

(10) Are self-concerned and self-involved without being selfish;

(11) Are sensitive to the signals their body gives; and

(12) Are expressive and good communicators.

As far as I can tell, I know more long-term AIDS survivors than anyone in the world. A notice I placed in the *PWA Coalition Newsline* has produced dozens of replies. Despite a persistent feeling that to talk about surviving is to jinx it, the prospect of meeting someone else who'd beaten the odds overcame all reluctance. If I had to describe in one word the common characteristic of the PWAs I interviewed, it would be grit. These people are all fighters: opinionated, incredibly knowledgeable about AIDS, stubborn, and passionately committed to living, they work hard to stay alive. And they are all involved in the politics of AIDS—some by becoming publicly identified, others counseling or operating hotlines. Politics can be an antidote to the self-obsession that comes with AIDS. To realize that there's someone worse off, whom you can help, is an incredible relief—and maybe even healing.

"If I had to describe in one word the common characteristic of the PWAs I interviewed, it would be grit."

In the course of two dozen interviews, I discovered patterns, but no single pattern. Some had returned to the bosom of their families; others were as obstinately alienated as ever. Some had noble, caring lovers; others were single (but considered themselves eligible). Some were working full-time and proud of it; others were working full-time at disability. Some had sworn off drinking, smoking, and recreational drugging—but not all. One of the longest surviving PWAs gleefully recounted doing and dealing cocaine from his hospital bed (while undergoing experimental treatment from an IV-unit attached to his arm).

Some survivors insisted that they owe their lives to experimental therapies, while others attributed their survival to the fact that they refused to be guinea pigs. Despite intense pressure among physicians to take AZT—the only federally approved treatment for AIDS—only one of the gay long-term survivors was on that drug when I interviewed him. When I asked why they hadn't hopped on the AZT bandwagon, most echoed PWA Bruce Zachar's quip: "If it ain't broke, don't fix it." On the other hand, all the blacks and Hispanics I interviewed are on AZT. State and federal subsidies that provide AZT for free encourage its use among the poor. If, as some of us suspect, this drug proves to do more harm than good, we will have another example of good intentions backfiring, costing the lives of minorities.

One long-term survivor of KS, who has completely turned his back on Western medicine in favor of macrobiotics, practically glows with health—proof that Western medicine hasn't cornered the market on AIDS treatments. And in fact, everyone I talked to had at least dabbled with holistic therapies.

More surprising to me was a rekindling of religious sentiment. A majority of long-term survivors spoke movingly about a return to the faith of their childhood. I hadn't expected to discover so much religious faith, because it certainly hasn't played any role in my own survival. I have filed safely away a signed, notarized document indicating that any request I might make for religious assistance is to be taken as prima facie evidence of dementia sufficient to invoke my power of attorney.

My own explanation for the recrudescence of religious sentiment among long-term survivors would be this: the psychoneuroimmunologists could be right; there may well be a will to live. Marshaling this will requires hope. And when rational systems offer no hope, we turn to those systems that do. In our culture, that means religious systems that speak of life after death, of meaning to suffering, of a caring, paternal god who will take care of you.

Luck

When asked why I think I've survived five and a half years after my diagnosis, I usually quip: "Luck, classic Coke, and the love of a good man." I'm only half joking. I have been lucky. I have never been that sick. Although my first opportunistic infection, cryptosporidiosis, nearly killed me, it didn't. And the complications I've had since then have been comparatively mild: bacterial pneumonias; shingles; chronic, often violent, diarrhea; blood tests that show a depletion of the T-cells that protect one from disease; and some strange immune complex problem, which has required that I receive transfusions periodically. But somehow (genetics, perhaps?) I've managed to avoid KS. And I've been lucky enough to tolerate Bactrim (a powerful sulphur drug) which I've taken as prophylaxis against PCP.

And I am lucky enough to have been a skeptic. For example, I have never believed that HIV, or any other, "new" virus, is the cause of AIDS. By the age of 27, when I was diagnosed, I'd had thousands of sexual contacts and as a consequence, developed dozens of sexually transmitted diseases—viral, bacterial, parasitic, and fungal. When I got AIDS, the question was not why, but rather how I had been able to remain standing for so long! Whether I'm right or wrong in my belief that AIDS is really the result of repeated assaults on the immune system by common infections, the important thing is that I always believed that if I stopped doing what I thought was making me sick, I could get better.

"Believing that I could survive is probably the precondition necessary for my survival."

Believing that I could survive is probably the precondition necessary for my survival. Unlike many other people with AIDS who considered themselves "ticking time bombs," my worldview admitted from the first at least the possibility of recovery. My doctor's shared skepticism about the etiological party line led him to discourage me from jumping on many a bandwagon of experimental treatments. This also probably saved my life.

My macrobiotic friends cringe when I credit classic Coke, and they're right. After all, as any Mom will tell you, a strip of bacon left overnight in a glass of Coke will "fry" by morning; imagine what it does to your gut. But in my survival strategy, Coke represents pampering myself—giving myself permission to enjoy.

The Love of a Good Man

My lover hates when I say that he's the key to my survival because it implies that if he leaves me, I'll die. Or that if I die, he must not have loved me enough. I met Richard at the absolute lowest moment of my life, in fact the week of my diagnosis.

The worst part about being diagnosed wasn't the thought of dying. It was believing that I would die without ever having known the love of another man. I'd had lots of sex; but I'd never really had a lover—as in living with someone and wanting to grow old and grumpy with him. And so, when the AIDS sentence was pronounced, I felt like factory seconds—damaged merchandise. It never occurred to me that anyone would risk loving me now. I couldn't believe he hung around. But he did. And we've been together for nearly six years. I don't think it's mere coincidence that I've survived as long as our relationship has lasted. Though he hates it when I say it, if I'd been alone, I'm not certain I'd still be here.

For weeks, I flailed about in search of a nice ending for this piece. Fate intervened. In February [1988], I was forced to swallow a TV camera (they called it an endoscope). Biopsies suggest that I either have lymphoma or may soon develop it. I'm back on the merry-go-round of inconclusive tests, disagreeing doctors, and expensive hospitals.

In the first years of AIDS, I had a pretty simplistic notion of hope. I thought that if one believed hard enough in the possibility of survival—if you were a "fighter"—you could beat AIDS. Then I watched some of the bravest and best fighters fall to AIDS. I've refined my belief: having hope won't guarantee that you'll survive, but not having hope seems to guarantee that you'll succumb quickly.

Although I'm winded from nearly six years of coexisting with AIDS, I must now readjust to the possibility of lymphoma. Even in dark moments, when doubt and hopelessness threaten to overwhelm, I am aware of an almost palpable will to live. The hysterical *joie de vivre* [joy for life] of Julia Child cooking videos, my cookie cutter collection, the imminent release of Streisand's next album, and the secure sensation of my lover coming to bed, sometimes make me want to weep with joy. I should miss them so, if I died.

Hope Is Rational

I'm convinced it's as rational to have hope as it is to give up. If 85 per cent of people diagnosed with AIDS are dead after five years, then 15 per cent are still alive. I intend to remain among that prophetic minority.

Michael Callen is a founding member of the People With AIDS Coalition and the editor of Surviving and Thriving with AIDS: Hints for the Newly Diagnosed.

"I have returned to support group after four years. I bring my pain to the group and let it go."

viewpoint 17

Support Groups Help AIDS Victims Cope with Death

Bob Russell

In April '83, I was diagnosed with Kaposi's sarcoma. My life was shattered. At this time, the first wave of AIDS hysteria had broken in the media—front page stories of men diagnosed on a Monday and dead by Friday. Poppers were thought to cause AIDS.

My friends were afraid to touch me or eat food that I had touched. My boss had never heard of the illness. I had to explain to my parents what it meant to have AIDS, and I feared I would not live to see my 31st birthday, a few weeks away. I felt totally alone with my illness.

Three days later, I went to Ward 86, the newly-formed AIDS Ward. While waiting to have my vital signs taken, Bobby Reynolds came into the examining room. Bobby was the first person with AIDS I ever met. He wore his sad, hangdog smile and said, "I heard you just got diagnosed." He spoke these soft words, tinged with sorrow, that I would hear him repeat time and again to other newly diagnosed men. Bobby touched me then, through my fear and pain, with his humanity and compassion and told me to come to the Shanti support group. I did.

The First Support Group

There was only one group back then—one Shanti group—one AIDS group. Sometimes as few as two or three people would show up. Now there are 15 Shanti support groups alone. Churches have also formed support groups for people with AIDS; metaphysical groups have formed; therapy groups exist. There are more kinds of AIDS groups than you can shake a stick at. But back then there was just this one little support group crammed into the Community United Against Violence (CUAV) office.

And Shanti was small. Jim Geary (just a name to me) actually lived in the Shanti office. Steve, who ran the support group, was Jim's one-person, part-time staff. Shanti was a shoestring operation.

I was still in shock two weeks later, when my counselor first arrived. I remember Marty, a very handsome, tanned blond nurse. I knew I had a crush on him (it turned out everyone had a crush on him). He was soft-spoken, had good listening skills and a smile that would make you melt. I never knew what to talk about. But I liked to look. Sometimes we'd go to the Patio Cafe for coffee and a goodie. I never called him because I didn't want to bother him. Within two months, Marty completed his volunteer commitment and left Shanti. I wonder about him often.

I continued going to the support group. There was Bobby again and Dale. Dale and I were diagnosed the same week and Marty was his counselor too (we used to compare notes). Cowboy Ron was there and a few others, at different places with their illness. All are dead now.

Scottie, from group, was the first man I knew to die of AIDS. He was in his mid-twenties, really cute, just diagnosed—a puppy dog. Scottie got sick real fast. He had an identical twin and the doctors wanted to do a bone marrow transplant. The twins agreed. Scottie went to Los Angeles and had it done. His body was bombarded with lethal doses of radiation. His immune system and everything else was wiped out. Before the transplant could take effect, Scottie caught an infection. He died like a baby.

Quitting Group

I stopped going to group shortly after that. And I didn't see another counselor. I never really associated myself with other people with AIDS, something many people who are diagnosed choose to do. I continued to work full-time, exercised daily and stayed healthy. I lived my life one day at a time

Bob Russell, "Heroes and Heroines of Our Time, Shanti Volunteers Who Are Also People with AIDS: Part II," *Eclipse: The Shanti Project Newsletter*, Fall 1987. Reprinted with permission.

and made every moment count.

In October '83, I attended a three-day workshop with [Elisabeth] Kübler-Ross for people with AIDS. It was at Wildwood. I bicycled there and back from San Francisco and became known as the "bicyclist with AIDS." The experience I got from the workshop profoundly affected me and I moved into a house with two other men with AIDS. We all appeared healthy but within three months, my first roommate had died. There was no will. Friends and family (born-again Christians from the Midwest) arrived, ransacking our home. Some of my possessions were taken as well. The family tried to set me down on my knees to be saved, renouncing my gayness and embracing their beliefs. That was fun!

My second roommate, Geoff, deteriorated more gradually. He developed lots of small infections and got weaker and weaker. When Geoff went into the hospital with Pneumocystis pneumonia one year later, I got my second Shanti counselor. I knew that Geoff would not be coming home, and I needed help dealing with his dying. Mike, my new volunteer, fresh from the training, was just what I needed. He really helped me through that terrible time. I was the executor of Geoff's will and held his health care power of attorney. The family came, wanting to make his health care decisions, wanting his property. Friends wanted to put him into a hospice. Geoff's last request to me was that everything that could be done by the doctors was to be done. I had to honor that request, despite what other people felt. I felt the wrath of his friends and family. I became very stressed out and got pneumonia a week after his death. Through all the pain and suffering of that process, Mike, my Shanti person, was at my side.

"I'm doing what feels right, . . . giving love and support where it's most needed."

Again, my life returned to normal. I continued working and exercising—both so important for my self-esteem. My only involvement with Shanti from Spring of '84 through the end of '86 was attending the people with AIDS weekends at Wildwood and seeing Mike, my counselor, who had grown into a close friend. From my weekends at Wildwood, I became known as "the piano player with AIDS." In November '86, I was diagnosed with early stage AIDS dementia. I had been exhibiting symptoms of disorientation, confusion, loss of memory, feebleness and general neurological impairment. I didn't know that dementia is a terminal illness but my friends knew I was dying. I went on AZT [an experimental anti-AIDS drug] at that time and left work. AZT brought me back. The symptoms faded. My brain, which had shrunk, returned to normal size. After three months, I returned to work. But even now, if I stop taking the AZT, I will soon die.

Becoming a Support Counselor

In February '87, I took the Emotional Support training as a community participant and fell in love with Shanti for really the first time. It was the most powerful two weekends I had ever lived. I knew that I had come home. Bobby appeared on the client panel and looked ashen. He didn't have long to live.

I facilitated the next training in May: so much more love; so many loving, caring men and women. Participating in the training continued to feel like the best thing for me to do. This training occurred as Bobby was dying. All of us grieved over losing this man; many of us still grieve for him. Bobby was followed by Dale, Cowboy Ron and Sean—men I had known since my diagnosis. Heroes that had chosen to fight AIDS with Shanti support. They are all gone now. My peer group has steadily died off. My grandfather must have felt much like this, watching his friends die.

Letting Pain Go

I have returned to support group after four years. I bring my pain to the group and let it go. Those men left such a legacy to me, to people with AIDS in San Francisco. The plan was to be involved in the August training, but pneumonia again reared its ugly head. I believe this was because of the stress I suffered from dealing with my friends' dying.

Mike and I are no longer counselor and client. Our lives have grown apart. I miss Mike deeply and still think of him so much. We shared two exciting wonderful years—fun times and painful times. Many friendships don't reach that level of intimacy. He'll always be a part of my life.

I have a new counselor now—Shirley. We're still getting to know each other. I'm happy I'm working with a woman and I get a strong sense that Shirley really wants to be there for me. That feels good.

I regret not having been more active in the fight with AIDS since my diagnosis. I feel like I wasted time. But I didn't know I'd have four and one half good, relatively healthy years. No one would have bet on that. I'm out there now . . . and fighting. I'm doing what feels right, doing what I should have done back in '83—giving love and support where it's most needed. I'm able to stand up in public forums now and say, "I have AIDS. I have been living with AIDS for four and one half years." I do it for one reason: so that the newly diagnosed have something to pin their hopes on. Maybe they will have eight and one half good, healthy, quality years!

Compassion and Caring

My heroes are gone. I carry them in my heart. And I, and others like me, must carry on for each of them. Wonderful men and women keep getting diagnosed with AIDS . . . and keep dying. There is so much pain and sadness in this work. People with AIDS come to me now (now I'm referred to as the "Grand Dame of AIDS") for support and encouragement. There's still so much work to do. AIDS is here to stay and getting worse. But compassion and caring, as manifested through Shanti, is the only thing that makes any sense in all this. As Thornton Wilder said in The Bridge of San Luis Rey: "There is a land of the living and a land of the dead . . . and the bridge is love."

Bob Russell is a volunteer counselor with the Shanti Project, a San Francisco organization that provides counseling and support services for AIDS patients.

"When AIDS came, I had no choice. There was something inside me that said, 'Look at yourself.' I began to do that, and that's how I got well."

viewpoint 18

Focusing on the Self Helps AIDS Victims Cope with Death

George Melton, interviewed by Lese Dunton

A growing number of people with AIDS and related conditions are viewing their diagnosis as a blessing in disguise, an opportunity to change their attitudes and their lives. Instead of accepting it as a blueprint for death, they've chosen to look at it as a stepping stone to health: mental, physical, and spiritual. . . .

In the following interview, George Melton tells his story of self-discovery and restored health. In the spring of 1985, Melton's lover, Wil Garcia, was diagnosed as having a dangerously low T-cell count, a pre-AIDS condition. The doctor told Garcia that if his count continued to decline, he probably would not live much longer. When Melton was tested, his count was even lower than Garcia's. He had AIDS-Related Complex/borderline AIDS. Two months later, Garcia developed Kaposi's sarcoma lesions, confirming that he had AIDS.

Melton and Garcia traveled to Mexico to obtain Ribavirin, but the drug failed to help them. They tried combining it with Isoprinozine, but this too failed to be effective. Throughout the summer and fall, their health declined as the visits to the doctor increased.

They decided to pursue alternative healing techniques. They started looking into books, meetings, and themselves, to find the answers. Now, over two years later, their health is excellent and they're leading happy, productive lives. Their doctor said their healing is "attributable to a remarkable life change of acquiring insight, aspiration, spirituality, and love of self."

Recovery for Melton and Garcia started within, and they believe that people who use AIDS to change their inner condition have much to teach others about living. Melton and Garcia are setting an example for this growing movement, bringing to light a new awareness and life in the face of this usually devastating disease. In the following interview, Melton talks in depth about his experiences.

Lese Dunton: *What was the turning point for you?*
George Melton: We were about to go to Mexico again to get more Ribavirin, but before we did we went to a bookstore to pick up a book a friend recommended, *Getting Well Again*. I started browsing through the metaphysical section [of the store] and discovered a book by Edgar Cayce. I figured I would have some time to read in Mexico, so I bought it.

That was the book that started all the changes. That was the first hint to us about the connection between the mind and the body. I got really excited, and when we came back I read all the Edgar Cayce books I could find. I got really turned on. Then I got into the *Seth* books. That was all about belief creating reality.

Feeling Good About Myself

How did your point of view start to shift?
I began to look at my relationship to this larger force and what it was. I started to see it as something that not only was me, but in which I was immersed and which was supportive of me. I began to feel good about myself, because I became aware of how I was using my mind. I looked at the beliefs I was operating under, the limitations I had accepted for myself, the feelings I had about myself—that I wasn't worthy or I wasn't a good person—for whatever reasons I had those feelings. I saw they had no basis in reality. They were just things I had accepted; either people had told me, or the way people reacted to me or whatever. I began to feel better about myself and looked for the ways I had not allowed what was inside of me to come out.

What did you find?
I looked at my job. I'd allowed myself to work at a

George Melton interviewed by Lese Dunton, "Getting Beyond AIDS: Some People Are Discovering that They Can Heal Themselves," *New York Native*, January 4, 1988. Reprinted with the author's permission.

job I enjoyed, but it was the ways I trapped myself in it. I thought this location was the secret to my success or that that company was the secret of my success. These are limitations and traps. Even though I needed to change, I couldn't allow myself, because I didn't know that my success came from me, and when I left I took it with me.

So I changed my job. I began to prove to myself that this was all me, that everything was coming out of me. I began in little ways to test that, to prove it to myself. It gave me the strength to see that there was more there, and to go further with it. It became like claiming my freedom.

We're all free, but if you don't know it, it doesn't do you any good. If you have a million dollars in the bank and you don't know it, it does you no good. It doesn't mean you don't have it, it just means you have no awareness of it. When you come into awareness, it's all there for you.

Using Sex Positively

What else did you discover?

Sex has been a great lesson for me, and AIDS made me face it, the way I used my sexuality. I didn't love myself; I looked for validation from other people. It took a sexual form for me. I didn't have enough confidence to walk up to someone, because I had these fears of rejection or whatever. But I knew I was kinda cute. I just used sex to communicate. I'd go to bed with someone so they'd tell me I was okay, or whatever I needed to hear. I felt good about myself through another person.

You can never be happy getting it from another person. It has to come from within. After a while, I could never get enough of that and I fell into promiscuity.

My behavior is not what needed to be changed. It was my feelings about myself that needed to be changed; my behavior was just an outward reflection of what was going on inside. Every time I was doing that, it was an invalidation of me. I couldn't tell me that I felt good about myself.

So healing begins with loving yourself.

Yes. That really comes down to the bottom line for everybody. I began to recognize the ways in which I was expressing the fact that I didn't love myself, through my behavior and the inability to trust myself. When you don't love yourself, you can't trust your feelings. You don't have the integrity to fall back on you own judgment. You don't know what's right for you, so you never trust what you feel. The funny thing is that your feelings are always right. It's that communication from yourself that's more than just the personality self, and it exists outside of time and space. It can see all the variables, and computes it all and gives you the feeling. You feel what you should do—and that's what you should do, whereas your intellect works with other variables—your sight, all your senses—and those are very limited. The two are sort of in opposition to each other.

We're so intellectually oriented that we go with the intellect and ignore our feelings. But our feelings come from a much larger picture of what's going on, and always give us the right answer. When you don't love yourself, you can't allow yourself to follow your feelings and trust the process.

"I began to heal the wounds inside of me and to knock down the walls."

That's where disease comes in.

Yes, illness comes from that. The soul knows what's right and gives you the feeling. That's its communication to you about the route you should take. It tells you about the activity you should do, how you could express yourself, whatever. Then the personality says, "No, this is not right." It has all these belief systems it's adopted. There are medical belief systems that say, "You die when you get AIDS," or, "I can't get well." Whatever you've accepted as a limitation becomes a limitation for you. But it's only as real as you have made it. The God within you allows you to form your experience by what you accept about it. When you accept that you can't get well or that germs are out to get you, then that's your reality and that's what you'll experience. Mass consciousness accepts this on a broad scale. When you're brought up under these belief systems, unless you consciously examine them and reject them, you sort of fall under this.

People ask, how can a child get sick? They don't know anything about this. It's because they're under the conscious umbrella of their parents and society at large. Until you come to an age where you can face that and reject it, you fall under it.

Healing Wounds Within

Medically it can't yet be explained, but on a spiritual level, how did your healing happen?

I began to heal the wounds inside of me and to knock down the walls. My experience began to reflect that, because life is experienced from the inside out. Everything out there is effect, and you are ultimate cause. That's what omnipotence is. There is only one power: God. You can distort that power and use it any way you want to, but it's you. It's coming from you. Everything that seems to act on you from "out there" is something you have empowered against yourself, and you can take it back any time you want to. I began to understand that, to lean on that and have faith in the whole process of life.

So, by looking at yourself and loving yourself you can change your reality?

Yes. And the universe is stacked in your favor. The impetus is towards fulfillment and expression. It's only through your mind—the filter on the whole thing—that you've stopped the process. When you start cleaning off these beliefs—"This is not possible"; "I can't do this"—then the flow comes in. It's like sun shining through a window. It can't shine through if you've got all this dirt on the window. If you start wiping off the window, the sun starts shining through. Your experience starts to reflect that. The inner becomes the outer. It all comes back to you. You have to go within. God is within.

If you don't love yourself, you're never going to find it, because he or she is you. I didn't know that. That's what I discovered. That's how I got well—by understanding that, and having the desire and willingness to change....

You saw AIDS as an opportunity.

That's what it was for me. Looking back on the progression of venereal disease in the gay community, first there was crabs, then a gonorrhea—all opportunities to look at behavior and not being aware of what disease was. I just took a pill and kept going. Finally, there was AIDS, and you're not going to take a pill. You're going to have to stop and look at yourself.

Some people will never allow themselves to stop and look, and they will die. But there's no such thing as an incurable disease. There is disease that can't be manipulated on a physical level. That's what AIDS was for me. When AIDS came, I had no choice. There was something inside me that said, "Look at yourself." I began to do that, and that's how I got well. Then it just became a self discovery. After a while, I didn't even think in terms of being sick. I got so excited about finding out that I was okay, and looked for ways to explore that. Life became full of growth through joy and fulfillment, rather than growth through crisis. It took a crisis for me to stop and look, because I wasn't thinking that way.

AIDS as a Message

What is AIDS trying to tell us?

AIDS is a message. It's your body speaking to you about an imbalance in the flow. Your soul wants to express and your consciousness becomes a filter that won't allow it to come through. When you won't let the flow come in, you get blockages, and these manifest in the body. I began to look at the ways I wasn't allowing that to happen. The role of illness is for you to spend a little time with yourself, enter into the disease, and say, "What is this disease about? What is my body telling me?" You'll always get an answer. The body is like a map, and you can learn to read it.

In our society, we don't deal with disease that way. We take a pill and keep going. I came to a point where I realized it was a gift. There was a lesson there. I prayed, "Not my will, but thine," and, "Please don't let me die without knowing what this is about. If I die, that's okay, I don't care, but just let me learn what this is all about." From that point on, things began to change. I quit searching for a physical healing. It was a spiritual healing. My spirit was sick and my body just reflected that.

Why hasn't the medical community come forward with this realization?

At first there weren't too many cases of people who were doing this. But now the numbers are increasing and the medical profession is having their beliefs challenged. Their understanding is science, and science measures all the stuff on the outside. It plays with the symptoms. It never touches the cause. That's not to knock science. It has a place. To understand the laws of the physical world is important. Obviously our lives have benefited in many ways. But to not understand that you're dealing with the outer is a great limitation, because the cause is within. All this is directed from within. When you don't know that, you're playing with a shadow. You're not playing with the real thing at all.

"When you realize everything is contained within you—all the confidence and the tools—then it doesn't matter where you find yourself."

Your health and expressiveness are very clear....

I'm doing it through speaking, opening my heart up. I've healed myself, but I want to take that further. I want to help enlighten people and heal them—through my own consciousness, by the way that I relate to them, speak to them. I pursue this actively. It's all the same process that I used to heal myself. It's just going further with the awakening. The success of life is not the result. The success is that you allow yourself to speak, that you allow yourself to write. If no one ever reads it or publishes it, or nobody ever listens, the success is that you allowed yourself to do it. Let go of the results. Being into the results is one of the ways the intellect tricks you into being a failure, when there really is no failure. The only failure is the failure to speak or write or express. Don't judge it, just do it. This thinking is exactly the opposite of how most of the world thinks. The world believes in struggle and attack and all those things.

Creating One's Own Reality

So it's up to each individual.

Yes. The concept that you're responsible for everything that happens to you—some people resist that greatly. When I heard that, it was the most hopeful thing I had ever heard, and I knew it was

death / dying

true, anyway. It was such a relief to see it written down in a book, so I could have some verification. I saw the opportunity there. I thought, well, if I did this, I can undo it. I'm the co-creator.

The more you can work on yourself, the more all transition becomes something wonderful and exciting. When you realize everything is contained within you—all the confidence and the tools—then it doesn't matter where you find yourself. You'll always have that within you. That's the only thing you take with you when you die—that essence, that understanding, those feelings. Death is not a defeat. For me, it was something that I was not ready to experience.

George Melton is the author of Beyond AIDS: A Journey into Healing. *Lese Dunton writes for* New York Native, *a weekly gay community newspaper.*

"Not only do those with AIDS benefit from . . . hospice programs, but the complexities of this devastating illness require this sensitive and humane approach."

viewpoint 19

Hospices Help AIDS Victims Cope with Death

Herman Kattlove and Jeannee Parker Martin

Editor's note: The following viewpoint discusses two hospice programs in California. Part I is by Herman Kattlove and Part II is by Jeannee Parker Martin.

I

Doctors have met their match in AIDS.

When patients with the disease first appeared, we were aggressive in providing them with treatment, using all possible high-tech interventions of modern medicine. AIDS patients with fevers were hospitalized and extensively evaluated; those with severe pneumonias were placed on respirators. Patients who developed Kaposi's sarcoma, that telltale purplish skin cancer, received chemotherapy. We tried to reverse their weight loss with complicated and expensive methods of intravenous nutrition.

But the patients died. The "thin disease," as it is called in Africa, prevailed.

This consistent failure has led to a pullback in the intensity of care directed toward AIDS patients. Today, physicians seldom place AIDS patients with pneumonia on respirators, fevers are evaluated in the office, hyper-alimentation is avoided, and chemotherapy for Kaposi's sarcoma is given only when absolutely necessary.

Indeed, we have reached a situation in which physicians often don't want to treat AIDS cases. I heard a dean at a large New York medical school complain that most top students in his recent graduating class no longer wanted to take training in internal medicine because they would be confronted with patients suffering from AIDS. The problem is not confined to new graduates, however. Physicians in my community have also expressed a reluctance to treat AIDS patients. These physicians are not insensitive to the needs of the patients. But they are overwhelmed by the enormous burden of the patients' many problems, both physical and social.

The patients themselves have also become disillusioned by aggressive medical interventions. Their friends, who received such treatment, still died. Furthermore, they saw that the price of this therapy—the prolonged hospitalizations, the frequent bloodlettings, the nausea and the hair loss of chemotherapy—was not worth it.

Thus a new institution, the hospice, has emerged for the care of AIDS patients. The concept of the hospice arose in England, where certain hospitals would designate a section of the building as a place to house terminally ill patients—usually those with cancer. Gradually a philosophy of care emerged, with the palliation of symptoms and the provision of comfort becoming the primary goals of the hospice program. All that mattered was the quality of life, not its length.

In the United States, the hospice concept was translated into a home-care program in which visiting nurses help patients deal with the symptoms of their diseases. In addition, the hospice program provides social workers, clergy and lay volunteers to help the patient and his or her family cope with the process of dying. Here, too, the emphasis has been on patients with cancer, since they can be clearly identified as terminal and often need treatment to relieve their pain as well as other symptoms of their disease.

Now, the hospice is beginning to care for AIDS patients as well. About one-third of the patients in the hospice program of St. Mary's Hospital in Long Beach have AIDS. Many other hospice programs in Southern California have a similar proportion of AIDS patients.

Although we in the hospice programs are willing to care for these patients, it is a hard job. One

---

Herman Kattlove, "AIDS Brings Urgency to Need for Hospice," *Los Angeles Times*, August 16, 1987. Reprinted with the author's permission.
Jeannee Parker Martin, "Ensuring Quality Hospice Care for the Person with AIDS," *Quality Review Bulletin*. October 1986. Copyright 1986 by the Joint Commission on Accreditation of Healthcare Organizations, Chicago. Reprinted with permission.

problem is financial. Many of these patients—most of them young, gay men—have lost their jobs and can't afford housing. Consequently, so-called AIDS homes have sprung up in Long Beach. These converted rooming houses have become a kind of unregulated hospice, where our hospice team makes rounds to oversee the care of our patients living there. I think that the only reason these AIDS homes are permitted to exist is that the city has found no adequate substitute to house its dying AIDS patients, whom nursing homes do not accept.

New York has begun to address this problem, and today about 50 beds are available for the care of terminal AIDS patients. This in no way will meet New York City's expected need, however. Experts have estimated that in 1991 between 2,000 and 7,500 AIDS patients will be hospitalized daily there. Although the number for the Los Angeles area will be lower, we need to begin to plan now what we will do when the full brunt of this epidemic strikes.

"Funds should be provided for supervisory home-hospice agencies and for caregivers to attend AIDS patients who can be kept at home."

New York has also designated a local hospital to devote itself exclusively to caring for AIDS patients. Such a move is inappropriate. Hospitals are necessary to treat acute problems of AIDS patients, but are an expensive and socially inadequate way to care for these patients on a long-term basis.

We need a better approach in the Los Angeles area. Our local governments will need to develop free-standing hospices for the care of these patients or face the enormous expense of hospitalizing them. Allowing more unregulated rooming houses to usurp what should be a governmental function is not the answer.

Funds should be provided for supervisory home-hospice agencies and for caregivers to attend AIDS patients who can be kept at home. All this must start now. The alternative might be chaos reminiscent of the great plagues of the Middle Ages.

II

As the number of cases of acquired immune deficiency syndrome (AIDS) continues to grow, so does the need for effective home care and hospice services. It has been estimated that more than 1.5 million people have been infected by the virus (formerly known as HTLV-III/LAV; now known as HIV—human immunodeficiency virus) and that 10% of these individuals will have fully developed cases of AIDS within three years. If these estimates are on target, more than 50,000 persons will have been diagnosed with AIDS by 1989. The current experience in San Francisco indicates that approximately 10% of people with AIDS who live in the community are receiving home care or hospice services. A projection of this figure would add up to more than 15,000 people with AIDS nationwide who will need home or hospice care by 1989. In San Francisco, which consistently has had approximately 10% of all cases nationwide, 1,500 would need these services. This would be challenging to even the most experienced administrators of home health agency or hospice programs.

An Unprecedented Challenge

Caring for the person with AIDS is an unprecedented challenge for those adhering to the hospice philosophy of care. Not only do those with AIDS benefit from the multidisciplinary approach adopted by most hospice programs, but the complexities of this devastating illness *require* this sensitive and humane approach. The AIDS patient's multiple physical and psychosocial problems are more intense than those of most traditional hospice patients. Hospice programs will be constantly challenged by the need for more support from homemaker-home health aides, nurses, social workers, therapists, and volunteers. However, reimbursement restrictions and staffing limitations mean that, although the need for care is great, the available resources are few. . . .

San Francisco has developed a communitywide approach to caring for persons with AIDS. In early 1982 the San Francisco Department of Public Health began to systematically organize, supervise, and fund projects to ensure quality care for community members who have AIDS. Since then, a continuum of services—including hospitals, residential care facilities, home health agencies, counseling groups, and volunteer organizations—has been developed to provide care for those who need it. The number of AIDS cases in San Francisco mandates this coordinated public health approach; other communities may find it unnecessary or impractical. But the problems of the individual with AIDS are the same whether there are a half dozen or a hundred cases diagnosed in any geographical area. Therefore, the San Francisco experience can help identify problems and explore plausible solutions nationwide.

Home care services were found to be a necessary part of the continuum of AIDS care in 1982, when the Shanti Project Residence Program identified an increasing need for housing. At the same time, the Visiting Nurse Association (VNA) of San Francisco began to receive referrals for AIDS patients. The city negotiated with VNA of San Francisco to provide limited homemaker-home health aide services to persons living in Shanti residences.

It quickly became evident that a full range of

hospice home care services was required to meet the needs of this population. In 1984 the city entered into a contract with Hospice of San Francisco (a subsidiary of VNA of San Francisco) to develop and implement a multidisciplinary approach to care for terminally ill persons with AIDS who require home and/or hospice care. Out of this effort evolved the AIDS Home Care and Hospice Program, a large multidisciplinary program for the care of persons with AIDS.

Since mid-1984, the AIDS Home Care and Hospice Program has cared for more than 400 persons with AIDS. Of these, 90% have died at home, and 10% have been discharged from the program to other settings. Some of those discharged returned to the hospital and remained there until they died. Others have returned to live with family members in other cities. The conditions of still others have stabilized, so they no longer require the program's intensive services. The average duration of care has been 57 days. The program's average daily caseload has increased from 18 patients in 1984 to 63 patients in 1986, and the program has a waiting list of 30 to 45 patients. Other home health agencies and the city's public health nursing department help provide services to these people until an opening occurs in the program.

The Multidisciplinary Approach

Although some home health or hospice programs may feel unprepared to provide care for persons with AIDS, all agencies have resources that can easily be adapted to caring for these patients. The most important of these resources is the existing multidisciplinary staff. Many agencies may not use the multidisciplinary team with all of their patients, but almost every person with AIDS has complex physical and psychosocial problems that require joint interventions by homemaker-home health aides, nurses, social workers, volunteers, therapists, and physicians.

"The palliative care or supportive care provided by a hospice team is essential from the first day of diagnosis."

Severe physical and neurological conditions may require assistance around the clock by a homemaker-home health aide. Complicated physical problems may require daily nursing intervention. Changes in physical status may require new medication orders from a physician. Diverse psychosocial concerns may need the skills of an experienced counselor or the expertise of a social worker. Individuals with complications, such as blindness, may benefit from intervention by rehabilitation therapists. When family and friends are unavailable to assist with activities of daily living, volunteers may be appropriate to attend to the person's needs. The entire multidisciplinary team is needed to intervene with these intricate problems.

A coordinated, multidisciplinary team approach should be instituted from the start of care. All team members should meet regularly to discuss the plan of care and to ensure that all needs are being addressed. In this manner, the person with AIDS will receive optimal care during the terminal stages of this devastating illness. . . .

Why Hospice Care?

Not every person with AIDS will elect hospice or home care as his or her illness progresses. Some may seek active treatment in an acute-care setting for each opportunistic infection or choose aggressive experimental regimes to help thwart the spread of their illness. These therapeutic interventions are often provided in a hospital but may be provided at home as home parenteral therapy becomes more available.

But for other persons with AIDS, the palliative care or supportive care provided by a hospice team is essential from the first day of diagnosis, irrespective of the patient's treatment decisions. There is currently no cure for the underlying immunodeficiency caused by HIV. Furthermore, the average prognosis for those with a diagnosis of AIDS is approximately 13 months. Since very few therapeutic interventions for opportunistic infections associated with AIDS provide more than temporary relief of symptoms, these treatments can be considered palliative in most instances. Although some individuals with AIDS have experienced dramatic stable periods for years after the diagnosis of and subsequent chemotherapy for Kaposi's sarcoma, these people are few in comparison with the thousands who have multiple and severe complications of opportunistic infections.

But when does aggressive curative therapy end and palliative care begin? Aggressive therapeutic intervention will serve to palliate the symptoms of severe or fatal opportunistic infections. Thus the patient may experience weeks or even months of improved quality of life. Not only will such palliation enable the individual to live his or her remaining life in comfort and dignity, but, when hospice services are available, the person with AIDS will benefit from the skilled and humane support provided by the hospice multidisciplinary team. When not threatened by a "terminal prognosis," most patients choose hospice home care over hospitalization since it allows them to remain in familiar and comfortable surroundings.

It therefore seems appropriate to modify existing hospice admission criteria so that persons with AIDS can be admitted without a prognosis of impending death. Still, the average duration of care of the 400 patients cared for in the AIDS Home Care and Hospice Program has been 57 days, and it is unlikely that many patients accepted for hospice care will exceed traditional prognosis limitations of six months or less.

Quality Care for AIDS Patients

Approximately 21,000 Americans have been diagnosed with AIDS, and many more are certain to be diagnosed before a cure or a vaccine is found. Never before in hospice care have patients been so ill or required so much intervention from every team member. It is the responsibility of all home health agencies and hospice administrators to meet this challenge by identifying resources, educating staff, and ensuring quality hospice care for all persons with AIDS. Regular community outreach will help augment the multidisciplinary team. Such a coordinated approach involving agency and community will ensure quality hospice care for all persons with AIDS.

Herman Kattlove is the medical director of the hospice program at St. Mary's Hospital in Long Beach, California. Jeannee Parker Martin directs the AIDS Home Care and Hospice Program in San Francisco.

"Abortuses, anencephalics and brain dead infants should be utilized as organ and tissue donors for the purposes of transplantation."

viewpoint 20

Infant and Fetal Tranplants Are Ethical

Arthur L. Caplan

The attempt to transplant the heart of a baboon into the chest of a human infant at Loma Linda University Medical Center stirred a great deal of debate and controversy both within and outside of the medical profession. A number of important ethical concerns were raised about the surgery. These included questions about the adequacy of the consent obtained from the baby's parents to the surgery, the thoroughness of the human subjects committee review of the research protocol, the scientific feasibility of the undertaking, the morality of using a live primate as a donor and the practicality of developing techniques for transplanting organs from animal sources to human beings given the scarcity and cost of primate sources.

The most serious criticism levelled against those involved in the Baby Fae case was that the transplant team had failed to make a serious effort to locate a suitable human donor before turning to a live animal source. Organ procurement officials in California indicated that they had not been contacted prior to the occasion of the surgery as to the availability of a heart from a human donor....

The shortage of organs and tissues available from human sources for infants is far more severe than the serious shortfall that exists for children and adults. The small size of newborns means that, for the most part, only organs from other infants can be used for transplantation. The gap between supply and demand is likely to grow greater in the years to come as transplantation techniques for infants are perfected. Unless a means can be found for increasing the supply of cadaver organs and tissues from newborns and infants, the only means of treating life-threatening congenital organ failure will be through the use of xenografts....

In most nations, those who serve as organ donors must be declared dead by medical authorities having no connection or affiliation with transplantation. In most Western nations the definition of death that is utilized is that of brain death—the total and irreversible cessation of all brain function. This definition was adopted in most American states and many other countries in order to accommodate the dilemmas posed by medicine's newly acquired abilities to prolong life through artificial, mechanical means.

Brain death definitions were also adopted in response to the desire of the medical community and the lay public to facilitate organ donation. A brain death standard allows for the maintenance of cardiac and respiratory function in cadavers for time periods sufficient to permit the harvesting of organs.

Organs can be harvested, at least for a period of a few days, from persons who remain attached to various mechanical forms of life-support. Under a brain death definition of death a person with no brain function can be declared dead on the basis of various neurological tests. The tests used to determine the occurrence of brain death are highly standardized and exceedingly reliable with the singular exception of one segment of the human population—newborns.

Unreliable Tests

The neurological determination of brain death in an infant is a much more difficult and complicated affair than it is in the adult or even the young child. The standard neurological tests used to determine the absence of brain function in adults, primarily EEG [electroencephalograph] measurements, are known not to be one hundred per cent accurate in newborns. Some infants have displayed no clinical evidence of brain activity and no EEG activity but have gone on to manifest such function twenty-four

Arthur Caplan, "Should Foetuses or Infants Be Used As Organ Donors?" *Bioethics*, vol. 1, no. 2, 1987. Reprinted with permission.

hours after the administration of the relevant diagnostic tests. The neurological criteria that are known to be adequate for the reliable diagnosis of brain death in adults and children have not proven to be so in the case of infants.

Determining Brain Death in Infants

Not only are there relatively few infants who die under circumstances that would make them suitable to serve as organ donors, the criteria for determining death for such children are difficult to fulfil given the technology and expertise available in most hospitals. The only completely reliable test for determining brain death in an infant is an assessment of blood flow to the brain. This is accomplished using contrast arteriography, a rather complex and expensive technique, which is not available in most hospitals in the United States or in other nations. If, over a significant period of time there is no blood flow to the brain, then it can be determined reliably and with certainty that the brain has lost all function. But without the technology to make such a determination, it is impossible to reliably diagnose brain death in infants.

> *"Children with anencephaly cannot survive without artificial life support for more than a few days. . . . There is no question that such children are incapable of any cognitive activity."*

Thus, while there is increasing interest in extending eligibility for transplantation to include newborns with congenital organ and tissue dysfunction, there is reason for concern about the availability of donors for such children and the capacity of medical personnel to accurately and reliably diagnose death in the pool of infants who are currently serving as, or may in the immediate future be, donor candidates.

Anencephalic Infants as Donors

There is at least one group of infants who, while not presently serving as the source of organs or tissues, might do so if existing laws and regulations governing organ procurement were modified. Each year in the United States approximately one of every 1,800 births results in a child who is afflicted with a fatal, incurable congenital defect known as anencephaly. Children with this condition are born with all but a small portion of their brain missing. If they possess any brain tissue at all it is at most only a small portion of brainstem and even this is often seriously malformed. Such children often have no skull above eye-level although this is not always the case.

Anencephaly is a disorder closely related to other defects of the neural tube such as spina bifida. There is no treatment for the condition. Children with anencephaly cannot survive without artificial life support for more than a few days. Many die in utero or are stillborn. There is no question that such children are incapable of any cognitive activity or any form of sentience.

Approximately 2,000 such children are born in the United States each year. Figures for the rest of the world are difficult to obtain. The number of anencephalic infants is likely to diminish somewhat in the future as various diagnostic tests such as ultrasonography and alpha-foetal protein (AFP) screening become more widely available. The only course of intervention for the condition is abortion. Anencephaly is one of the few conditions for which late (third trimester) abortions are performed in the United States.

Anencephaly, unlike brain death, is simple to diagnose. There are two types; in one the skull and brain do not form above the brainstem, in the other the skull does form but except for the brainstem the brain does not. In the former case the condition is obvious both to the layman as well as the medical professional. In either case the prognosis is always fatal.

A Source of Organs for Other Infants

Anencephalics could provide a source of organs and tissues for other infants. But since some of these children possess some brain function, they do not meet the definition of death which exists in most Western nations—the total and irreversible cessation of all brain function.

Laws in many jurisdictions require that death be pronounced using brain death criteria or the cessation of heart and respiratory functions before organ procurement can occur. Anencephalic infants do not meet these requirements. At the same time if physicians were to wait until all electrical activity from the small portion of the brain present in such infants ceased, there is grave concern that the vital organs and tissues of the infant would be severely damaged. The physiological function of the circulatory and respiratory systems of these infants is so poor that unless organs and tissues are harvested within a short time after the birth of such an infant there is a grave risk that they will not prove suitable for transplantation.

As a result of the uncertainty of the medical profession about the legal status of anencephalic infants, no more than a handful of such children have served as tissue or organ donors in the United States or anywhere else in the world. This is so in spite of the fact that many parents of such children express an interest in organ donation. While the abortion of such children even in the last weeks of a pregnancy is accepted by health care providers and legal authorities, the prevailing laws and regulations governing organ donation make it highly unlikely that these infants will be utilized as organ donors.

The failure to utilize anencephalic infants is made all the more ironic in light of the difficulties and uncertainties that surround the diagnosis of brain death in the newborn. No such uncertainties cloud the diagnosis of anencephaly and there is no difficulty whatsoever in predicting the outcome of the condition among those children so afflicted.

Abortuses as Donors

Aborted foetuses, with few exceptions, cannot serve as the donors of organs. Abortion is usually conducted early on in pregnancy at a time when the major organs have not developed. However, aborted foetuses can serve as the source of various tissues including nerves, brain tissue, stem cells taken from bone marrow or the developing liver, and islet cells from the pancreas. The present techniques utilized in abortion do not obviate the possibility of using tissues for the purposes of transplantation or research.

The use of foetal tissue derived from abortuses is a practice that is shrouded in secrecy in the United States and most other nations. Research utilizing foetal tissues in such areas as bone marrow transplantation is ongoing in many nations but the methods for obtaining such tissues are rarely discussed publicly. One recent exception to the general policy of silence about tissue procurement is the policy statement of the Swedish Society of Medicine. This statement recommends that no procurement of organs or tissues from foetuses take place without the consent of the mother and an ethics committee. But such discussions are the exception where public policy concerning the use of abortuses is concerned.

There are prohibitions in place in the United States against experimentation on foetuses in utero. However, such regulations do not apply to the use of tissues and organs derived from cadaver sources. In American law and regulation, only living human beings have the capacity to serve as the subjects of medical research. Federal and state laws governing the procurement and distribution of foetal tissues from abortuses, be they the product of spontaneous abortions or not, are, at best, vague.

The Need for Donors

The need for organs and tissue for infants, while not extensive, is nonetheless quite real. Approximately one in 5,000 infants is born with end stage renal disease. In the United States this means that somewhere between four and five hundred children are born every year who require a substitute for their lack of kidney function.

There are a similar number of children born with congenital defects of the heart each year in the United States. While surgeons have had limited success utilizing corrective surgery, the so-called Norwood procedure, in some of these children, for most there is no alternative except a transplant or a mechanical substitute.

Well over a thousand infants are born each year around the world with congenital liver failure of various types for whom no alternative is presently available except some form of transplantation. Thousands more are born with life-threatening deficiencies in their immunological, endocrine and enzymatic systems which require tissue transplants of various sorts if survival is to be possible.

There are three possible sources of human tissues and organs for these infants—infants who suffer brain death, anencephalic newborns and abortuses. If it is morally justifiable to devote medical and social resources to the attempt to save the lives of infants born with congenital life-threatening conditions (a premise I shall simply presume for the sake of my analysis without any further argument or justification), then the question of whether or not existing public policies should permit the use of brain dead infants, anencephalics or abortuses as the donors of organs and tissues must be addressed....

The Family's Request

Perhaps the most convincing argument favouring the use of brain dead infants, anencephalics and abortuses as organ or tissue donors is that parents of such children sometimes raise the possibility of donation on their own. Anencephaly is usually diagnosed *in utero*. It is not uncommon for parents, upon hearing of the diagnosis, to ask if their child might serve as an organ donor and to request that the treating physician and hospital take such steps as are necessary to maximize the chances for successful organ recovery.

> "Many parents of anencephalic children would find some consolation in the donation of organs and tissues to help others."

The donation of organs and tissues is often an act that provides some solace to families who find themselves confronting the sudden and often unexpected death of a baby. Many parents of anencephalic children would find some consolation in the donation of organs and tissues to help others. Since the diagnosis and prognosis regarding anencephaly are indisputable, it is difficult to see on what grounds donation should continue to be denied to those families who voluntarily request it.

The potential benefits of transplantation for infants, children and adults of fully utilizing infants and foetuses as donors are enormous. Many parents are eager to have their dead or anencephalic child used as a donor in the hope that something good might come of a tragic situation. Yet uncertainty as to the legality and morality of organ procurement from such sources places the parents in a terrible dilemma.

The parents of an anencephalic or dying baby are often well aware through reports in the media that there are other families desperately seeking organ donors for their children. Upon volunteering they learn that legal and policy uncertainties prevent hospitals from using many foetal or infant donors. Thus, not only are families asked to cope with the death of a child: the absence of a clear public policy with respect to foetal and infant donations makes it impossible for them to help others with whose plight they can well empathize. Perhaps the strongest argument for reexamining public policy with respect to donation from infants is that existing policies make it impossible for those families who wish to have an anencephalic or dying infant serve as a donor to do so. . . .

Organ Donation and Abortion

Mothers are not free to terminate their pregnancies whenever they wish to do so. In the United States and many other Western countries abortion is only legally permitted during the first twenty-four weeks of a pregnancy.

There has been wide debate in the United States, the United Kingdom and other nations as to the morality of abortion. Many critics of abortion are opposed to the creation of any public policy that might directly or indirectly legitimate the practice. For example, some opponents of abortion have also opposed the enactment of laws recognizing a brain death definition of death, on the grounds that such laws might legitimate the destruction of foetuses prior to the time at which they possess brain activity. It is likely that similar arguments might be raised against the practice of allowing organs and tissues to be procured for transplantation or research from abortuses.

It is possible to conceive of circumstances under which parents might seek an abortion only to obtain organs and tissues for transplantation. For example, poor women in nations where markets are permitted in organs and tissues might seek abortions solely for financial gain. Since abortion on-demand in the first trimester is legal in most countries the possibility does exist, even if it is an exceedingly remote one, that policies aimed at maximizing the utilization of infants as donors could lead to increases in the numbers of elective abortions.

While these concerns are valid, it seems no more morally palatable to ban or discourage the use of infants as donors in order to decrease the attractiveness of abortion than it does to try and control the costs of transplantation by creating an artificially low supply of organs and tissues for transplant. Instead, it makes more sense to try and discourage the sale of organs and tissues for profit and to enact legislation carrying criminal sanctions against those who knowingly transplant organs and tissues that were obtained for economic consideration.

"It seems no more morally palatable to ban . . . the use of infants as donors . . . than it does to try and control the costs of transplantation by creating an artificially low supply of organs."

Similarly, those concerned about the legitimating effect organ donation from foetuses might have upon child abuse or abortion should support efforts to restrict the rights of parents to control the disposition of bodily remains in circumstances where they are believed to have, or known to have, caused the death of the infant. Decisions to initiate donation ought be made by third parties having no previous relationship with the mother or with recommending or performing abortions. Those serving in such roles also ought to have no connections or interests in tissue or organ transplant programmes.

Doubt about Death

It has already been noted that where infants are involved, the determination of the occurrence of brain death is a difficult task. The transplant community must insist that organs and tissues be procured only from infants diagnosed as brain dead by reliable and accurate methods.

Obviously, it would be immoral to take organs from an infant when there was uncertainty as to the occurrence of death. The public and the legal system has supported organ procurement to the extent that they have been persuaded of the absolute accuracy and reliability of the brain death standard. In the United States legal authorities have on occasion threatened to prosecute physicians who removed organs from bodies being maintained by artificial life-support in jurisdictions where no law recognizing a brain death standard has been enacted.

At the same time, doubt as to the reliability of definitions of death invoking the cessation of brain activity and as to the goodwill of those involved in the process of organ procurement continue to haunt the entire field of transplantation. Many people refuse to carry donor cards for fear that they will receive less than optimal care should they appear to be candidates for organ donation. Others simply misunderstand the concept of brain death and refuse permission for donation on the grounds that the deceased is 'still alive.' There is a very real fear present in the minds of the public concerning the motives and virtues of those involved in the determination of death and the procurement of organs. This fear has been fuelled by books such as *Coma* and television programmes such as that produced on BBC's Panorama series a few years ago which suggested that not all organ donors were in fact dead at the time of donation.

Overcoming Fear of Organ Donation

Such concerns are especially important in understanding organ procurement from infants. Families are sometimes unwilling to allow physicians to remove life support from infants who are dying or who have died in neonatal intensive care units. While much concern has been expressed about the possibility of undertreatment of the handicapped in neonatal intensive care units, the issue of overtreatment or pointless medical treatment is also a problem for both health care providers and families. Since the prospects for successful organ procurement diminish the longer an infant is maintained on artificial life-support, fears about prematurely ending treatment for infants who are undoubtedly dead can and do hinder organ donation.

At the same time, infants born with most of their brain missing raise particularly difficult emotional and moral problems for parents and for health care providers. Such children may live for a few days supported by their own spontaneous breathing and cardiac function. If given food, fluids and antibiotics, as is the case in some American neonatal units, they may survive for weeks. While some neonatologists are willing to classify all anencephalic infants as dead, many possess brainstem activity which in itself is sufficient to disqualify them as brain dead.

"It is difficult to mount an argument against the utilization of anencephalic infants . . . on grounds other than psychological ambivalence."

Some nurses and neonatologists believe that all anencephalic infants ought to be given food and fluid support. Often the nursing staff finds it cruel not to feed and hydrate a baby who appears normal in all respects except for the absence of a brain. Some physicians agree, although many who do support the administration of food and fluids in the hope that they may actually hasten an anencephalic's death as a direct result of aspiration or the infections that often follow upon such an incident.

The need to assure the public about the motives and concerns of those doing organ procurement would seem to weigh heavily against any attempt to utilize anencephalic infants prior to the occurrence of brain death. The prospect of taking organs or tissues from a human being who is breathing and performing other bodily functions without mechanical assistance would be repugnant to many both within and outside the medical community. Such activity, even if done with the full consent of parents, might totally undermine the public's faith and trust in organ procurement and those who engage in it.

An Unconvincing Argument

Nevertheless, it is difficult to mount an argument against the utilization of anencephalic infants who are not brain dead on grounds other than psychological ambivalence. Adult donors who have been declared brain dead give every appearance of life to those unfamiliar with technology such as mechanical ventilators and total parenteral nutrition. While the procurement of organs and tissues from anencephalics who still manifest signs of life may seem macabre, it seems just as macabre or even more so to permit such children to serve as donors only when they have met a definition of death that is not entirely reliable, and have then been resuscitated and placed upon artificial life-support for the sole purpose of harvesting organs!

The case against using anencephalic infants as donors must be based not upon the interests of such children, but upon an argument to the effect that to do so is a violation of respect for human life. Many commentators have noted that policies aimed at maximizing the procurement of organs from human beings must take cognizance of the symbolic importance of the body in Western society.

The notion that respect ought be accorded the body, either living or dead, regardless of the presence of sentience or consciousness is one that has a long tradition in Western theology and culture. The roots of such a view seem to lie both in a desire to respect the autonomous wishes and desires of persons who once possessed sentience or consciousness with respect to the disposition of their bodies, and to respect the desires and wishes of family members.

It is difficult to see how an argument based upon respect for persons can be used to discourage organ procurement from anencephalic infants. These are human beings who cannot be said by any stretch of the imagination to have had desires, wishes or thoughts concerning the fate of their bodies. Unlike an adult such as Karen Ann Quinlan who has fallen into a permanent vegatative state as a result of illness or injury, there is no meaningful sense in which anencephalic infants can be said to have any of the properties associated with interests, self-respect or personal dignity.

Respect in the case of anencephalics must therefore be grounded solely in the desire to acknowledge the general interest family members and society have in the dignified treatment and disposition of the human body. If this is the basis for insisting upon respectful attitudes and practices where bodies are concerned, then the moral question that requires resolution where anencephalics are concerned is whose interests ought to take precedence; the desires and wishes of parents and family, the needs of those seeking organs and tissues for transplantation or research, or general societal sensibilities regarding the treatment of the bodies of such children?

The claims of those in need of organs and tissues would appear to command great weight when juxtaposed against the sensibilities of strangers with respect to the procurement of organs from anencephalics. Respect for the dead and the imminently dying is important but when the parents of a dying child feel that respect is best shown by donating tissues and organs so that others may live, it seems hollow sentimentality to prohibit such gifts on the grounds that it is repugnant to certain sensibilities to do so.

The fact that some members of the general public may feel squeamish or even be horrified at the thought that organs and tissues might be removed from a body which is still capable of spontaneous cardiac and respiratory functions surely must be taken into account in formulating public policy, but such feelings ought not be given more weight than they are due. Similar concerns were expressed in the last century about the practice of invasive surgery, and in this century about the procurement of organs from bodies maintained by mechanical means. Society has modified its attitudes where both practices are concerned and may come to do so in thinking about organ procurement from anencephalics.

Nor does the use of anencephalics as donors legitimate the utilization of those in permanent vegatative states as organ or tissue donors. Societal policies governing organ procurement from those who have lost their personhood may be influenced by, but are independent of, the reasons supporting the policies that are adopted to govern those who have never had and, more importantly, cannot develop, any semblance of personhood.

The Family's Claim

It seems morally correct to recognize that family members have a far more powerful claim to have their wishes and desires respected where matters of treatment of the bodies of children are concerned than do unrelated third parties. If parents understand that organ procurement from an anencephalic infant may involve taking organs from a living but brain-absent body, and wish to have their child serve as a donor, it would seem ethically wrong to prohibit donation on the grounds that it may violate the sensibilities of other members of society. The case against such donations becomes even less persuasive once the interests and needs of those awaiting transplants are brought into the picture. . . .

Abortuses, anencephalics and brain dead infants should be utilized as organ and tissue donors for the purposes of transplantation or research. Existing law and public policy in every nation should be modified to allow organ procurement from foetuses and infants. The definition of 'donor' ought to be modified so that donors may be either those who are brain dead or those suffering from anencephaly. The criteria for brain death must be modified to reflect the technical requirements necessary for making an accurate diagnosis in infants. Brain death should not be pronounced without blood flow measurements of circulation to the brain by means of contrast arteriography.

"It is difficult to see how an argument based upon respect for persons can be used to discourage organ procurement from anencephalic infants."

Procedures must be developed for ensuring that family permission for donations is sought in all cases in which expert medical opinion holds that tissues or organs might usefully be procured. And procedures must be created for allowing the transfer of authority for making donations in those instances in which a parent is known or believed to have been responsible for the death of the infant.

The general public must be educated as to the need for and anticipated benefits of organ transplantation utilizing infant donors. Doubts about the morality of infant organ and tissue donation need to be addressed by those in the best position to articulate the benefits of social policies aimed at encouraging donations: patients, their families, and health care providers.

Arthur L. Caplan is the director of the Center for Biomedical Ethics at the University of Minnesota.

"Fetal tissue transplants and organ retrieval from live anencephalic infants . . . involve the use of body parts at least potentially obtained by the deliberate killing of a human being."

viewpoint 21

Infant and Fetal Transplants Are Unethical

Leslie Bond

"The law does not prescribe motivations for conceiving a fetus. Most of us grew up with an understanding of why one conceived. Most commonly, it is to have a baby. When one says, 'Let's have a fetus so we can get substantial nigra [brain tissue] after we abort it,' that somehow strikes us as alien. But by what grounds can we say it is wrong? It is not illegal. We have a law that says we cannot stop a woman from having an abortion for whatever reasons she finds necessary."

Dr. Robert Levine
Yale University School of Medicine

"I realize this opens up a Pandora's Box, a can of worms, or whatever you want to call it, but I foresee growing fetuses someday for spare parts."

Antonin Scommengna
Michael Reese Hospital

"I know it sounds macabre. It sounds like you're sawing organs out of a live human being. I don't think that should stop you from talking about it. You can take advantage of a death to make something good happen."

Arthur Caplan
Center for Biomedical Ethics
University of Minnesota

Prior to 1987, the possibility that the bodies of aborted babies would be "harvested" or that anencephalic newborns would become a prime target for organ transplants was for the most part confined to the pages of novels such as *Brave New World* and *Coma*, and journals or publications specializing in "bioethics," such as the Hastings Center's *Hastings Center Report*. But . . . both of these extraordinary proposals have rapidly moved out of the realm of novelists and specialists and into the arena of medical ethics and public policy.

As we shall see, these new transplant techniques are inescapably caught up in the questions of abortion, infanticide, and euthanasia—the protests of proponents to the contrary notwithstanding. Alas, because the issues, both technical and moral, are so complicated, we can do no more here than skim the surface. Above all else, we wish to show three things: First, how these proposals themselves horribly violate pro-life principles; second, how the rationale being used to support them—that if a person "is going to die anyway," why not get some "good" out of his death—in the present environment represents an open invitation to kill millions of other medically dependent people; and third, how the contention that *any* human being may be used solely as a "means" to benefit another person (a "means to an end" rather than an end in him or herself) is totally alien to accepted legal, medical, and ethical mores. . . .

Paving the Way

We note at the outset that, *for now*, the targets are aborted babies and babies born with brain stems only. For now, "only" tissue, apparently, is being taken from aborted babies (as opposed to whole organs, as is the case with babies born with anencephaly). *For now*, most researchers more or less concede that both these categories of babies should be "dead" before their bodies are scavenged.

But the logic of the principle being established unquestionably paves the way for a host of other atrocities: exploiting other categories of disabled newborns, such as those born with Down's syndrome, hydranencephaly, and other neural disorders; encouraging later abortions to produce the "ideal" stage of tissue (or organ) development; deliberately taking the tissue/organs from undeniably living unborn babies and anencephalic infants; and—since abortion is legal throughout the *entire* 40 weeks of pregnancy—aborting near-term perfectly healthy babies in order to guarantee "undamaged" organs.

If this sounds farfetched ("slippery slopeism") take note that: while some researchers insist that tissue would "only" be harvested from "early" abortions,

Leslie Bond, "'Harvesting' the Living," from *A Passion for Justice*. Washington, DC: National Right to Life Committee, 1988. Reprinted with permission.

reportedly the highest success rates have resulted from transplants performed in China using tissues taken from unborn infants at seven to eight months gestational age; already, at least four women have offered to become pregnant, specifically so they could abort and harvest the resulting "tissue," either for themselves or for an ailing relative; some proponents have predicted that "fetuses" will be grown specifically to provide "spare parts"; others have announced plans to market a treatment derived from the tissue of aborted babies' bodies which they estimate will generate $3 billion in revenues; and still others have suggested expanding the live donor "pool" to include patients in persistent vegetative states.

Debate about the new techniques has been intense, capturing the attention of programs such as *Nightline*, *Crossfire*, the *Today* show, (Phil) *Donahue*, and even (Geraldo) *Rivera*. But throughout the controversy, doctors have continued their research, not waiting for a consensus to emerge on the issues. Already, in fact, patients have received transplanted tissue from the bodies of aborted babies as treatment for diabetes, radiation-induced blood disorders, and Parkinson's disease. Thousands more are clamoring for their turn. And [in October 1987] an infant known only as "Baby Gabrielle" became the first infant born with anencephaly to be accepted as an organ "donor" at a U.S. hospital.

A "Fountain of Youth"

As an indication of where we are headed with respect to these technologies, researchers have indicated that treatments using fetal tissue transplants may be on the horizon for conditions such as Alzheimer's disease, sickle cell anemia, Huntington's chorea, leukemia, epilepsy, and mental retardation, to name just a few. One researcher has predicted that a full twenty percent of the U.S. population could potentially benefit from transplants using fetal neural cells alone; twenty percent of the current U.S. population translates to 40-50 million potential "beneficiaries" of this kind of transplants.

No wonder, then, that another researcher claimed that fetal transplant techniques are "to medicine what superconductivity is to physics," while a reporter touted the transplants as a veritable "fountain of youth."

In the case of anencephalic infant organ transplants, within weeks of performing the first such operation in this country in October 1987, officials at Loma Linda University Medical Center in California announced plans to accept more anencephalic infants in the near future for similar purposes. In fact a second infant intended to be used for transplant was born at the hospital in December. However the baby was stillborn, making her organs useless for transplantation.

Officials at the hospital say that they do not forsee having more than one or two anencephalic infants admitted for transplant purposes at the facility at one time. But according to media reports, the hospital receives about 50 calls a year from parents of anencephalic infants wishing to donate their child's organs. In addition, according to the *Minneapolis Star Tribune*, some officials have predicted a need for up to 5,000 infant hearts and kidneys each year in the near future. (It should be noted that Loma Linda also has been at the forefront of the trans-species [animal-to-human] transplant movement. Dr. Leonard Bailey, who performed the transplant operation on Baby Gabrielle, also was the lead physician in the controversial 1984 case in which a baboon heart was transplanted into "Baby Fae.")

"Endless ethical questions arise from both techniques at issue—from commercial exploitation of these babies' bodies, to women conceiving babies expressly for the purpose of aborting them."

Endless ethical questions arise from both techniques at issue—from commercial exploitation of these babies' bodies, to women conceiving babies expressly for the purpose of aborting them to obtain tissues or organs, to making abortion seem "noble" by using the unborn infant's death for the "good" of others, to harvesting many other neurologically impaired patients beginning with those diagnosed as being in a "persistent vegetative state." As we explore these enormously controversial questions, it will be helpful to place these two transplant controversies in perspective. Let us also examine, therefore, some of the reasons physicians are eyeing fetal tissue and the organs of anencephalic infants, and offer a brief history of each to show how we arrived at the present moment.

Fetal Tissue Research

Fetal tissue has long fascinated researchers as a source of transplant material, in part because fetal cells, being soft and pliable, are easier to work with than tissue taken from adult cadavers. Fetal tissues also have incredible regenerative abilities which allow them to continue to develop in the recipient's body. Equally important, the immune system in unborn children is not fully developed, making fetal tissue less likely to "reject" the foreign tissues in a recipient's body. (Transplant "rejection" is customarily a two way street—the recipient's body can reject the transplant, or the transplanted tissue can activate its own immune system and "reject" the recipient's body. It is only this second possibility which is lessened in fetal transplants. As fetal tissue transplant surgeon Robert Gale of the University of California/Los Angeles put it, the fetal tissue is "tricked" into behaving as if it were still developing in its own body.)

Early fetal tissue transplant work involved transplanting tissue from the bodies of fetal animals to the bodies of adult animals. Such experiments began at least as far back as the late 1800s. But, apparently, research did not pick up speed until decades later, when a Swedish and American medical team began to use the technique to treat animals with a chemically-induced version of Parkinson's disease. Parkinson's disease is a severe nervous disorder which currently affects an estimated 1.5 million patients in the United States alone. Symptoms of the disease, including shaking, stiffness, an inability to initiate movement, and difficulty with speaking, walking, and swallowing, eventually progress to an almost total loss of movement control.

In the 1970s, researchers reportedly succeeded in alleviating some symptoms of Parkinson's disease in rats by transplanting dopamine-producing brain cells from rat fetuses to the brains of the affected adult rodents. (Dopamine is a chemical which is thought to be related to Parkinson's disease.) But according to a 1979 issue of the research journal *Science*, the medical team then decided to forgo further experiments with fetal brain tissue in animals. The reason, they said, was that it would be "ethically impossible" to apply the research to human beings *because the source of the cells would be human fetal brain tissue.*

The scientists then turned instead to a less controversial source of transplant material also thought to produce dopamine: the adult rat's own adrenal gland.

"As more tissue is needed, pressure will mount to use the tissue of intentionally aborted infants."

The usual scientific protocol would have dictated that, as scientists continued research in these so-called "auto-transplants" (that is, transplanting of tissue from one part of the animal's body to another part of the same animal's body) they test next in mammals, then in primates, and finally in human beings. However, instead, in 1982 researchers at the Karolinska Institute in Sweden skipped these intermediate steps and began testing the technique in humans.

Treatments involving auto-transplants to patients with Parkinson's disease continued with varying levels of success. At the same time, research in animals continued on both tracks: auto-transplants, and transplants using fetal tissue.

From Animals to Humans

Then in December 1985, Denver researchers Dr. Everett Spees and Kevin Lafferty brought the fetal tissue debate into the human arena when they performed the first fetal tissue transplant in humans—using tissue from human aborted babies. (Recall that the earlier human trials had involved auto-tranplants.) Using the babies' pancreatic tissues, the two researchers separated out special insulin-producing cells and transplanted them into the body of a 51-year-old diabetic patient. According to the researchers, the transplanted fetal cells soon began producing insulin in the body of the diabetic patient. By the end of 1987, at least 15 other adult diabetics had received similar transplants. Others had received fetal liver cells as treatment for a radiation-induced blood disorder. Since 1985, in fact, the field of fetal tissue transplants has virtually exploded, prompting one proponent to claim that we have reached "a new age of science" and one journalist to predict "a new form of surrogate motherhood, in which women get pregnant for the purpose of getting abortions and selling the victim's remains."

One of the latest—and most controversial—developments in fetal tissue transplant research came in September [1987], when doctors in Mexico became the first to apply the fetal-cell treatment for Parkinson's disease to human beings. (The Parkinson's treatment is even more controversial than other kinds of fetal tissue transplants because some of the cells used are *neural* cells—taken from the brain of the unborn infant. The added controversy arises both from the Frankensteinian overtones of brain tissue transplants, and from the sheer number of projected "uses" for fetal neural cells.)

In the Mexico transplants, doctors removed tissue from both the brain and the adrenal gland of a reportedly spontaneously aborted 13-week-old baby and transplanted the tissues to the brains of two patients with Parkinson's disease—one receiving the fetal brain tissue, and the other the fetal adrenal tissue.

It is interesting that the Mexican doctors used the two different types of dopamine-producing fetal tissues in the two transplant operations, for it would appear that they simply did not know which technique would be more successful—not surprising, since very little is known about the causes of the disease in the first place. In fact, interviewed on *Nightline*, lead surgeon Rene Drucker Colin admitted that doctors do not even know if the fetal transplants will be more useful than the auto-transplants, although the fetal transplants do save the patient the trauma involved in the auto-transplants of undergoing two major operations (one to obtain the adrenal tissue, and the other to transplant the tissue into the brain) simultaneously.

Pressure To Use Aborted Infants

Another interesting aspect of the Mexico transplants was the emphasis that Drucker Colin tried to place on the fact that the unborn infant whose tissue was used had died from a miscarriage, rather than an induced abortion. But under questioning by *Nightline's* Ted Koppel, Drucker Colin acknowledged that as more tissue is needed, pressure will mount to use the tissue of intentionally aborted infants. And apparently to Drucker Colin, this is not a major problem when it is weighed against what he called the "right" of the patients to receive the treatment.

"You also have to talk about the rights of the people who are, who have a degenerative disease. And if you're faced with these people, you have to give them solutions," he said. Society must contend with the fact that "you're going to eventually need organ donations from fetuses or from any other source," and the legal and ethical problems have to be "looked at," he said.

"But as a physician, you have to solve the problems of the patients," he added.

Proponents of fetal tissue transplants, such as transplant surgeon Gale, who used tissue from aborted babies to treat six victims of the 1986 Chernobyl nuclear power plant disaster, adamantly insist that the use of these babies' tissues is totally separate from the question of the legality or morality of abortion. Gale argues that as long as abortion is legal, doctors in fact have an "obligation" to use the aborted infant's tissues for the benefit of others, and, he says, it would be "irresponsible" for them not to do so. Indeed, appearing on the (Geraldo) *Rivera* program, Gale asserted that transplant physicians may "play a role" in offering the aborting woman "some consolation" after an abortion by using her infant's tissues to help others. (Rivera himself offered the remark that using tissue from aborted babies could provide a "happy ending" to an abortion.)

Patricia King, a professor at Georgetown University Law Center and a proponent of fetal tissue transplants, also has attempted to disassociate the issue of abortion from the issue of using aborted babies for transplant tissue.

Referring to a conference she attended on the issue held at Case Western Reserve University, Ms. King told *NRL News*, "I don't think that we had to stop and have a big discussion about our views about abortion, because we were talking about dead fetuses. Not everybody is concerned about how the fetuses got to be dead."

By contrast, ethicist Arthur Caplan does not even bother to try to separate the harvesting of fetal tissue from the abortion issue, choosing instead to argue that using the aborted baby's tissue is more "pro-life" than disposing of the body in another manner. In fact, he claims that "a society that would throw fetal remains into a dumpster or an incinerator without offering them to save other young lives is morally suspect."

"What is more respectful of life?" he asked a panel at the International Organ Tranplant Forum in Pennsylvania. "Incinerating [the aborted fetuses] or treating them as we do other human cadavers, which is to say we offer the option of organ donation and tissue donation?"

"The killing of an unborn infant is a violation of the child's civil and human rights . . . and scavenging the remains of that child . . . can only compound that injustice."

Pro-lifers working to protect these most innocent of victims say it is impossible—nay, even dishonest—to pretend that the use of the tissue can be separated from the manner in which it becomes available. Because if the slaughter of the unborn were not going on in the first place, they stress, the issue would not even be before us now. The killing of an unborn infant is a violation of the child's civil and human rights, they insist, and scavenging the remains of that child—even to "help" others—can only compound that injustice.

The most oft-cited opponent of fetal tissue transplants is Dr. J.C. Willke, President of the National Right to Life Committee.

"The argument is that these tiny babies are 'going to die anyway,' so why not get some 'benefit' from their organs or tissues. 'After all, abortion *is* legal,' they say," Dr. Willke noted. "The best analogy here is with the Nazi Holocaust." In Nazi Germany, he explained, concentration camp doctors freely experimented on Jewish prisoners before and after death, and used their tissues for the 'benefit' of others and the 'advancement' of science.

"The argument then was the same," he stressed. "They said, 'These Jews are going to die anyway; why not get some benefit from their body parts? After all, it *was* legal to kill Jews.' But peoples of all nations now agree that what happened in Nazi Germany was a disgrace to mankind, a revolting and shameful example of the deplorable levels to which man could sink. The judges at Nuremberg had Nazi doctors hung for their participation," he said.

Another point of major concern, Dr. Willke said, is the question of whose "permission" will be required for an aborted infant's tissue to be "donated." Early indications are that many researchers would require only that the mother of the child—the aborting woman—consent to the harvesting of the child's body parts.

"Here again an analogy is helpful," Willke said. "When a patient's organs are 'donated' by a parent, spouse, or next of kin, it is fully understood that the surrogate authorizing the donation loved and cared for the deceased, tried to do what was best for him or her, provided the best medical care, etc. But if a wife say, shot and killed her husband, she would have no legal or moral right to make such a decision. By participating in that killing, she impunes any right she may have had to 'donate' those organs," he stressed.

"So it is with the use of body parts from an aborted infant," Willke said. "That mother was a part of the killing of that child, and such lethal activity totally disqualifies her—or anyone involved in the abortion—from *any* moral right to 'give' those organs or tissues away."

Harvesting Tissue Before Death

Other critics, such as Jeremy Rifkin, founder and president of the Washington, D.C.-based Foundation on Economic Trends, cite still other reasons to oppose the use of fetal tissues.

According to Rifkin, at least one federally-funded organ distribution center may be harvesting fetal tissue in violation of a 1985 federal law because it does not verify that the aborted infants it harvests are dead before the organs or tissues are removed. The law prohibits federal funding for the harvesting of fetal parts while the unborn child is still alive.

Rifkin's organization has filed a petition with the National Institute of Health (NIH) seeking the immediate cessation of funds for the organization in question, the Philadelphia-based National Disease Research Interchange (NDRI). For her part, NDRI founder and president Lee Ducat told the *Washington Post* that it is not her job to verify that the unborn child is dead before tissues are removed. But Ducat said she believes hospitals and clinics supplying NDRI with fetal tissues are following the law.

Rifkin's allegations highlight one of the major ethical questions surrounding the fetal tissue debate—one which even gives some transplant proponents pause. Specifically, should it be required that aborted infants be dead before their tissue is harvested? According to an article published in the February 1987 issue of the *Hastings Center Report* written by ethicist Mary Mahowald and transplant researchers Jerry Silver and Robert Ratcheson, all of Case Western Reserve University Medical School in Cleveland, the most successful experiments using fetal tissue to treat drug induced Parkinson's disease in primates have involved transplanting tissue from *live* primate fetuses. In their report, the three authors noted that it is not yet known "whether the same results can be obtained through use of neural tissue from dead fetuses." They contended that the use of nonviable *living* aborted infants "is morally defensible if dead fetuses are not available or are not conducive to successful transplants."

Mahowald and her cohorts also have suggested that, in the future, the timing and the method of abortions "may need to be altered" in order to ensure availability of fetal tissue at the optimum stage of development. "Maintaining the pregnancy is comparable to maintaining vital functions of a cadaver donor through mechanical support," they argued....

According to some, many patients or families of patients in need of treatment for the various diseases fetal tissue could potentially alleviate want to obtain fetal tissue transplants no matter what the source of the tissue may be. "The majority of people with the disease [Parkinson's] could care less about the ethical questions," said Frank Williams, national director of the American Parkinson Association.

But other patients and families recoil from the thought of being made well by tissue harvested from the bodies of innocent unborn children killed by abortion. "My father was in bed with a nerve disease for five years," said John Cardinal O'Connor, Catholic Archbishop of New York. "If I had said to him that I would put a baby to death to keep him alive, he would have put me in jail."

"Harvesting" Anencephalic Babies

The concept of harvesting anencephalic infants arouses deep-seated emotional and intellectual debates principally for two reasons: First, the question of whether a dying patient—or one whose "quality of life" is deemed low—must be dead before his or her organs are used for the benefits of others; and second, whether the patient's death may be hastened—or his life prolonged—solely for the purpose of preserving his body parts for the benefit of another.

"Other patients and families recoil from the thought of being made well by tissue harvested from the bodies of innocent unborn children killed by abortion."

Anencephaly is a rare condition which occurs in between two and three thousand infants born in North America each year. Children born with anencephaly usually have a fully functioning brain stem (the portion of the brain which controls breathing and other basic life functions). However they lack all or part of the upper portion of the brain—that which controls cognitive function.

Anencephalic infants are often stillborn, and

death / dying

among those born alive, many have serious problems with other major organ systems. But some are born with healthy organs such as heart, liver or kidneys. Since most of these infants die within the first few days after birth, they have become prime targets for organ transplant proponents.

> *"It is considered totally unethical to treat any patient—including an anencephalic infant—solely as a something to be used to benefit another patient."*

Over the past 15 years, researchers in other countries have reported several cases in which doctors have transplanted the organs of anencephalic infants. But until Loma Linda decided to transplant the heart of the Canadian newborn "Baby Gabrielle," U.S. medical facilities—including Loma Linda—had refused to accept these infants as organ donors. And the reasons behind their refusal then stem from the same issues which today make the practice so controversial: While the infants were breathing, they could not be classified as "dead," and their organs could not be taken; but unless they were put on a respirator—a move which was considered unethical for reasons we will discuss in a moment—by the time they stopped breathing on their own, their organs and tissues (except for their corneas) were useless for transplant. . . .

Flawed Proposals

Researchers have understood from the beginning that taking organs from anencephalic infants who are—as one Loma Linda medical ethicist who supports transplants put it—"crying, swallowing, [and] flinching" would generate "reverberating thunder." In an attempt to tone down this public outcry, proponents have come up with what amounts to a sort of compromise: Treat the anencephalic infant like "other organ donors" by placing him on a respirator, waiting for brain death to occur, and then taking the organs. But such proposals are seriously flawed in two respects: First, because it is considered totally unethical to make one patient's treatment decisions—in this case, the use of a respirator—solely for the benefit of another individual, rather than for the benefit of the patient himself; and second, because medical experts agree that it is virtually impossible to determine death in a newborn infant using "brain death" criteria—the only criteria available if a patient's breathing is being maintained on a respirator.

Let's examine the first of these problems. Under commonly accepted medical practice, it is considered totally unethical to treat *any* patient—including an anencephalic infant—solely as a something to be used to benefit another patient, rather than as a valuable individual in and of him or herself. In addition, critics stress, putting an anencephalic infant on a respirator could well prolong the child's death—again, solely for the benefit of another.

"Is it right for us to threat these children solely as a means to an end, even if the goal is otherwise good?" asked Los Angeles pediatric neurosurgeon Dr. Alan Shewmon and UCLA medical ethicist Leslie S. Rothenberg in an article written for the *Los Angeles Times*. "The purpose of such treatment is not to help the infant; it is to keep the desired organs intact," they stressed. "Compassion for the parents certainly includes giving the information that under existing law they can authorize the removal of their children's corneas, after death, for the benefit of other children.

"It should not include trading off life—however fleeting—for another."

Determining Death

The second concern about using a respirator to preserve an anencephalic infant's organs for transplant stems from the fact that, for technical reasons, it is virtually impossible to determine death in a newborn infant using "brain death" criteria. This leaves open the very real possibility that organs will be harvested from an anencephalic infant who is on a respirator *before* death has actually occurred. This, in fact, is the concern over cases like that of Baby Gabrielle—as we will see in a moment. First, let us take a brief look at some of the reasons it is so difficult to use "brain death" criteria in newborns.

Brain death criteria, as mentioned above, are used to determine death when a patient's breathing is being maintained by a respirator. The criteria involve measuring the activity of the upper brain. But apparently, the upper brain does not function in newborns in the same way that it does in adults because most of the newborn's activities—crying, sleeping, sucking, etc.—are controlled by the brain stem. Currently, doctors do not have a method to assess the function of the brain stem.

In the case of "ordinary" organ donors who are put on respirators, say, after a traffic accident or other trauma, doctors are able to determine total brain death because the patient's brain stem "swells" due to the trauma, causing brain death. The anencephalic infant has suffered no such trauma and therefore the brain stem normally is not swelling. Additionally, even if the infant's brain stem *did* swell, a newborn's skull structure is much more resilient than that of an adult, allowing it to expand with the brain and avoid brain death.

Proponents of using anencephalic infants as organ "donors" dismiss both of these concerns on the grounds that anencephalic infants are not "persons" or "moral agents"—or, as ethicist Arthur Caplan put it, that they are "incapable of feeling." "I see no basis for making an argument that somehow we're going to harm them or hurt them or lose sight of what these children's interests are," he stressed on *Nightline*. "I don't think they have any." Anencephalic infants have "insufficient brain to support such a statement," he said. . . .

The Preference for Live Donors

In anencephalic infant organ transplants, as in all other such operations, physicians want to transplant the organs while they are still fresh. The "fresher" the tissue, the more likely the transplant will be to "take." Since organs deteriorate as a patient dies, the obvious temptation is to remove the organs before death has occurred.

Far-fetched as this may sound, several proposals already have been offered—two of them in state legislatures—to facilitate the removal of organs from anencephalic infants who are breathing on their own, whose hearts are beating, and who are very much alive. . . .

While none of these proposals has been adopted in the U.S., it is interesting to note that the courts of at least one country—West Germany—reportedly have "accepted" the concept that anencephalic infants have "never been alive despite the presence of a heartbeat." It is also interesting that, according to the *New England Journal of Medicine*, in making its determination, the West German court cited the U.S. Supreme Court decision in *Roe v. Wade*.

One of the most thorough critiques of proposals to allow the harvesting of organs from living anencephalic infants comes from ethicist [Alexander] Capron.

"There are some who say anencephalics never had brain function and can't feel pain," he asserts. "But I argue, why use a group that is most vulnerable and least able to express its own wishes on the situation?" Anencephalic infants "may be dying patients, but they are still alive and breathing," he stresses.

Further, he warns, the use of anencephalic infants as organ "donors" would also "amount to the first recognition of a 'higher brain' standard [of death]—and a first step toward a broader use of this standard."

"To state that such patients are dead would be equivalent to saying that the late Karen Quinlan was 'dead' for the more than ten years that she lay in a coma," he emphasized. A law to allow the harvesting of organs from live anencephalic infants, then, would either treat two similar groups—anencephalic infants and patients in persistent vegetative states—very differently, or it would "lead to a further revision in medical and legal standards under which the permanently comatose would also be regarded as 'dead' despite the fact that many of them can survive for years with nothing more than ordinary nursing care."

Capron also noted that allowing the removal of organs from anencephalic infants would severely undermine the public's confidence in organ transplant programs as a whole by introducing "new elements of uncertainty." This uncertainty would lead families of patients to ask if any particular patient is "really dead" or if physicians "mean only that the outlook for the patient's survival is poor, so why not allow the organs to be taken and bring about death in this (useful) fashion?"

Medical ingenuity should be directed toward finding ways to care for dying patients so that their organs can be used after death, Capron said. But "medicine should not embark on a course of sacrificing living but incompetent patients for the admitted social good of transplanting organs.". . .

Harvesting the Living

On the surface, fetal tissue transplants and organ retrieval from live anencephalic infants seem to be very different issues. But in many more ways, these two techniques are inextricably linked.

As we have seen, both techniques involve the use of body parts at least potentially obtained by the deliberate killing of a human being; in one, the undeniably living unborn infant is killed by abortion, while in the other, since doctors cannot be certain that the anencephalic newborn is "brain-dead," the infant may well be alive when his vital organs are removed. And of course, if proponents were to have their way, these babies' organs would be harvested while they were, without doubt, very much alive.

"Several proposals already have been offered . . . to facilitate the removal of organs from anencephalic infants who are breathing on their own, whose hearts are beating, and who are very much alive."

In both techniques, too, proponents hail the use of the tissues or organs as a way for some parents to overcome the negative emotions they may feel after an abortion or the birth of a disabled child: doctors can alleviate the guilt felt by the aborting woman and assuage the grief felt by the parents of the anencephalic infant by reassuring them that their child's death ultimately served to benefit others. Advocates of both techniques also rest their arguments on the precarious logic that if a patient is "going to die anyway," it is acceptable to use or even hasten his death for the benefit of others.

Proposals such as the two we have discussed here

are in fact a logical extension of the utilitarian ethic adopted by those who support killing in other contexts—such as abortion, infanticide, and euthanasia. For as Rothenberg put it, "As one becomes more nonchalant about taking life, it becomes easier to advance the boundaries, or to add other categories to the initial, narrower conception of those circumstances when it is 'appropriate' to end a life."

Leslie Bond is the assistant editor of National Right to Life News.

"If organs from ... anencephalic fetuses can be obtained ... the family should be allowed to salvage from their tragedy the consolation that their loss can provide life to another child."

viewpoint 22

Anencephalic Infants Should Be Used as Organ Donors

Michael R. Harrison

Organ transplants could give an increasing number of children with fatal childhood diseases the chance of a full life. However, most children die waiting for an appropriate donor organ.

The need for small organs is acute and the demand is likely to grow. In the United States 300-450 children with end-stage renal disease could be taken off dialysis regimens if they received renal transplants. The only hope for the 400-800 children with liver failure (biliary atresia, cholestatic syndromes, and inherited metabolic defects) is liver transplantation; for the 400-600 children with certain forms of congenital heart disease such as hypoplastic left heart syndrome it may be cardiac transplantation; and for an increasing number with childhood haemopoietic and malignant diseases, it is bone-marrow transplantation. Finally, enzymatic, immunological, and endocrine deficiencies may be corrected by the use of cellular (rather than whole-organ) grafts.

For many childhood diseases, biological tissue replacement may be the only satisfactory solution because the transplant must be able to grow and adapt to increasing functional demand over the potentially long life span of the recipient. But the logistics of organ transplantation are very demanding for the young recipient, in whom rapid organ failure and lack of interim support measures make the "time window" for transplantation narrow.

The present system of obtaining vital organs from "brain-dead" accident victims cannot meet the demand for small organs. It is also logistically complex and very expensive. The cost of a new heart or liver often exceeds $100,000. Unless donor material becomes simpler and less costly to procure and transplant, these life-saving procedures will have to be rationed.

Fetuses with defects so hopeless that they meet the requirements for pregnancy termination at any gestational age may be ideal donors. With anencephaly termination is justifiable even in the third trimester, and vital organs other than the brain are usually normal. It occurs once in every 1000-2000 births, is easily detected by screening for raised alphafetoprotein levels in maternal serum and amniotic fluid, and can be confirmed by sonography. When screening programmes capable of detecting 90% of all anencephalic fetuses are instituted, we can expect to detect around 2000 anencephalic fetuses in the United States each year. Even if only a small proportion proves suitable as source of donor material, it could go a long way towards satisfying estimated needs.

Advantages of Fetal Organs

It is unlikely that a functionally immature fetal organ can immediately replace and sustain vital organ function in a child; continued partial function of the native organ or availability of interim external support for organ function will be crucial. With support by dialysis, kidneys transplanted from newborn babies with anencephaly can show remarkable growth in size and function. Technical difficulties with small-vessel anastomoses are now surmountable. Since there is no method of providing good interim support for failing liver and cardiac function, total orthotopic replacement with fetal heart or liver would be limited to neonatal recipients and near-term donors. The fetal organ would have to be large enough to fit the recipient and functionally mature enough to immediately replace life-sustaining function. But traditional whole-organ orthotopic replacement may not be necessary or even desirable. Auxiliary transplantation of immature organs that can develop until they take over the life-sustaining function of the failing native organ may prove safer,

Michael R. Harrison, "Organ Procurement for Children: The Anencephalic Fetus as Donor," *The Lancet,* December 13, 1986. Reprinted with permission.

simpler, and less expensive. . . .

If fetal organs prove suitable, transplantation for children may be greatly simplified biologically, technically, and logistically. But the most important potential advantage is that use of fetal organs may need less immunosuppression than will use of mature organs. Fetal organs are not less "antigeneic" and thus less subject to rejection than mature organs because histocompatibility antigens are expressed early in fetal life. However, fetal grafts in general survive longer than do more mature grafts, and the use of fetal donors allows the immunological manipulations that improve graft survival. The fetus can be tissue-typed by examining amniotic fluid or fetal blood, so the best possible recipient can be chosen by cross-matching. In addition, recipients can be pre-treated with donor cells (amniotic fluid or blood) by the same strategy that has led to improved graft survival in clinical renal transplantation.

"Families are surprisingly positive about donation; they clutch at any possibility that something good might be salvaged from a seemingly wasted pregnancy."

In the future, perhaps the unique immunological relation between mother and fetus can be exploited to facilitate graft acceptance. When the need for transplantation can be predicted before birth (e.g., hypoplastic left heart, thalassaemia) it may be possible to induce specific unresponsiveness in the potential recipient antenatally, for transplantation either before or after birth. Although transplantation immunity develops early in all mammals, in early gestation the fetus is uniquely susceptible to induction of tolerance by donor cell suspensions. Also, graft rejection and graft-versus-host disease may be less likely if grafting is done before the recipient becomes immunocompetent and/or the donor organ becomes populated by "passenger" leucocytes.

The diagnosis of fetal anencephaly is always devastating. Once the family has worked through their grief and decided how the pregnancy will be managed, the possibility of organ donation may be brought up. In my experience families are surprisingly positive about donation; they clutch at any possibility that something good might be salvaged from a seemingly wasted pregnancy. Sometimes families even bring up the subject themselves, or they become upset when organs cannot be donated because of a legal ambiguity.

Would allowing organ procurement from an anencephalic fetus increase maternal risk? To be successfully transplanted, the organs must be oxygenated and perfused until harvest. If labour were induced by the usual techniques (for example, by cervical dilatation and ripening, pitocin) rather than by the more violent techniques often used in late abortion (for instance, prostaglandin injection), most anencephalic fetuses can be delivered vaginally without increased risk to mother. Caesarean delivery would ordinarily not be considered except for maternal indications, even when labour is difficult to induce, or when the anencephalic fetus seems to be in distress.

Ethical and Legal Issues

If further research and clinical experience shows that use of fetal organs is a biologically sound and cost-effective treatment for otherwise hopeless childhood diseases, society will have to decide what attitude to adopt towards the anencephalic fetus.

One attitude is that the anencephalic baby is a product of human conception incapable of achieving "personhood" because it lacks the physical structure (forebrain) necessary for characteristic human activity, and thus can never become a human "person". The idea that a product of human conception is biologically incapable of achieving "humanness" seems radical until we consider the many products of conception lost by early miscarriage or stillbirth because of gross abnormalities. Although this approach makes organ procurement simple by denying the anencephalic baby the legal rights of personhood, there are compelling reasons for avoiding this stance. First, it is difficult to reach a consensus about personhood and what constitutes humanness. Secondly, denying personhood denigrates the pregnancy itself and may lead to a less respectful approach to the grieving family and to medical care of the fetus and newborn. Finally, there is the possibility of abuse; other fetuses or newborn babies, possibly with less severe handicaps, might be denied personhood.

Another attitude is that the anencephalic fetus is a dying person and that death is inevitable at or shortly after birth because of brain absence. The first point in favour of this attitude is that brain absence can be clearly defined and limited only to anencephalics, so individuals with less severe anomalies or injuries cannot be classed with anencephalic babies as exceptions for brain death guidelines. Another point in favor of this attitude is that the anencephalic fetus is considered a person, albeit one doomed to death at birth. To consider the anencephalic baby as a person who is brain absent is to recognise his devastating anatomical and functional deficiency without demeaning his existence. He has rights and deserves respect, so removal of organs must not cause suffering, detract from the dignity of dying, or abridge the right to die. This is best done in the operating theatre as is currently being done for brain-dead subjects. This approach also provides a sound ethical rationale for the present practice of allowing the family to choose termination of an anencephalic pregnancy at any gestational age, and would eliminate potential incongruities, such as insisting on care of aborted anencephalic subjects.

Current laws seem to forbid removal of organs from an anencephalic subject until vital functions cease, by which time the organs and tissues are irreparably damaged. This is because anencephalic babies are not brain dead by the widely accepted whole-brain definition of death which requires "irreversible cessation of all functions of the entire brain, including the brain stem"; anencephalics may have lower-brain-stem activity capable of maintaining vital functions, although precariously, for hours after birth.

Defining Death

The whole-brain definition of death was drafted to protect the comatose patient whose injured brain might recover function. However, failure of the brain to develop is clearly different from injury to a functioning brain, and it was simply not considered when the brain-death definition was formulated. The extreme caution and safeguards needed in pronouncing brain death after brain injury should not apply to anencephaly, in which the physical structure necssary for recovery is absent. If failure of brain development, or brain absence, is recognised as the only exception to present brain death statutes, society and the courts can then concentrate on the legal implications of regarding the anencephalic subject as being brain absent. I believe that brain absence will come to have the same medicolegal implications as brain death, but this will have to be recognised by society and confirmed by the courts.

"If the anencephalic fetus is considered to be equivalent to brain-dead subjects ... the family should be able to allow organ donation after delivery."

If the anencephalic fetus is considered to be equivalent to brain-dead subjects for legal purposes, the family should be able to allow organ donation after delivery and to arrange the timing and place of delivery to facilitate transplantation. Obstetrical decisions about how and when to end the pregnancy must be independent of plans to use the organs for transplantation. Members of the transplant team should not be involved in counselling or perinatal management, and the diagnosis of anencephaly should be confirmed by a panel independent of the transplant team and including a neurologist, a bioethicist, and a neonatologist. The family should also be able to decide before delivery whether they wish to see and hold the newborn.

Because many fetal disorders can now be diagnosed and even treated antenatally, we are learning to accept the fetus as an unborn patient. We are also identifying fetuses so fatally damaged that survival outside the womb is impossible. The ability to transplant fetal organs may now give us the chance to recognise the contribution of this doomed fetus to mankind. If organs from prenatally diagnosed anencephalic fetuses can be obtained with safety for mother and respect for the fetus, the family should be allowed to salvage from their tragedy the consolation that their loss can provide life to another child.

Michael R. Harrison is a pediatric surgeon at the University of California San Francisco Medical Center.

"Once an exception is made to include babies with anencephaly as 'dead,' the list would be expanded to include the comatose, . . . the retarded, the brain damaged, and the senile."

viewpoint 23

Anencephalic Infants Should Not Be Used as Organ Donors

Mary Senander

The muddy waters of debate surrounding transplant and research ethics are becoming murkier, even sinister—and the debate, uglier and rather schizophrenic. On the one hand, a bill before Congress would prohibit the use of animals from pounds and shelters by any researcher who holds a grant from the National Institute of Health, the largest single source of support for biomedical research in the U.S. The bill is supported by animal rights proponents. On the other hand, researchers are announcing, with great pride, breakthroughs in the use of cells and tissues of aborted human babies for research and transplants. (The physician who transplanted fetal liver cells to victims of the Chernobyl explosion has been treated in hero-like fashion in frequent media interviews.)

"Harvesting" Organs

Nothing reflects this ethical quagmire so much as the issue of using anencephalic infants as organ donors. An anencephalic infant has little chance of survival beyond a few weeks; most will die within days. By the time these babies die, they usually have infections or deterioration that make them unsuitable as heart, liver or kidney donors.

However, prenatal testing (amniocentesis) can, in some cases, diagnose a fetus with anencephaly, giving transplant surgeons advance notice of a potential donor. Newly born, the young donor will have fresh, useful organs, which can be successfully "harvested." The "dilemma" is that the newly born child, though critically ill, is still breathing and is very much alive. The "solution" is to manipulate the law—or at least definition—to consider the baby "dead." Changes in the laws have been attempted; experiments in other countries indicate that newly born infants with this tragic handicap are considered alive enough to be useful, but dead enough to be used.

As early as 1979, Dr. Paul Kinnaert of Brussels, Belgium, reported that kidneys from anencephalic newborns "function quite satisfactorily when placed in adult patients." At a joint congress of the International Surgical Society and the International Cardiovascular Society, he stressed that, in light of the current shortage of kidneys for transplant, anencephalic infants should not be overlooked. Noting that there are no legal or ethical problems in Belgium with removing kidneys from anencephalic infants, he told about a 23-year-old patient who had received two kidneys from such a child. The grafted kidneys had shown impressive growth during the 2 1/2 years since surgery. But the panel chairman, Dr. John Najarian of the University of Minnesota Medical School, stressed that such transplants would pose enormous legal and ethical problems in the U.S.

More recently, physicians from the Departments of Ob-Gyn and Surgery at Wilhelms University in Muenster, Germany, reported three "successful" kidney transplantations from two anencephalic babies—they called them "fetuses," although they were delivered live (one at 38, one at 36 weeks gestation) and stabilized on life support systems until the surgeons slit open their bellies to remove the kidneys about an hour later. (In the second case, the donor was a twin. The healthy sibling, delivered at the same time, was not selected as a donor.)

In both instances, the parents, aware that their child would have a condition incompatible with life, elected not to have an abortion (the parents of the twins found selective abortion morally unacceptable). They chose, instead, to wait the remaining weeks and to present their infants as donors. "In both cases, the parents drew psychological benefit from the organ transplantations," the doctors reported. "No additional moral dilemma was apparent beyond that

---

Mary Senander, "Dead or Just 'Dead Enough'?" *Human Life Issues*, Spring 1987. Reprinted with permission from *Human Life Issues*, a publication of the Human Life Center, University of Steubenville, Steubenville, Ohio.

with a brain-dead child whose life support is withdrawn and whose organs are retrieved when informed consent is provided by the parents."

Legislation Against Infants

It is estimated that there is an annual "need" in the U.S. for 400 to 500 infant hearts and kidneys, and up to 1,000 infant livers. About 3,500 infants are born with anencephaly each year, a potentially large supply of organ donors. But, under current law, this would be illegal—the infants, though dying, are still very much alive. It would be considered homicide, a direct causing of death, to remove vital organs from these human beings.

A bill considered in the California Legislature would have amended the Uniform Determination of Death Act (UDDA) to include a provision that states: "An individual born with the condition of anencephaly is dead." Introduced by State Senator Milton Marks (R-San Francisco), the bill would add a third category to two current standards used to determine death: irreversible cessation of circulatory and respiratory functions, and/or irreversible cessation of all function of the entire brain, including the brain stem. The new standard would recognize those who have lost higher (neocortical) functions of their brain as dead. After public testimony against the bill, including commentary from the U.S. Department of Health and Human Services, made it clear that significant medical, legal, and ethical effects would result from such legislation, Marks withdrew his bill. (He then co-sponsored a second bill which called for a new, state-wide bio-ethics task force which would, among other duties, recommend policy changes for infant organ donations, including use of anencephalic infants.) . . .

"Anencephalic infants may be dying patients, but they are still alive and breathing."

Dr. Michael Harrison, a pediatric surgeon at the University of California at San Francisco, insists that anencephalic infants differ from other brain damaged children by being "brain absent." He deplores the waste of useful organs, and maintains that anencephaly is the "only exception to brain death that should ever be made . . . it is not a first step to a slippery slope."

Others, while agreeing that the anencephalic brain is very limited, do not accept Harrison's sweeping definition of brain absence and fear abuses. Alexander Capron, a professor of law, medicine and public policy at the University of Southern California at Los Angeles, who was instrumental in framing the UDDA policy, testified against Marks' California proposal. "Calling a person dead wouldn't make them stop breathing." Anencephalic infants may be dying patients, but they are still alive and breathing, and "we don't usually bury breathing people!" he said. . . .

Defining Humanhood

In a 1972 essay, Joseph Fletcher, "father of situation ethics," wrote, "It's time to spell out the 'which' and 'what' and 'when' of humanhood." He set out, "in no rank order at all," a list of 15 criteria or indicators of humanhood, including minimal intelligence, self-awareness, self-control, a sense of time, a sense of the future and of the past (memory), the capability to relate to others, control of existence, concern for others, communication, curiosity, change and changeability, balance of rationality and feeling, idiosyncrasy, and neo-cortical function (this being the "cardinal indicator"). It is certain that Fletcher, who maintains that "What has taken place in birth control is equally imperative in death control," understands that these definitions include huge numbers of our neighbors who are pleasantly senile, chemically dependent, mentally ill or brain damaged. (For that matter, how many of us meet *all* indicators, even on a "good" day?) . . .

There is legitimate concern that, once an exception is made to include babies with anencephaly as "dead," the list would be expanded to include the comatose, those in persistent vegetative states (PVS), the retarded, the brain damaged, and the senile.

It is not popular to point out that the slippery slope has precedent, but it is a fact that should not be ignored. Commenting on the Muenster experiment, Dr. Joseph Stanton of The Value of Life Committee in Brighton, Massachusetts, wrote, "It was [also] in Germany a half century ago in the Third Reich that the 'congenitally defective' infants and children were among the earliest victims in the euthanasia programs which ultimately took the lives of 275,000 patients. At Nuremburg, this was held to be a 'crime against humanity.' For the anencephalic, advocacy of abortion [or] donor transplant to 'make some good come out of tragedy' is a siren song."

It is symptomatic of our secular society, the contemporary "therapeutic state," to justify any means to achieve a socially desirable end. It is both ironic and ominous that the voices of animal rights enthusiasts often appear louder and more visible than those in defense of vulnerable humans. Still, no matter how much an individual patient or even society might benefit from a practice, civilized people must continue to object when human beings are used or abused as a means to that end.

Mary Senander is the public information director of the Human Life Center's International Anti-Euthanasia Task Force.

"It is . . . possible to oppose abortion on moral grounds, and still approve the use of fetal tissue for . . . therapy."

viewpoint 24

Aborted Fetal Tissue Should Be Used for Transplants

Mary B. Mahowald, Jerry Silver, and Robert A. Ratcheson

As if the ongoing abortion controversy were not complex enough, recent developments in neuroscience have exacerbated the situation. At this point, the following scenario may be anticipated:

> A fifty-year-old patient, debilitated from Parkinson's disease, is unable to work or live independently. He and his family have suffered from the economic and emotional effects of the disease. Physically, he experiences rigidity of his arms and legs; he has lost facial expression; his extremities shake; he walks with a shuffling gait; he has difficulty swallowing and speaking. As the disease progresses, these symptoms are becoming more pronounced. Although some symptoms can be alleviated by medication, successively larger doses are required, to a point where the doses may actually trigger symptoms. Since no cure is presently available, the patient can only look forward to further deterioration and premature death.
>
> An experimental treatment has recently been demonstrated to be effective in relieving symptoms of parkinsonism induced in primates. The technique involves obtaining neural tissue from viable or nonviable fetal primates and transplanting this tissue into the brain of an afflicted adult animal. It is unlikely that American neurobiologists who developed the technique will be able to pursue the work with humans—unless legal restrictions on the use of fetal tissue are modified. Whether the same results can be obtained through use of neural tissue from dead fetuses is as yet unknown.

This scenario describes the situation that faces a number of American researchers. Impressive advances have made it impossible to avoid the thorny ethical questions surrounding potential use of fetal transplantation in human beings. The issue exemplifies what [Philosopher] William James terms a genuine option—a choice between alternatives that are live, momentous, and unavoidable.

The new technique is based on the relatively old idea that specific fetal tissue transplants can replace or repair adult tissue. Fetal tissue can be transplanted with greater success than adult tissue because it is less immunologically reactive, thereby reducing the incidence of rejection. Fetal tissue also has a greater capacity to develop than adult tissue. This may be attributed to the relative lack of differentiation and rapid growth of fetal tissue, which develops both physically and functionally after transplantation.

The age of the fetus may be critical to success: mid-gestation or earlier has thus far produced the best results in rodents, while transplantation in primates has produced survival and growth from both viable and nonviable donors. A nonviable fetus may survive for a short time before death occurs. During that time, and for several hours after, the tissue is still living, and is thus capable of further development and function if transplanted to a viable organism. This is comparable to the viability of organs or tissue obtained from cadaver donors, except that the fetal brain may not yet be dead.

The process is straightforward. Abortion is induced and performed through a method intended to preserve the desired fetal tissue. A specific segment of brain tissue is then removed from the fetus and placed in a strategic area of the recipient's brain. Within weeks, the healthy tissue begins to function as part of the organism into which it was transplanted, and symptoms of the disease decline. . . .

The Abortion Issue

Despite the significant therapeutic possibilities of fetal neural tissue transplants, the process raises enormous ethical problems. Old questions must now be reexamined in light of new knowledge: What are our moral obligations (if any) to a fetus that has been or may be aborted? What are our obligations to the pregnant woman who undergoes abortion, whether spontaneously or electively? What are our

Mary B. Mahowald, Jerry Silver, and Robert A. Ratcheson, "The Ethical Options in Transplanting Fetal Tissue," *The Hastings Center Report*, February 1987. Reproduced by permission. © The Hastings Center.

obligations to an individual whose health can be restored through transplantation? What are our obligations to the larger society, in which many may benefit through research support and therapeutic applications? . . .

The way in which fetal tissue becomes available [is] through abortion. Spontaneous abortions (noninduced pregnancy loss occurring before twenty completed weeks of gestation) are less problematic than induced abortions because they are analogous to the circumstances through which life-saving organs ordinarily become available—the cessation of brain function in trauma victims. But the number of spontaneously aborted second-trimester fetuses is relatively small, and many of these lack sufficiently healthy tissue for successful transplantation.

Induced abortions during any stage of pregnancy are legally permissible if the procedure is undertaken for the sake of the pregnant woman's life or health. Although 1.3 million fetuses are aborted yearly in the United States, the number of healthy fetuses that might thus be obtained is again quite small. The more advanced the gestation, the less likely abortion is to occur, whether spontaneously or electively. Some second trimester abortions are induced after prenatal monitoring has indicated fetal defects; the defects themselves tend to reduce the probability of successful transplant.

Clearly, electively aborted, healthy fetuses are the primary source for transplantation of fetal tissue. But these abortions, unlike situations in which transplantation is made possible because of trauma or spontaneous abortion, carry the onus of deliberateness—i.e., fetal death appears to be intended. If intent is morally relevant, this feature is problematic. Accordingly, those states that have proscribed research with fetuses obtained through elective abortions, while sanctioning research with fetuses obtained through spontaneous abortion, have argued that a woman who chooses abortion thereby forfeits the right to make further decisions relevant to the abortus. By not choosing abortion, she retains the right to make such decisions—even as a parent may give permission for research involving his or her child.

The Question of Intent

However, the fact that abortion is "induced" or "elected" (terms often used synonymously in the clinical setting) does not imply that fetal death is directly intended. In some cases, abortions are induced because the continuation of the pregnancy poses a serious threat to the woman's life or health. What is intended then is to restore the woman's health or save her life by interrupting the pregnancy, severing the tie between the woman and her fetus. If the tie could be severed without terminating fetal life, this would be the preferred outcome. Fetal death may thus be a foreseen but unintended consequence of an abortion that is therapeutic for the pregnant woman.

Even where fetal death is intended, one could argue that the pregnant woman should determine the fate of her fetus—whether living or dead, viable or nonviable, *in utero* or *ex utero*. As we have already suggested (in remarking about closer approximation to "uncontroversial personhood"), this argument is least persuasive if the fetus is living and viable, or possibly viable. Court orders and legal decisions have maintained the obligation of practitioners to provide care for these fetuses or abortuses.

"A transplant surgeon who is morally opposed to abortion may morally use the tissue of a nonviable fetus, obtained through an abortion, in order to cure serious diseases in other patients."

The UAGA [Uniform Anatomical Gift Act] allows use of tissue obtained from dead fetuses so long as one parent consents, and the other does not object. Several possible requirements of the technique make it even more important to respect the autonomy of the pregnant woman: gestation may need to be prolonged, and the method of abortion may need to be altered, in either case in order to increase the chances of therapeutic success for the recipient. If midgestation is the optimal time for human transplantation (a possibility that has not been established), a woman who would otherwise undergo abortion during the first trimester might be asked to continue her pregnancy until the second trimester. Maintaining the pregnancy is comparable to maintaining vital functions of a cadaver donor through mechanical support. However, while the latter practice is legally permissible, prolonging vital functions of a living fetus for research purposes is prohibited by federal guidelines.

Choosing the Right Method

Among alternative methods of abortion, the procedure used in the primate experiments (hysterotomy) is least directly damaging to the fetus but entails greater risk for the pregnant woman. In contrast, the method which is most directly damaging to the fetus (dilation and evacuation, or D&E) is statistically safest for the pregnant woman if performed at the appropriate stage of gestation. Other abortion procedures (e.g., prostaglandin or saline infusion) may be both medically indicated and productive of viable fetal tissue. In light of the different effects of different methods, however, the pregnant woman's free and informed consent is morally appropriate not only with regard to when, but also with regard to how, her pregnancy will be terminated.

Just as it has been possible to enact liberal abortion laws in conjunction with laws restricting fetal experimentation, it is also possible to oppose abortion on moral grounds, and still approve the use of fetal tissue for research and/or therapy. It is only possible, however, if the procedures of abortion and transplantation are practically and intentionally distinct, rather than integrally related as means and end.

Theoretically, abortion may be undertaken as a means of facilitating research or clinical applications for others; in fact, however, abortions are typically chosen by individuals as ends for themselves. The end of transplantation is achieved by the means of retrieving tissue from an already nonviable fetus. The physician who performs an abortion, whether therapeutic or elective, is doing something for the pregnant woman; the physician who transplants fetal tissue into the body of another patient is doing something for that person. These two individuals ought to be distinct, just as they are in the analogous situation of organ retrieval from living related or cadaver donors. Real or apparent conflicts of interest are thereby avoided.

The Physician's Responsibility

The physician who performs an abortion may have moral responsibilities to the fetus that are secondary to those toward the pregnant woman. For example, from methods that present an equal risk to the pregnant woman, the physician may be obligated to choose the one least directly destructive, or least painful to the fetus (if the fetus can experience pain). This is comparable to a situation in which capital punishment is viewed as morally justifiable, while torture is clearly an objectionable means of implementation. Or, physicians may be morally obligated (as they are already legally obligated) to treat a viable abortion survivor. In *Planned Parenthood of Kansas v. Missouri*, the majority opinion of the U.S. Supreme Court affirmed the following: "Preserving the life of a viable fetus that is aborted may not often be possible, but the State legitimately may choose to provide safeguards for the comparatively few instances of live birth that occur." But this array of obligations applies to the physician involved in the abortion, not the transplant surgeon. A transplant surgeon who is morally opposed to abortion may morally use the tissue of a nonviable fetus, obtained through an abortion, in order to cure serious diseases in other patients, *so long as both practical and intentional distinctions between the two procedures are clearly maintained.*

Whether or not abortion is a morally acceptable option, further moral considerations are applicable to fetal tissue transplantation. Two of these are specific to evolving knowledge regarding the technology: (1) the requirement of consent on the part of the pregnant woman; (2) the avoidance of pain to the fetus (for example, by insuring that the fetus is already dead, or by using anesthesia). Two other conditions apply here, as they would to other transplantation situations and to any experimental use of human subjects: (3) other modes of research or therapy are not available, and (4) the good expected is at least proportionate to the risk and/or harm that is also expected.

"[Slippery slope] arguments . . . are no more compelling than arguments about the permissibility of abortion or withdrawal of life-sustaining treatment."

History furnishes convincing examples of the moral uses of results that have been obtained by questionable, illegal, or immoral means. In fact, the argument that it is immoral not to use such results for good purposes is more compelling than its counterargument. For example, although many consider the American bombing of Nagasaki immoral, no one seems to question the morality of utilizing the information thereby provided to learn about radiation (a research goal) and to benefit future victims of radiation fallout (a therapeutic goal). Much earlier, dissection of human corpses was an illegal act; yet those who practiced dissection may have justified it as a form of "civil disobedience," essential to the successful treatment of others or to developing an adequate understanding of the human body. Their posterity undoubtedly used the knowledge thus obtained for moral purposes, without incurring the accusation that they were acting immorally.

A Good Goal

Admittedly, these examples involve our use of knowledge rather than tissue or organs. They thus address the research goal of fetal tissue transplants, not their therapeutic goal. Yet the therapeutic goal provides the more persuasive case for use of the new transplant technology, based partly on its analogy with use of organs and tissue from cadaver donors or from living donors. Crucial principles that apply to both sides of the analogy are: respect for autonomy (of pregnant woman or donor); beneficence toward both donor and recipient, and justice or fairness (an equitable distribution of harms and benefits among those affected).

Obviously these principles may also be considered in defending the position that transplantation of fetal tissue is morally wrong, even though the procedure might save a life or cure a debilitating illness. Unless we subscribe to a crassly utilitarian (even eugenic) ethic, scientific progress and therapeutic effectiveness are not adequate grounds for *using* people. It may be objected that nonviable fetuses are not persons anyway, at least not legally. If established personhood is a sufficient basis for opposing transplantation, however, organ transplantation from living adults should also be rejected.

The crucial role of informed consent, as [Ethicist] Han Jonas has suggested, is to transform the situation from one in which a donor is used to one in which the donor's or proxy's autonomy is respected. Or, as [Ethicist] Richard McCormick has argued with respect to the participation of children in low-risk experimentation, membership in a community may justify the procedure. The situation may be considered "low risk" on the basis of the donor's inability to survive, regardless of whether the transplantation takes place.

As with many troublesome ethical issues, the slippery slope argument is applicable to transplantation of fetal tissue. For example, we may initially permit only the transplantation of tissue from dead fetuses. If this does not prove successful or adequate, we may then transplant tissue from nonviable (living) fetuses or abortuses. Routinization of the practice could lead to transplantation of larger and larger portions of the brain, to transplantation of entire brains from viable fetuses, or to harvesting organs from other donors who are not dead, but are dying or chronically ill. In those circumstances too we may have the moral benefit of consent, whether direct or proxy, but consent alone is not sufficient warrant for using human organs or tissue. Moreover, while the technology might at first be used purely for convincing therapeutic reasons (to heal or save lives in situations of seriously debilitating disease, for example), morally questionable motives such as profit making could eventually take over. That possibility has of course existed throughout the history of organ and tissue transplantation. Here one could envision a situation in which women would be paid to become pregnant and undergo abortion exclusively for the sake of fetal tissue transplantation. The moral problems thus raised parallel those that may occur in surrogate motherhood.

Placing Wedges

While arguments of this sort are valid and important, they are no more compelling than arguments about the permissibility of abortion or withdrawal of life-sustaining treatment. The roadway travelled by those who make ethical decisions is unavoidably a slippery slope. To traverse it successfully requires placing wedges at the right places, in order to restrict or stop travel at those points where one is most likely to fall. Accordingly, if transplantation of fetal tissue is permitted, there must be reliable checks against extending the technique to living, viable individuals, and against commercialization, which would trivialize human life in its nonviable stage. Such checks are neither new nor ineffective; they have been successfully applied to organ and tissue retrieval from cadaver donors.

"If transplantation of fetal tissue is permitted, there must be reliable checks against extending the technique to living, viable individuals."

There is no doubt that fetal tissue transplantation evokes ghoulish images of the procedure itself as an assault and a mutilation of immature human beings. Similar images arise with regard to organ retrieval from cadaver donors. However, recent suggestions for alleviating psychosocial problems associated with organ retrieval are applicable here also. These include educating the staff regarding the procedure, its therapeutic possibilities, and applicable moral guidelines; showing consideration for families, and allowing for refusal to participate in the procedure; recognizing the legitimacy of "emotional discomfort and cognitive dissonance" regarding the issue. While these steps may facilitate the use of fetal tissue where it is morally defensible, they need not and should not obviate the need for continuing scrutiny of its moral basis in particular cases. A degree of aversion will serve as a wedge, helping to maintain our moral balance along the slippery slope.

Mary B. Mahowald is associate professor of medical ethics and co-director of the Center for Biomedical Ethics at Case Western Reserve University School of Medicine and University Hospitals of Cleveland. Jerry Silver is associate professor of developmental genetics and anatomy at Case Western Reserve University School of Medicine. Robert A. Ratcheson is professor of neurology and director of neurological surgery at Case Western Reserve.

"The core objection [is] that the source for these transplants is aborted babies unjustly killed by a society which . . . cannot wait to feast on their remains."

viewpoint 25

Aborted Fetal Tissue Should Not Be Used for Transplants

Dave Andrusko

Editor's note: In the following viewpoint, Dave Andrusko addresses readers of National Right to Life News, *a weekly publication of the National Right to Life Committee.*

Headlines in newspapers from Connecticut to Washington tell the story. Although there is some controversy, reporters say, transplant surgeons are developing a "miracle cure" for everything from slight hearing loss to Parkinson's disease.

The source of this cure-all, described as a veritable "foundation of youth"? Tissues taken from the bodies of aborted babies.

Researcher after researcher, hospital after hospital, medical school after medical school are jumping on the bandwagon. There are perfunctory remarks about "ethical issues raised" and the like but there is an aura of inevitability to their comments. And why not, if as one exuberant proponent put it, fetal tissue techniques are "to medicine what superconductivity is to physics"?

Making what is already an ethical minefield even more explosive is that transplant researchers have gone beyond taking cells and tissues from the organs of aborted babies. A transplant team in Mexico "harvested" fetal *brain* tissue from an infant who reportedly was miscarried and transplanted the tissue into the brain of a patient with Parkinson's disease.

Since then similar fetal brain tissue transplants have been done in Sweden and Cuba, according to fetal tissue transplant proponent Dr. Abraham Lieberman of the New York University School of Medicine.

The reasons for the added controversy are complex. For some, it is the "Frankensteinian" overtones of any kind of brain transplant. For others,

Dave Andrusko, "More Medical Facilities Preparing to Make Jump Into Fetal Brain Transplants," *National Right to Life News*, April 7, 1988. Reprinted with permission.

it is the fact that brain cells, unlike some other cells, theoretically might not be able to be successfully transplanted *unless* taken from the "donor" while he or she is still alive. (In fact, most fetal tissue transplant experiments in primates in the U.S. have involved tissue harvested from live, anesthetized fetal monkeys.)

For still others, the problem lies in the sheer numbers of projected "beneficiaries" of fetal neural tissue transplants—and the corresponding numbers of abortions which will be seen as necessary to supply the needed tissue.

For many in the scientific community, the Mexican and Swedish transplants caused even greater controversy because of the disturbing fact that apparently none of the physicians involved in the human fetal brain tissue transplants conducted any preliminary experiments in any animals except mice and rats. Normal scientific protocol would have called for a gradual progression from rodents up through primates before a human application were even considered.

But all these reasons are amplifications of the core objection: that the source for these transplants is aborted babies unjustly killed by a society which has no use for them alive but which cannot wait to feast on their remains.

Later in this story, we shall discuss the use of other-than-neural fetal tissue. But let us first examine fetal neural tissue usage, "where the action is" for transplant surgeons and researchers.

Advancing Research

Thus far, scientists in the United States reportedly have confined their experiments with fetal brain tissue transplants to animal models. But in an interview with *NRL News*, Yale University School of Medicine fetal tissue researcher Dr. D. Eugene Redmond Jr. said that at least seven hospitals in the U.S.—which he declined to name—already have approved protocols for the harvesting of fetal neural tissue.

Yale is not one of these, he asserted. But researchers at the university are among those working on primate models in the hope of someday applying the techniques to human beings.

Interestingly enough, however, the primary transplant method Redmond uses in his experiments on primates would be, he says, totally inapplicable to *human* fetal transplants. The reason is that Redmond's experiments involve performing a Cesarean section abortion on the pregnant monkey, then anesthetizing the aborted monkey, opening the animal's skull, and harvesting the desired tissue *while the baby monkey is still alive.* Redmond says he would be totally opposed to harvesting tissue in a similar fashion from live aborted human babies.

"No number of benefits to other patients will change the fact that that first patient—the unborn child—was mercilessly killed."

But, not all researchers agree on this point. In fact ethicist Mary Mahowald and researchers Jerry Silver and Richard Ratcheson, all of Case Western Reserve University School of Medicine, wrote in an article for the February 1987 issue of the *Hastings Center Report* that the use of nonviable *living* aborted infants "is morally defensible if dead fetuses are not available or are not conducive to successful transplants." And readers of *NRL News* will recall the several attempts of state legislators in California, New Jersey, and Ohio to legalize the harvesting of whole organs from living *born* infants who have severe neurological disabilities. . . .

Citing his opposition to the harvesting of tissue from living aborted infants, Redmond said he also is working with frozen fetal tissue in his transplant experiments. In these, he said, researchers perform the Cesarean abortion, allegedly allow the live monkey to die, then harvest the tissues and freeze them for later use. These transplants appear to work as well as the live transplants, he says.

Ethical Questions Abound

But again, medical and ethical questions abound. For example, in customary organ transplants—say, from an accident victim—tissues can be kept viable after the patient is brain-dead with the use of a ventilator. But how certain can we be that, if the aborted child were *genuinely* brain-dead, it would be possible to obtain viable, transplantable *brain* tissue? Brain death involves the total and irreversible cessation of all blood flow to the entire brain. Redmond's tests for death in the aborted monkey—which he said involve observation of the stopping of respiration, heartbeat, and muscle response—apparently do not include criteria to determine brain death.

Serious ethical questions also would arise if this practice were used on humans: that is, allowing a live intact aborted infant to die in order to harvest his or her tissues. In addition, changing the timing or method of abortion in order to procure an intact or more developed unborn baby possibly at greater risk to the aborting woman also would cause serious ethical dilemmas. In response to the latter problem, Redmond said, "It's hard for me to see a position where I would think [increasing the risk to the mother] was reasonable," as far as the mother was concerned, but that "as far as the fetus is concerned, it doesn't make a whole lot of difference because the fetus is going to be dead anyway."

Interestingly, Lieberman told *NRL News* that Swedish researchers have devised a method by which they are able to extract fetal neural tissue for transplant from the remains of an unborn infant torn apart by a suction abortion—although it doesn't work with every aborted infant. "Sometimes the fetus is so macerated that you can't see anything," he said.

Lieberman added that a potential future "problem" in these transplants might arise if abortifacient drugs such as RU 486 gained wide acceptance. Use of the drugs would necessarily cut down on the number of surgical abortions and, therefore, on the amount of available tissue, he said.

The Source of Fetal Transplants

Like many other fetal transplant proponents, Redmond says there is "no reason at all for the fetal tissue issue to get intermixed in the debate about elective abortions." But as others associated with the transplants have quickly learned, it is virtually impossible to separate the "miracle" tissues—said to possess the key to curing Alzheimer's disease, leukemia, sickle-cell anemia and epilepsy, to name just a few of the applications—from their source.

"No number of benefits to other patients will change the fact that that first patient—the unborn child—was mercilessly killed," stresses Dr. J.C. Willke, president of the National Right to Life Committee and one of the best known opponents of the transplants. Proponents argue that these tiny babies are "going to die anyway," Willke notes. "But that argument was used at Nuremberg as a defence for the atrocities committed by doctors in the Nazi death camps," he recalls. "It was rightly rejected then, as it must be rejected now."

Other critics, such as Jeremy Rifkin, founder and president of the Washington, D.C.-based Foundation on Economic Trends, cite still other reasons to oppose the use of fetal tissues.

According to Rifkin, at least one federally-funded organ distribution center may be harvesting fetal tissue in violation of a 1985 federal law because it does not verify that the aborted infants it harvests are dead before the organs or tissues are removed. The law prohibits federal funding for the harvesting of fetal parts while the unborn child is still alive.

Rifkin also has filed a petition with the U.S. Department of Health and Human Services (HHS) on a separate matter—this one regarding the possible sale of fetal tissues. In his petition, Rifkin requests that fetal tissues be included in the list of organs and tissues banned from commercial sale by the 1984 Organ Transplant Act. Currently, the law lists several organs and tissues which may not be sold, and allows the Secretary of HHS to specify other body parts to be banned from commercialization.

"The notion of harvesting and commercially exploiting tissues and organs from thousands of human fetuses for transplant surgery is abhorrent and contrary to the ethical canons of a civilized culture," Rifkin insists.

An Abusive Technology

The irony is that no sooner do some proponents tell the public that they, too, oppose "abuses," then do other supporters make the case that, in effect, there is no such thing as an "abuse."

For example, supposedly "everyone" agrees that it would be inappropriate to take the tissue before the baby is dead; that fetal tissue should not be commercialized; and that women should be prohibited from becoming pregnant with the intention of aborting and either selling the resulting "tissue" or designating it for transplant to an ailing relative or even themselves.

But, everyone *doesn't* agree, which points out the fact that, assurances aside, there can be no way to "contain" the way fetal tissues are secured or distributed.

"Patients and families recoil from the thought of being made well by tissue harvested from the bodies of innocent unborn children killed by abortion."

For example, as noted above, Mahowald and her cohorts contend that the use of live aborted infants is "morally defensible." Already, at least one U.S. company has announced plans to market a treatment for diabetes derived from the tissue of aborted babies' bodies which it projects will generate $3 billion in revenues. Medical ethicist Marjorie Shultz has suggested that since doctors and hospitals are making money off the transplants, why shouldn't the "origin point"—the aborting woman—do so as well.

And thus far at least six women have requested assistance in becoming pregnant for the sole purpose of aborting the child for his or her tissue. Perhaps the most well known of these accounts is that of Ray Leith. Leith appeared on *ABC*'s nationally aired *Nightline* program and said that she wanted the tissue transplanted to her father, who suffers from Parkinson's, to "be my fetal tissue."

In still another instance, a diabetic woman who had had 14 miscarriages before she had two live births, announced on a San Francisco TV news program *Express* that she would like to get pregnant again and use her aborted child's tissues because she wanted "not to have this disease anymore and that's it. I'll do whatever I need to."

The History of Fetal Transplants

The concept of fetal tissue transplants is not new to the medical world. In fact it has long fascinated researchers as a source of transplant material, in part because fetal cells, being soft and pliable, are easier to work with than tissues taken from adult cadavers.

Fetal tissues also have incredible regenerative abilities which allow them to continue to develop in the recipient's body. Equally important, the immune system in unborn children is not fully developed, making fetal tissue less likely to "reject" the foreign tissues in a recipient's body.

(Transplant "rejection" is customarily a two way street—the recipient's body can reject the transplant, or the transplanted tissue can activate its own immune system and "reject" the recipient's body. It is only this second possibility which is lessened in fetal transplants. As fetal tissue transplant surgeon Robert Gale of the University of California/Los Angeles put it, the fetal tissue is "tricked" into behaving as if it were still developing in its own body.)

Early fetal tissue transplant work involved transplanting tissue from the bodies of fetal animals to the bodies of adult animals. Such experiments began at least as far back as the late 1800s.

But, apparently, research did not pick up speed until [the] 1970s, when a Swedish and American medical team began to use the technique to treat animals with a chemically-induced version of Parkinson's disease. Parkinson's disease is a severe nervous disorder which currently affects an estimated 1.5 million patients in the United States alone. Symptoms of the disease, including shaking, stiffness, and inability to initiate movement, and difficulty with speaking, walking, and swallowing, eventually progress to an almost total loss of movement control.

Ethically Impossible

However, according to a 1979 issue of the research journal *Science*, after working with the fetal transplants in rats, the medical team decided to forgo further investigations. Why? Because it would be "ethically impossible" to apply the research to human beings: the source of the tissues would have to be *human* fetal brain tissues.

The scientists then turned to a less controversial source of transplant material which they theorized could have the same effect as the fetal brain tissue: the adult rat's own adrenal gland (known as "auto transplants"). By 1982, researchers were applying the auto transplant technique to human beings, with mixed success. At the same time, in animals research continued on both tracks: auto transplants and transplants using fetal neural and non-neural tissue.

In December 1985, Denver researchers Dr. Everett Spees and Kevin Lafferty brought the fetal tissue debate into the human arena when they performed the first fetal tissue transplant in humans—using tissue from human aborted babies. (Recall that the earlier human trials had involved auto transplants.)

Using the babies' pancreatic tissues, the two researchers separated out special insulin-producing cells and transplanted them into the body of a 51-year-old diabetic patient. According to the researchers, the transplanted fetal cells soon began producing insulin in the body of the diabetic patient.

By the end of 1987, at least 15 other adult diabetics had received similar transplants. Others had received fetal liver cells as treatment for a radiation-induced blood disorder.

A New Age of Science

Since 1985, in fact, the field of fetal tissue transplants has virtually exploded, prompting one proponent to claim that we have reached "a new age of science" and one journalist to predict "a new form of surrogate motherhood, in which women get pregnant for the purpose of getting abortions and selling the victim's remains."

Yale, the University of Washington, the University of Rochester, and Case Western Reserve University are just a few of the medical schools and hospitals which have stated an interest in or begun to prepare for work in fetal tissue transplants using animals or human beings.

According to some, many patients or families of patients in need of treatment for the various diseases fetal tissue could potentially alleviate want to obtain fetal tissue transplants no matter what the source of the tissue may be. "The majority of people with the disease [Parkinson's] could care less about the ethical questions," said Frank Williams, national director of the American Parkinson Association.

But other patients and families recoil from the thought of being made well by tissue harvested from the bodies of innocent unborn children killed by abortion. "My father was in bed with a nerve disease for five years," said John Cardinal O'Connor, Catholic Archbishop of New York. "If I had said to him that I would put a baby to death to keep him alive, he would have put me in jail."

Dave Andrusko is the editor of National Right to Life News, *published by the National Right to Life Committee, a pro-life organization based in Washington, DC.*

bibliography

The following bibliography of books, periodicals, and pamphlets is divided into chapter topics for the reader's convenience.

AIDS

David Brand — "Surviving Is What I Do," *Time*, May 2, 1988.

Edward N. Brandt Jr. — "What Lies Ahead?" *The World & I*, November 1987.

Anthony S. Fauci — "The Scientific Agenda for AIDS," *Issues in Science and Technology*, Winter 1988.

Steven Findlay — "Unlocking the Key to AIDS," *U.S. News & World Report*, February 29, 1988.

John Fortunato — *AIDS: The Spiritual Dilemma*. New York: Harper & Row, 1987.

Chris Glaser — "AIDS and A-Bomb Disease: Facing a Special Death," *Christianity and Crisis*, September 28, 1987.

Louise L. Hay — *You Can Heal Your Life*. Farmingdale, NY: Coleman Publishing, 1984.

David Margolick — "At the Bar," *The New York Times*, April 22, 1988.

Barbara Peabody — *The Screaming Room: A Mother's Journal of Her Son's Struggle with AIDS*. San Diego: Oaktree Publications, 1986.

Quality Review Bulletin — "Quality of Care for AIDS Patients," (special issue) August 1986. Available from the Joint Commission on Accreditation of Healthcare Organizations, 875 N. Michigan Ave., Chicago, IL 60611.

Jerome Schofferman — "Hospice Care of the Patient with AIDS," *The Hospice Journal*, Winter 1987. Available from The Haworth Press, 35 Griswold St., Binghamton, NY 13904.

Scott Schrader — "AIDS and Suicide: The Burden of Choice," *The Advocate*, March 15, 1988. Available from 6922 Hollywood Blvd., Tenth Floor, Los Angeles, CA 90028.

Earl E. Shelp and Ronald H. Sunderland — *AIDS and the Church*. Philadelphia: The Westminster Press, 1987.

Douglass Shenson — "When Fear Conquers," *The New York Times Magazine*, February 28, 1988.

Robert M. Swenson — "Plagues, History, and AIDS," *The American Scholar*, Spring 1988.

Bill Thomson — "A Bioelectric Approach to AIDS," *East West*, February 1988.

Michael Woods — "The War on AIDS," *The World & I*, November 1987.

Euthanasia

Brian Bird — "Voluntary Suicide May Make California Ballot," *Christianity Today*, April 8, 1988.

Harold O.J. Brown — "Euthanasia: Lessons from Nazism," *The Human Life Review*, Spring 1987.

Daniel Callahan — *Setting Limits: Medical Goals in an Aging Society*. New York: Simon and Schuster, 1987.

Karen Grandstrand Gervais — *Redefining Death*. New Haven, CT: Yale University Press, 1987.

Denise Grady — "The Doctor Decided on Death," *Time*, February 15, 1988.

The Hastings Center — *Guidelines on the Termination of Life-Sustaining Treatment and the Care of the Dying*. Briarcliff Manor, NY: The Hastings Center, 1987.

Sidney Hook — "In Defense of Voluntary Euthanasia," *The New York Times*, March 1, 1987.

Derek Humphry — "Legislating for Active Voluntary Euthanasia," *The Humanist*, March/April 1988.

JAMA: The Journal of the American Medical Association — "It's Over, Debbie," January 8, 1988.

Allen Jay — "The Judge Ordered Me To Kill My Patient," *The Human Life Review*, Fall 1987.

Perri Klass — "Deathwatch," *Discover*, October 1987.

George D. Lundberg — "'It's Over, Debbie' and the Euthanasia Debate," *JAMA: The Journal of the American Medical Association*, April 8, 1988.

Richard John Neuhaus — "The Return of Eugenics," *Commentary*, April 1988.

Kathleen Nolan — "In Death's Shadow: The Meanings of Withholding Resuscitation," *The Hastings Center Report*, October/November 1987.

Allan Parachini — "The Debate Over Death," *Los Angeles Times*, March 9, 1988.

Nellie Pike Randall	"My Father's Best Gift," *Reader's Digest*, January 1987.
Judith Wilson Ross	"Act Now, in Health, on 'Pulling the Plug,'" *Los Angeles Times*, May 6, 1987.
Thomas Scully and Celia Scully	"Playing God," *Glamour*, January 1988.
Mark Siegler	"The A.M.A. Euthanasia Fiasco," *The New York Times*, February 26, 1988.
Kenneth Vaux	"Debbie's Dying: Euthanasia Reconsidered," *The Christian Century*, March 16, 1988.

Infant Euthanasia

Matt Clark	"Doctors Grapple with Ethics," *Newsweek*, December 28, 1987.
Matt Clark	"Should Medicine Use the Unborn?" *Newsweek*, September 14, 1987.
Commonweal	"Manipulating Death," January 15, 1988.
Joan Frawley Desmond	"Should We 'Harvest' Fetal Tissue?" *The Human Life Review*, Winter 1988.
Christine Gorman	"A Balancing Act of Life and Death," *Time*, February 1, 1988.
Leon Jaroff	"Steps Toward a Brave New World," *Time*, July 13, 1987.
Charles E. Rice	"The Harvest of Abortion," *The New American*, February 29, 1988.
Emanuel Thorne	"Trade in Human Tissue Needs Regulation," *The Wall Street Journal*, August 19, 1987.
Robert J. White	"The Aborted Fetus: A Commercial Prize?" *America*, January 23, 1988.

Organ Donation

John D. Arras and Shlomo Shinnar	"Anencephalic Newborns as Organ Donors: A Critique," *JAMA: The Journal of the American Medical Association*, April 15, 1988.
Sandra Blakeslee	"New Attention Focused on Infant Organ Donors," *New York Times*, December 14, 1987.
Alexander Morgan Capron	"Anencephalic Donors: Separate the Dead from the Dying," *Hastings Center Report*, February 1987.
Rodney Clapp	"Prolonging Life To Promote Life," *Christianity Today*, March 18, 1988.
Leslie S. Rothenberg, D. Alan Shewmon, and James W. Walters	"Anencephalic Infants: Means to an End or Ends in Themselves?" *Los Angeles Times*, December 10, 1987.
Janny Scott and Louis Sahagun	"Baby Called Brain-Dead; Organs OK for Donation," *Los Angeles Times*, February 19, 1988.
Shawna Vogel	"Anencephalic Babies," *Discover*, April 1988.

index

abortion, 96
  mother's rights in, 114-115, 118, 119
  promotes disrespect for life, 99, 102-103, 117
  see also organ transplants from infants
AIDS, 44
  among children, 71-73
  and hospices, 89-92
    benefits of, 91-92
    costs of, 90
  and sexuality, 58, 79, 86
  as curable, 86-88
  as fatal, 64, 67
    con, 55, 75-77, 79, 87
  coping with
    accepting death
      as positive, 61-65
      benefits of, 67-73
      harms of, 75-79
    psychological methods, 56-60, 85-88
      being hopeful, 55-60, 79
      expressing emotions, 61-65, 68, 71-72
      group therapy, 81-83
  description of, 68
  doctors' advice about, 55, 62, 64, 77, 79, 87
  doctors' reluctance to treat, 89
  families' role in, 62, 69-71, 82
  media portrayal of, 55, 57, 67, 75-77
  survivors of, 77-78
  treatments for, 85, 89
    AZT drug, 78, 82
    costs of, 90
    improvements in, 75
    side-effects of, 62, 70, 81
  victims' support services, 67-69, 81
Alexander, Leo, 21
American Medical Association, 27, 28-29, 37
Andrusko, Dave, 117

Baby Gabrielle, 100, 104
Barry, Robert, 47
Bond, Leslie, 99
Bouvia, Elizabeth, 21, 23, 39, 40, 47-48
Brandt, Richard, 9-10

Callen, Michael, 75
Cantor, Norman L., 31
Caplan, Arthur L., 1, 93, 99, 102, 105
Capron, Alexander, 105, 112
Cassell, Eric, 19
Colin, Rene Drucker, 101, 102

death
  and grieving process, 71
  and visualization techniques, 56-57, 59-60
  as natural, 18, 45
  as unpleasant, 34, 41
  definition of, 93
    and anencephalic infants, 94-95, 96-97
  denial of, 61-65, 67-73
    as beneficial, 75-79
    as harmful, 44
    society promotes, 44-45
  fear of, 63, 72
  technology's impact on, 1, 7, 20, 29, 37, 43, 45
death with dignity
  as a right, 18, 20
    con, 37, 43
  as unclear standard, 12
Down Syndrome, 3, 7-8, 9
Dunton, Lese, 85
dying patients
  and health care costs, 27
  doctors' responsibilities toward, 25, 27, 29, 34-35
    to preserve life, 49
    to respect patients' wishes, 43, 52
  family attitudes, 25, 38
  legal rulings on, 30, 32, 37
    Barber case, 25-26, 33, 38, 40
    Brophy case, 25, 39, 40-41
    Conroy case, 33-34, 39, 40, 53-54
    Rodas case, 21, 48-49
  palliative care for, 91-92
  rights of, 30, 31, 34
    are not absolute, 37-38, 39, 50
    to refuse treatment, 43-45
      as limited, 51-54
      con, 41, 47-50
    to treatment, 41, 48
  withdrawing nutrition from
    as form of suicide, 40, 49
    as humane, 32, 34-35
    as immoral, 37, 39-40, 48
    as valid, 31-35
      con, 37-41
    physical effects of, 41
    respects autonomy, 31-32
      con, 39, 48, 50
    rulings on, 30, 37
    threatens professional ethics, 25-27, 40
      con, 29-30

Engelhardt, H. Tristam Jr., 18-19
euthanasia, 11-12
  active
    reasons against, 21-24
    reasons for, 17-20
  and communal values, 17-18, 24, 48
  and Elizabeth Bouvia
    should be allowed to die, 43
      con, 21, 23, 39, 47-48
  and pro-life movement, 44, 47-48
  and withdrawing treatment, 15-16
    as valid, 29-30, 31-35
      con, 25-27, 37-41
  as a right, 19-20, 43-45
    con, 21-22, 47-50
  doctors' obligations in, 12, 16
    to hasten death, 19-20
      con, 22-23
    to preserve life, 16, 24, 25, 27
  in Holland, 47
  infant
    as sometimes justified, 1-5
      con, 7-10
    for anencephalics, 105, 112
  legal rulings on, 21
  standards for deciding
    death with dignity, 12, 18, 20, 37
    for comatose patients, 13-14, 20, 34, 38, 41, 53
    quality of life, 19
    sanctity of life, 12-13
  threatens morality, 22, 24, 48-50

Fletcher, Joseph, 112
Forsythe, Clarke D., 25
Fowler, Marsha D., 29

Gale, Robert, 101, 102, 119
Gert, B., 14
Grant, Edward R., 25

Harrison, Michael R., 107, 112
Hemlock Society, 21, 22, 23, 48
homosexuals
  and depression, 58, 63
  parents' attitudes toward, 69-71
  support systems among, 61, 67
  see also AIDS
hospices
  development of, 89-90
  for AIDS patients, 89-92
  need for, 21, 24
  services provided by, 91-92

infants, disabled
  Baby Doe case, 5, 7
  society's responsibility toward, 9-10
  treatment of
    and improved technology, 1, 7, 44
    as moral decision, 8
    may be discontinued, 1-5
      con, 7-10
    ways to decide, 2-5, 7-10, 50

death / dying I-1

parents' role in, 5, 8, 97
see also organ donation

Kane, Francis I., 44
Kass, Leon, 18, 19, 20
Kattlove, Herman, 89
King, Patricia, 102
Kübler-Ross, Elisabeth, 61, 77, 82

Lafferty, Kevin, 101, 120
Levine, Robert, 99
Lifton, Robert, 23, 40

Macklin, Ruth, 51
Mahowald, Mary B., 103, 113, 118, 119
Martin, Jeannee Parker, 89
Melton, George, 85
Miller, Phillip J., 17
Moody, Howard, 43
Morriss, Frank, 47

Nolan-Haley, Jacqueline M., 37

O'Connor, Tom, 55
organ donation, infant and fetal, 44
  and Baby Fae case, 93, 100
  and Nazi Germany, 102-103, 112, 118
  as ethical, 93-98, 116
    con, 99-106
  as moral, 115-116
    con, 102-103, 105-106
  as murder, 105-106, 112
  determining death in
    difficulties in, 103, 104-105
    must be closely regulated, 93-94, 96-98
  parents' role in, 95-96, 97, 98, 105, 108-109
  public opinion of, 97, 98, 100, 103, 120
  regulation of, 103, 114
    as too restrictive, 94-96, 109
      con, 111-112, 119
  shortage of donors for
    justifies use of infants, 93, 98, 107
      con, 102, 104
  use of aborted fetal tissues
    description of, 100-101, 117-119
    from live infants, 115, 118
    proposed regulations for, 96, 116
    reasons against, 117-120
    reasons for, 113-116
    sale of, 96, 100, 116, 119
  use of anencephalics, 94, 103-104
    and overtreatment, 97
    description of, 107, 111
    reasons against, 111-112
    reasons for, 107-109
    regarded as dying persons, 108-109

Parkinson's disease, 101, 103, 113, 117, 119, 120
People of California v. Barber, 25-26, 33
President's Commission for the Study of Ethical Problems in Medicine and Biomedical and Behavioral Research, 4, 21-22, 24, 29-30, 37, 44

Ramsey, Paul, 2, 3, 18
Ratcheson, Robert A., 103, 113, 118
Redmond, D. Eugene Jr., 117-118
Rifkin, Jeremy, 103, 118-119
right to die
  as false, 41, 47-50
  as legitimate, 43-45
  as limited, 51-54
  promotes teen suicide, 48, 49
Rothenberg, Leslie S., 104, 106
Russell, Bob, 81

Scommengna, Antonin, 99
Senander, Mary, 111
Shanti Association, 81-83, 90
Shaw, Anthony, 9, 10
Shewman, D. Alan, 21, 104
Silver, Jerry, 103, 113, 118
Spees, Everett, 101, 120
Stanton, Joseph R., 37, 112
suicide
  community attitudes toward, 44, 51-52
  doctors' role in, 22-24, 37, 40
  must be proscribed, 47-50
  teenage, 48, 49

US
  Department of Health and Human Services
    Baby Doe regulations, 2-3, 7
    organ transplant regulations, 103, 112, 119
  President's Commission for the Study of Ethical Problems in Medicine and Biomedical and Behavioral Research, 4, 21-22, 24, 29-30, 37, 44

Whitmore, George, 67
Willke, J.C., 102-103, 118
Wiseman, Patrick, 7

Zucker, Arthur, 11